SHERRY
THE NOBLE WINE

Sherry
The Noble Wine

Manuel M. González Gordon, KBE

MARQUÉS DE BONANZA

New and revised edition edited by
John Doxat

Quiller Press
LONDON

To the memory of
two grand old men of the wine trade
in Jerez and in London,

my father

PEDRO N. GONZÁLEZ DE SOTO,
1st Marqués de Torresoto
(born Jerez 26.9.1849, died Jerez 3.7.1946)

and his partner

ROBERT WILLIAM BYASS
(born Dalesford 1.10.1860, died London 18.8.1958),

whose outstanding personalities and lifelong devotion to Sherry deserve
the gratitude of all who today enjoy this wine. They were partners in the
firm of González Byass, in which they worked unceasingly from their
youth, they drank Sherry in moderation all their lives, and they died in
harness in their 97th and 98th years respectively, which proves that hard
work and Sherry are no obstacles to longevity.

As a tribute to the long association between the González and Byass
families, and as a token of sincere and deep affection.

Jerez, 1972   BONANZA

My father, Manuel M. González Gordon, Marqués de Bonanza, author
of this book, wrote the above dedication in 1972, when the first English
edition was published. Like the 'two grand old men of the wine trade' to
whom he dedicated his book, he also died in harness, as was his wish,
eight years later, when he was in his ninety-fourth year, and enjoyed
Sherry with his friends right up to the last days.

He was an extraordinarily human and much loved man of uncommon
personality, who made countless lasting friends for Jerez and for Sherry,
the wine he loved so well and for which he worked so hard throughout
his life.

As a tribute to his memory, in admiration and with deep affection.

Jerez, 1990   Mauricio González-Gordon
Marqués de Bonanza

First published 1935. This Edition published 1990 by Quiller Press Ltd, 46 Lillie Rd, London SW6 1TN

© Manuel González Gordon, 1948. This translation and new material © Manuel González Gordon 1972 and 1990

ISBN 1 870948 40 8

Printed in Great Britain by Butler & Tanner Ltd, Frome and London

Contents

Part One – The Story

Part Two – The Viticulture

Part Three – The Viniculture

Part Four – The Other Industries

Part Five – Supplementary Notes, Addenda & Appendices

Acknowledgements

I wish to express my gratitude in this English version of my book to my nephew Manolo González Diez, Mr Brian Murray and Mr Floyd MacNeille Dixon, all of whom had a hand in the translation—not forgetting my good friend the late Mr William Bulman. In writing this book I have been concerned as much with the historic and traditional art of Sherry-making as with the more recent technical and scientific approach to viticulture and vinification, and this has caused the translation into English to become rather involved. I wish to express my very sincere appreciation to all these kind friends for the many hours of untiring effort they have devoted to this work: without their assistance it would not have been possible for this English version to be published.

My thanks are also due to Mr R. W. M. Keeling for his summary of the 1967 Sherry case, and to Mr Anton Massel who very kindly read the English version of Part Two. Last but not least, I am very much indebted to my friend Mr Cedric Salter, whose books about Spain have been widely read, and my son Mauricio; without the help of both of them I doubt if I would have been able to finish this labour of love.

M.M.G.G.
1972

My very special thanks to Mr. Robert W. M. Keeling for writing a new foreword to this edition and also for the new data on how the defence of the Denomitation Sherry stands at present in this rapidly changing Europe. My thanks also for the help my father received, and I also on this occasion from two other very good friends who have done so much for Sherry: Dr. Justo Casas Lucas for his notes updating those he wrote for the first English edition and D. Cesar Peman Medina for the excellent line drawings that so well illustrate the Jerez viticultural practice, and his data and notes on recent changes in vineyard cultivation in the Jerez district.

Thanks are also due to D. Isidro Garcia del Barrio for the new map of vineyards and to D. Antonio Martinez Oliva for coordination. Thanks to Enrique F. Bobadilla, my son-in-law, to whom we owe many of the beautiful photographs in the book, to Alfredo Garcia Gonzalez-Gordon for permission to use some vineyard pictures from his collection, to Milagro my wife, Gabriel Gonzalez-Gordon, Andrew Calder, and Paula the author's first great granddaughter, for their patient proof reading. My gratitude also to Mr. Michael Cottrell, to Mr. Bryan Buckingham, and to my son Mauricio for help in many ways. To the editor Mr. John Doxat my gratitude for his forebearance with someone who knows so little about writing and producing books. Finally very many thanks too to Mr. Jeremy Greenwood of Quiller Press Ltd for his patience and for the fine job he has done.

M.G.G.D.
Jerez, 1990

Foreword

There must be some sadness in writing this foreword to the second edition of Manolo González's book because he is no longer here to talk about it. But one can easily picture him in one's mind's eye, checking each page, each date, each reference, each set of figures, with meticulous care, holding up the pages close to those twinkling but rather short-sighted eyes; one can see him in that high-ceilinged room of his at the Bodega, crammed full of photographs and mementos of friends all over the world. Did anyone ever have more friends in more places? He seemed to me to have to an extraordinary degree that Pauline characteristic of being all things to all men yet remaining himself quite constant and unchanging, and I think it shows in his writing and in the shape and form of this book.

He could spend hours in learned conversation with university professors, or in analysing sets of figures; he could receive and entertain visitors from all over the world and from every walk of life, and each would feel he had been given 'special treatment'; he could spend all day getting from Jerez to Seville because he would stop so many times with so many friends on the way, and none would willingly see him go.

I have always regarded him as the 'Pope of Sherry'; and indeed he had a kind of mystical reverence for what he has called 'the noble wine', which is quite hard for an outsider fully to comprehend. It fitted well with yet another side of this many-sided man: he was full of charity and good works, and he would often replenish himself not only with a copita of his favourite fino, but also with a quiet visit to his beloved monastery, not far from Jerez, to see his friends there. The monks had taken a vow of silence, and I used to guess that he particularly like this 'escape' because the only person allowed to speak in the monastery was the abbot.

Back in the ordinary world, Manolo González was an irrepressible enthusiast for everything to do with Sherry. Lawyers tend to tell their witnesses to answer questions in court as briefly and succinctly as possible. With Manolo Gonzalez, the star witness in the 1967 Sherry case in London, I gave up trying to stem the flood of eloquence, first with some apprehension, then with relaxed delight. Judge and Counsel found his enthusiasm and commitment engaging, infectious, and compelling. The perceptive reader will, I am sure, sense the complex, subtle and unique flavour of both the man and his wine as he turns the pages of this book.

When the long preparations for the trial of the Sherry case were dragging on, in the middle of the nineteen sixties, Manolo González used sometimes to suggest that abuses of the name Sherry in England would all be cured by European laws which would in due course become binding even on the British. This seemed in those days an unfamiliar and somewhat unattractive concept; yet when, in 1973, the United Kingdom became a member state of the European Economic Community, abuses of wine names like Chablis and Burgundy, which had been widespread in England for many decades, did indeed disappear. Suddenly regulations issued from Brussels were found to over-ride the old common law of England in a way which was as novel as it was, to many, disconcerting.

The benefit which flows from this incoming tide of European law has not yet fully reached the shores of Jerez. Manolo González's prediction has not yet come true. But some advantages are already apparent. 'South African Sherry' and 'Australian Sherry' are no longer so called. Yet 'British Sherry' and 'Cyprus Sherry' remain – locked, to be sure within the confines of the United Kingdom, but nevertheless still present and vigorous. There is a time limit for these descriptions, set at 1995. What happens then, is a matter for the European Commission to decide. No-one knows with certainty what the decision will be.

Times change, and nowhere more so than in Jerez: but it is satisfactory and pleasant to be able to record that, as always in the past, the González family and the González Company—and the two are inseparable—are in the front of the struggle to secure for Sherry its rightful place among the great wine names of the world. Manolo González was the leader in this struggle, and I am proud and honoured to have been asked by his family to write this foreword.

Robert Keeling
Chadlington, Oxford
May 1990

Introduction
to Original Edition

It was my good fortune to be born in Spain—and especially in Jerez, which isn't a bad spot at all. It was also my good luck that both my father's and my mother's families were Sherry shippers and that my father should have left me an interest in a Sherry-shipping business.

I suppose all this put it into my head to write a book about Jerez and its marvellous wine. It is a pity—from the reader's point of view—that the book could not have been written by one of my elders, who would surely have made a better job of it since they knew more about Sherry than I can ever know. However, I have done my best.

There is one very good reason why I should have written this book, however unskilled I may be in the art of writing, and that is to do my best to repay a debt, for had it not been for Sherry I am sure I should not now be alive. Here is the story, as told to me many years later by my mother.

When I was four months old—in January 1887—I became very ill; my life was despaired of by the Jerez doctors, who gave me one week at most to live. My father decided to call in a famous child specialist from Seville, but his opinion was even more disheartening, for he told my father that I could scarcely live another four days.

My father invited the doctors into an adjoining room and ordered a servant to bring glasses and a bottle of Sherry. As the servant passed in front of us with the decanter on a tray, the sun's rays shining on the golden wine must have caught my eye, because I raised my tiny hand and it occurred to my mother to give me a spoonful of Sherry. This she did, and as I smacked my lips and appeared to relish it she repeated the dose—a 'treatment' she went on giving me for several weeks.

Only my mother could explain my miraculous recovery, and although many years have passed since then, Sherry has continued to be my favourite medicine.

Although I drink moderately, I must confess that I do not take Sherry any longer in teaspoonfuls. In my opinion it is an excellent medicine for people of all ages.

Should any chapter in this book seem a little long, let me prescribe a glass of Sherry as a 'halfway house'. It will help you along should you wish to continue.

M.M.G.G.

This Edition
Note from the Editor

The first glass of alcoholic beverage I recall drinking contained Amontillado Sherry. I was a schoolboy. Within three years, I was taking a lot of Sherry. The London office of the *Yorkshire Post*, for whom I principally worked as a young journalist, was situated in Fleet Street, almost immediately opposite the famous El Vino wine house. It imported Sherry direct and it was served from the cask—in considerable quantities. I usually took the least expensive El Vino medium Sherry: it cost the equivalent of 4p a dock-glass (6 to the bottle).

I could not then have dreamt that I was much later to enjoy a close professional association with the Sherry trade, and, later still, to be privileged to be given a commission to prepare a fresh edition of the definitive classic in the literature of Sherry.

It became evident that I was not asked to perform a re-write operation. My rather daunting task was to preserve the book's character while bringing it up to date, to modernise its presentation, yet to retain intact nearly the whole original text. It is a work of intense erudition: some reorganization was needed to enhance its appeal beyond specialists, beyond reference shelves, to a wider readership amongst the ever-growing wine-loving public. What might the author have insisted on retaining? What might he now have omitted or wished to add? The book is *his*, not the editor's.

I outlined various suggestions. With one exception, my basic plan was accepted. I would rearrange the book, bring certain topics into line with today's conditions, keep the text virtually unaltered—if not necessarily in the same sequence as earlier printings. Some technical data have been removed from chapters where they interrupted narrative flow and transferred to appendices. A few now superfluous statistical tables have been deleted or curtailed. I have sectionalized former long chapters and inserted sub-headings in successive pages of unbroken print in the interests of readability.

My intention has been that, for all practical purposes, this important book is now as if the distinguished author had just completed it. His deep research, his intimate knowledge, form its basis. All the main text is in his words. The only major additions appear in Part Five: his posthumous approval is assumed to coincide with the requirements of contemporary readers.

My revision has been greatly aided—indeed, made possible—by the active co-operation of the author's son, Mauricio González-Gordon, Marqués de Bonanza, who provided vital ancillary information and agreed with me that it is of genuine historical interest to preserve on record the efforts and the drive that so many men of different generations have dedicated to Sherry and to show how, over the years, they have contributed towards a wider knowledge, understanding and appreciation of this noble wine.

Therefore, virtually all the historical, technical, commercial, economic and legal information about Sherry has been kept as written by his father; and I accepted most of his courteous stylistic criticism of what might be described as adjectival exuberance in my own small contributions.

John Doxat
Camberley, Surrey
1990

Part One:
THE STORY

Chapter 1

Jerez de la Frontera

The town of Jerez de la Frontera has played an important role in the history of Spain and is unique for many reasons, above all as the centre of the Sherry industry. It seems appropriate therefore, in this opening chapter, to examine the origins and ancient history of Jerez itself. As it would be difficult to deal exhaustively with the subject without straying beyond the terms of reference of this book, these notes will be confined to a brief résumé of the extensive material already written, for which I am indebted to Juan Moreno de Guerra and Hipólito Sancho, both authorities on the history of Jerez.

Little or nothing is known with absolute certainty about the foundation, original site and earliest history of Jerez, nor do we know whether it actually existed at the time of the Tartessians,* prior to the coming of the Phoenician settlers, although there is a wealth of supposition on the subject. Some early historians affirm that it is more than likely that, before the Greeks reached Jerez, it was founded by the Phoenicians, natives of Chaldea, who, driven from the land of Canaan by the Israelites, reached the Iberian shores in about 1100 BC, or perhaps as early as the fifteenth century BC, and founded the town of *Gádir* (afterwards called *Gades* by the Romans, and known today as Cadiz); then later on, moving inland, established the town of *Xera*. This is perhaps the most likely theory, bearing in mind the essentially commercial outlook of the Phoenicians, who had probably heard reports of these fertile coastal lands and come more in search of new outlets for their merchandise than as conquerors intending to impose their rule and customs on the country.

In the fifth century Stephen of Byzantium quotes a reference by Theopompos to

---

* The oldest indigenous people in Southern Iberia, whose territory was bounded by the Duero in the north and the Salado de Conil in the south.

'the town of Xera near the Pillars of Hercules'. This is apparently the earliest known reference to Jerez. Although some authorities believe that 'Xera' almost certainly refers to the Jerez of today, others, among them César Pemán, a reliable authority on such matters, are of the opinion that it was really some distance away, on what is now the deserted site of *Cera* (Torrecera), about ten miles from Jerez; in each case the topography is similar: that is, high ground near a river. The root of the name, *Xer* or *Cer*, may be derived from one of the ancient languages of the country, Ilberian, Punic or Turdetano, and probably signified an encampment or fortification by a river. This could apply to other places in the region, such as *Bexer* (now Vejer).

Attempts have also been made to try to fix satisfactorily the location of Tartessos, which, according to early historians, lay between two arms of a river. It is possible that they assumed that the Guadalquivir and Guadalete were in fact two branches or arms of a single river; if so, then Tartessos could have stood exactly where Jerez does today.

Nothing has been preserved regarding the history of Xera in those remote times. This obscurity which surrounds the beginnings of Jerez has led historians to debate whether it might not be the site of the Roman settlement of Asta Regia, believed to have been founded originally by the Phoenicians. The ruins of this settlement are still to be seen on the Asta plateau, within the present municipal area of Jerez. Another suggestion is that Jerez may originally have been the town called Asidona.

Both theories are difficult to substantiate. It is true that Jerez did in fact appear in certain ecclesiastical documents as *Asidona*, but this is thought to be because the see of the Bishop of Asidona was temporarily centred there during the Moorish domination, Jerez affording greater security than the rightful episcopal see of Sidonia, which was constantly in the forefront of battle. *Xera* was almost certainly distinct from both Asidona and Asta Regia, and probably of greater importance than either; it is believed to have been laid waste by the Vandals in 409–14.

Ancient Relics

The city of Asidona may possibly have been situated very near to the modern site of Jerez, at the place called Las Huertas de Sidueña near El Portal, where there still stands a small fort or tower known as the Castle of Doña Blanca. In the immediate neighbourhood of this tiny castle various objects have been unearthed which relate to varying periods from primitive to mediaeval times. In 1936 shards of Roman pottery and a fragment of a Visigothic burial-stone were also found there.

It is certain that Sidonia (or *Sidueña*) still existed in the Middle Ages. The name appears in the 'White Book' of Seville Cathedral (the official census of parishes of that diocese, compiled in 1411), in which Sidueña is mentioned as an inhabited place, with the note that its church was served by four beneficiaries from Puerto de Santa María, who levied their tithes there.

Sidueña had probably been abandoned by 1472, because in that year it was considered a suitable site for the foundation of the Jerez Charterhouse of Our

Lady of Protection, and the Carthusian Order customarily establishes itself away from populated areas. Incidentally, the site was ultimately rejected on the grounds that it did not belong to Jerez.

In the seventh century B.C. the Tartessians took advantage of the decline of the Phoenicians to wage war on them, and defeated them in battle. The Phoenicians, for their own protection, sought the help of the Carthaginians, who later turned against the Phoenicians and likewise vanquished them. They also routed the Greeks, who, according to some historians, were already in Spain when the Phoenicians arrived. In 240 B.C. began the struggle between the Romans and the Carthaginians which ended, after a century of continuous strife, with the victory of the Romans in 133 B.C. It was in this year that Scipio reduced Numantia and proclaimed Spain a Roman province.

Other historians believe that Jerez was the Roman city of *Ceritium* or *Seritium*, citing as evidence the discovery in Jerez of many coins of the Roman era; inscriptions on stone tablets found in the neighbourhood seem to corroborate this. In the Jerez archaeological collection there is an interesting piece of Roman mosaic found near the town with—significantly—a decorated border depicting vine-leaves and tendrils.

With the information and records available today it is impossible to prove that any one of these theories is correct. It is known, however, that the district has seen cities built by many different cultures throughout the ages, and it is reasonable to suppose, since the Jerez which we know today has come to be the most important town in the area, that it has developed directly from these early settlements.

What can more positively be asserted is that the town of Jerez is the *Sherish* of the Moors, and that it is mainly of Arab origin.

The Roman domination of Spain came to an end when the barbarian peoples entered the country in 409. The Vandals then settled in the south, in the Roman province of Bætica, which they called *Wandalusia*; the same name (without the initial W) is still used today. In 414 the Visigoths came to Spain as allies of Imperial Rome. They made themselves masters of the country, which they ruled for three centuries, until in 711 the celebrated Battle of the Guadalete—'the River of Forgetfulness', as this Arabic name is sometimes translated—was fought.

This encounter marked the beginning of the Moorish domination of Spain, which was to have such a profound influence on the country and its customs during eight centuries (711–1492). It is not possible to pinpoint where this battle between Goth and Moor took place, but there are strong indications that it was either on the Plains of Aina, by the Guadalete three or four miles outside the boundaries of modern Jerez, or on the Barbate. Diego I. Parada y Barreto suggests that the Moors, in their advance from Gibraltar and Algeciras, followed the Roman road along the coast and halted within sight of Medina Sidonia, whilst the Goths came down from the centre of the peninsula, through Córdoba and Seville, until they reached Jerez, where the two armies faced each other across the Guadalete. The battle is said to have lasted eight days. The armies of the Goths were led by their King, Rodrigo, and the Saracens by Tariq ben Zeyad at the orders of Muza ben Noseir, Governor of Africa for Caliph Walid I. Contemporary chronicles relate that the Goths had a force of ninety or a hundred thousand men, the greater part armed only with slings and staves, and that the Moors numbered a hundred and thirty thousand. It is also recorded that this battle, which saw the end of the Gothic greatness in Spain, was the most bitterly fought of the period.

So far, no special research has been carried out into the years of Visigothic domination. Archaeological discoveries have brought to light various relics of the time in this district: for example, a font, classified as Visigothic in an article by Manuel Esteve in the *Archivo Español de Arte y Arqueologia*, was unearthed some years ago on the Peñuela estate, about nine miles from Jerez.

Since the Spanish version of this book was published, Señor Esteve has continued his research work, and it was only recently that he discovered a Greek bronze helmet (Corinthian style) of the seventeenth century B.C. on the banks of the Guadalete near Jerez, this being the oldest Greek artefact so far found in Spain. A memorial tablet, also of the Visigothic period, was discovered in the Sidueña valley; it bears the epitaph of a Christian woman called Fidenda. These and many other similar items from various parts of the province reveal the importance of places whose real names and precise locations are unknown owing to the lack of contemporary documents.

Origin of the Name

As regards the name which Jerez bore in the time of the Goths, Manuel de Bertemati, in an address delivered to the Jerez Royal Society of Economics and published in 1883, remarked that it was strange that there should be no Gothic document extant which made any reference to Jerez, although the rule of the Goths lasted for three centuries. However, there are some Arabic and Hispano-Latin texts on the closing stages of the Visigothic domination which give to Jerez the names of *Seritium* and *Scheris* referred to earlier. There is no doubt that the name of *Xerez* is a corruption of the Roman *Ceret*. Bertemati goes on to say:

> During the Emirate of Yussuf el Fehri a number of new political divisions were created, as a result of which Jerez began to assume greater importance, and from that date, 747–8, there is a trend towards independent government in Jerez. The area between the rivers Wad el Kebir [*Guadalquivir*] and Wad Iana [*Guadiana*] was the first of the large regions into which Moorish Spain was divided. Its capital was *Medina Corthoba* (Córdoba), and the principal provinces in this southern region included *Eschbilia* (Seville), *Yajen* (Jaén), *Scheduna* (Sidonia), *Elvira* (Granada) and *Malacca* (Málaga). Of lesser importance than these, but at the same time the seats of governors of relatively high rank, were *Esteija* (Ecija), *Carmuna* (Carmona), *Scheris* (Xerez) and others. . . .

It can thus be said that the Moors were the first to use the name of *Xerez*, which itself is a variant of *Xeryx*. Jerez is a more modern spelling. Other versions have been *Xares*, *Xereto* and *Xeres Sadunia*, the latter name being changed again, after the expulsion of the Moors, to *Xeres Sidonis* or *de Sidonia* or *de Sedueña*. These additions to the name imply that Jerez was indeed near to or actually within the jurisdiction of the Bishop of Asidona.

No real grounds exist for ascribing to Jerez any other names than the above, although many others have been suggested—indeed, there is probably no other place in Spain with such a wealth of hypothetical names. There is practically no ancient city of unknown or doubtful location which has not been identified with Jerez. Father Martín de Roa, writing on this subject of the origins, antiquity and name of Jerez, remarks that the only people who did not attempt to give a name to the city were the Jews—it is perhaps remarkable that in the long list of names ascribed to the town there should be no hint of a connection between Jerez and Jericho!

Since the publication of the Spanish edition of this book a complete study of the etymology of the name of Jerez and its wine has been carried out by an eminent professor of Arabic, Dr. Jaime Oliver Asín, a member of the Spanish Major Scientific Research Council.

Of interest in this respect is a fragment of an Arabic map of the known world in 1154, drawn by El Idrisi, a Moorish writer of the twelfth century, and Geographer Royal to King Roger II of Sicily. This map was published by Konrad Miller* and is a reproduction of the original '*Mappae Arabica, Idrisi*', which are in Oxford and Paris; as it was made well over three centuries before America was discovered it must have been one of the first 'world' maps known. The old name of *Seris* can be clearly seen on the present site of Jerez.

The period of Moorish-Arab domination which gave Jerez its present name is the most interesting of all. From it stem the legacy of buildings and monuments, the popular music and customs of the district, and indeed the temperament of its people, endowed as they are with their own very distinctive characteristics.

The known history of Jerez in those times can be divided into six main periods. First, that marked by the destruction of the armies of Rodrigo in 711 and the resistance of the city of Sidonia, which was besieged, conquered and possibly destroyed: this marks the first stage of Moorish domination, and numerous references exist to the action of the Moorish cavalry from Jerez in their skirmishes against the Christians. Secondly, the period following the invasions of the Normans, who reached the coast in about 844 and 858 and destroyed Sidonia, through which they passed on their way to Seville. It would seem that, then as now, the natives of the colder countries of the north were attracted back irresistibly again and again by the warmth of the Spanish sun and the glow of the wine. Thirdly, the uprising against the Caliphate and the formation, in about 1009, of small independent Moslem states known as the Taifa Kingdoms. These included the Kingdom of Seville, established from 1023 to 1091 under the rule of the Moorish dynasty known as the Abbadids, who little by little brought under control the lesser neighbouring kingdoms, including Sherish (1053). This was a

* *Atlas*, Stuttgart, 1927.

period of marked advancement in literature and the arts. The fourth period, 1056–1146, is covered by the occupation of the Almoravids, an Arab tribe from the Atlas. The most outstanding event relating to Sherish during that time was the incursion as far as Cadiz of Alfonso VII ('the Emperor'), who besieged and destroyed Jerez in 1133. In the fifth period, that of the ascendancy of the Taifa Almoravids, rebel Arab chieftains assumed sovereignty over the towns and cities where they were acting as satraps. During this time the Arab leader Abengarrun proclaimed himself ruler of Jerez and the neighbouring town of Arcos.

The sixth and last period is the most important. It saw the rise to power of the Almohads, the Moorish race which succeeded the Almoravids. Their domination, which began in Jerez on 25 May 1145, was marked by great progress in the arts, literature and general culture. A well-known and highly esteemed historian, Yussuf ben Omar, often quoted by his contemporaries, was born in Sherish during that time. Some of the buildings destroyed by the Christians during the siege of 1133 were rebuilt, including the gateways and the fortified keeps defending them. (These towers were called *albarranas*, from the Arabic word meaning 'unmarried,' because their guardians were all celibate.) The Alcázar fortress, which still stands, no doubt also dates from that period. The Almohads may well have minted their own money, to judge by the large number of square-shaped coins found near Jerez.

As a local historian, Joaquín Portillo, has pointed out, Jerez and its surrounding countryside have known and experienced, in turn, the courage of the Phoenicians, the skill and guile of the Greeks and Carthaginians, the resourceful enterprise of the Romans and the valour of the Goths and Vandals. And it was here that Spain mourned the passing of the Gothic grandeur and the ascendancy of the savage Moslem, whose crescent banners rode high and unchallenged until the town was finally retaken by the Christians in 1264.

The Defeat of The Moors

The *Reconquista*—that is to say, the reconquest of Spain from the Moors—started at Covadonga, in the northern province of Asturias, in 717 (six years after the Battle of Guadalete), when Pelayo regrouped the remnants of the forces of his kinsman Rodrigo. But the movement had no effect in Jerez until the reign of Ferdinand III ('el Santo', 1217–52). In the *Crónica General,* the Moors' own record of their domination of Spain (as edited by Ramón Menéndez Pidal)*, there is a chapter entitled 'An Account of the Conquests which the King, Don Fernando, made after taking Seville'. It reads in part:

> After the King had conquered Seville and it was again inhabited and at peace . . . he then took Xerez, Medina, Alcalá, Beier and Sancta Maria del Puerto and Calez which lies in the sea and Solucar de el Alpechin, then Arcos and Lebrixa, Rota and Trebuxena. All places from the coast inland he captured, either in combat or by act of surrender, save Niebla, which was taken from him.

* Madrid, 1906.

This happened in 1251: that is, 241 years before the final stage of the *Reconquista*, which ended when Granada was taken by the 'Catholic Monarchs', Ferdinand and Isabella, on 6 January 1492. According to the Arab chroniclers, whose versions agree entirely with that of the *Crónica General*, Jerez submitted by an act of surrender and no actual fighting was involved. Nor did Ferdinand III come to Jerez: instead Sanchit, the King of Jerez, went to him to pay homage. This Moorish ruler thus became a vassal of the King of Castile, and as such confirmed certain privileges which the Castilian monarch had granted to Jerez.

Alfonso the Wise

The account in the *Crónica de Don Alfonso* X ('The Wise', who succeeded his father Ferdinand III) differs somewhat from the above, for in Chapter IV, entitled 'Of how the King Don Alfonso conquered Sherish and Arcos and Lebrixa and of Matters which befell in that Year [1255]', we read:

> And as there were very near to this city [Seville] the King of Niebla and the Algarve who was called Abenabad and another who was lord of Xerez and was called Abenabit . . . the King Don Alfonso considered it wiser first to subdue the town of Xerez and he thereupon gathered together his forces and went to take the town and laid siege to it for one month. The Moors of those parts, to prevent the King's men from cutting down or destroying their olive groves and orchards, being desirous of keeping and safeguarding their properties . . . and also bearing in mind that they were discontented with their present lord, before the King should make use of arms or do hurt to their lands and possessions . . . sent word to him that if he would but leave them in their homes with all their chattels they would yield the town to him and would pay to him each year the tribute they paid to their master. . . . And the King . . . consented and granted their request and afterwards . . . the Moorish lord of the town who was in the Alcázar was told to leave that place and to reach an agreement with Alfonso, it being arranged between them that he should have safe conduct thence with all that belonged to him. And the Alcázar was surrendered to the King who revictualled and rearmed it and delivered it to Don Nuño de Lara to hold in fief for him and Don Nuño set in charge of it one Garci Gómez Carrillo and the King permitted the Moors of the city to reside there and to retain their homes and possessions.

It would appear from this that in any event neither Ferdinand III nor his son Alfonso X took the city by force of arms but that it was surrendered to one or the other after negotiations and that the inhabitants became vassals of the King of Castile.

Arab Evidence

Arab chroniclers confirm this in two texts which have survived, the *Cartár* (translated by A. Huici*), and the *Anonymous Chronicle of Madrid* (or of

* Barcelona, 1917.

23

Copenhagen, as it is sometimes called), also translated by Huici. The authors of both Chronicles lived at the time of the events related. The second refers to the truce concluded by Ferdinand III shortly after the conquest of Córdoba in 1236, saying that after the battle of Las Navas de Tolosa the arms of Castile had always triumphed over the Moslems. It also refers to the separate peace made by Jerez for twenty years (from 1242), by the terms of which the Christians were allowed to live together with the Moslems while paying tribute to the Kings of Castile. This continued until the Christians rose in rebellion against the Moors and were expelled from the town as a punishment in 1261. As the *Anonymous Chronicle of Madrid and Copenhagen* relates it: 'In this year [1261], the Will of God was fulfilled in Xerez. The Christians had entered the fortified city on the condition that they should live at peace therein. It came about that, blinded and misled by the counsels of Satan, they rose up within the city against the Moslems who cast them out . . .' The document adds that later (in 1264) the Christians allied themselves with the forces of a dissident Arab tribe called the Benimerins, who, led by Mohamed ben Idris ben Adbelhac, had crossed the Strait of Gibraltar. The Chronicle continues:

> The Emir Abu Abdullah Alahmar, through his son the Emir Alaslah, made peace with Alfonso, leader of the Christians [in 1267]. By the terms of this peace, forty fortified places under Moorish rule were yielded up this being the greater part of Andalus including Xerez, Medina, Alcalá. . . . I was told, on good and reliable authority, that the total number of towns and large, well-defended fortresses ceded by Alahmar to Alfonso was 105 . . .

Tradition has it that on 9 October 1264, the Feast of St Dionysus Areopagiticus, the Christians launched a general offensive on Jerez and succeeded in entering the city, raising the symbol of the Holy Cross on its walls and battlements. From that time Jerez became the principal fortress in the area and the residence of the Captains General and *Adelantados* (or Governors) of the *frontera* (border territory) between the Moslems and the Christians.

In his unpublished history of Jerez the Spanish writer Spínola says:

> [King Alfonso X] granted as a coat of arms to the city the waves of the sea, azure and argent, telling his knights that, just as the waves of the ocean are in constant motion, beating against the cliffs, so would their constancy be perpetually attacked by their enemies; and he ordered also that the lions and castles of his own royal coat of arms should appear thereon, as an orle, saying that they were a symbol of strength. And although this is known only by ancient tradition, it is described in a letter which the King sent later to one of the knights he left in command of the Olive Tree Gate at Xerez, known today as the Rota Gate, which letter is still in the possession of his descendants. . . .

This letter, which is copied in its entirety by Spínola, contains the reference:

> . . . as a guerdon and reward, it is granted that you add to your device the waves, castles and lions which we gave to our City of Xerez as its device, being a

symbol and token of constancy. Given at the Royal Siege of Toro on 22 August, Era 1307, in the Year of our Lord 1269.

The addition of the words *de la Frontera* to the name of Jerez came about because, for many years after the conquest of the town by Alfonso the Wise, it was on the frontier which separated the Moslem army from the domains of the Kings of Castile. The use of this suffix was a privilege granted by John I on 2 April 1380.

Royal Recognition

During the ensuing century, the knights of Jerez and their followers took a prominent part in the many battles and skirmishes between the conquering monarchs and the Moors, and distinguished themselves in many feats of arms. For this reason Jerez figures among the cities of Spain which have merited the prefix of '*Muy noble y muy leal Ciudad*' ('Most Noble and Most Loyal City'). It was granted to Jerez by Henry IV (1451–74), who also decreed that its citizens should 'for all time be exempt from the exaction of loans and demands for money, both those living within the walls and those without'. Spínola remarks that there is no instance of any other Spanish town's receiving such privileged treatment.

Since 1860 the members of the Town Council of Jerez have had the right to be addressed as 'Their Excellencies', and the waves surrounded by the castles and lions of Castile are still to be seen on the town's coat of arms.

From the time of the recapture of Jerez by the Christians its citizens have taken part in many important battles. Amongst these mention must be made of Tarifa (1291); the Plains of Aina (1335); the famous encounter on the Salado (1340), where the city gained its historic banner; and Jimena (1431). Jerez also played a part in the taking of Utrera in 1477 when that town refused to receive Ferdinand and Isabella, who at the time were resident in the Alcácar of Jerez.

The *Jerezanos* (citizens of Jerez) also took part, under the command of the Marqués de Cádiz, in the taking of many towns such as Alhama, Zahara and Cardela (1314 to 1472) and Montefrío, during the reconquest of Granada in 1492. Jerez also always had the special duty of coming to aid the coastal towns when they were threatened by attack, whether from Moors, Turks or English. Sir Francis Drake attacked Cadiz in 1574 and 1596. Another British squadron which raided the town in 1625 also called for the mobilization of a troop of Jerezanos. During the reign of Charles V Jerez also contributed men and ships for the expeditions to African territory, and for the great fleets of Philip II, including the illfated Invincible Armada of 1588, in which Barahona, an illustrious citizen of Jerez, was among those who lost their lives.

Tradition relates that Columbus visited Jerez before setting out on his first voyage on 3 August 1492 and is believed to have stayed for a time in the Mercedario Convent. In a document signed by Isabella, dated May 1493 and now preserved in the Municipal Archives of Jerez, the Queen gives an order for 804 *fanegas* (about 1,300 bushels) of wheat to be supplied by the city to Admiral Colón (Columbus) for his second voyage of exploration, which he began on 25 September 1493 with a fleet of fourteen galleons and many smaller craft. Jerez also supplied its quota of men for the enterprise, and the chaplain who accompanied Columbus was Friar Jorge de Santiago, Prior of the Mercedario Convent in Jerez, who later became head of his Order in Castile and chaplain to Ferdinand and Isabella.

Whenever that period of Spanish history is recalled it brings to mind to the people of Jerez the famous explorer Alvar Núñez Cabeza de Vaca, born in 1490. He took part in the conquest of Florida and of the River Plate, and was renowned both for his valour and for his probity in the face of privation and hardship for the greater glory of Spain. An American writer, Morris Bishop, has published a fine account of the hazardous exploits of this distinguished Jerezano.* The author was apparently unaware, however, that the family of Núñez Cabeza de Vaca owned property and vineyards in Jerez and were producers of Sherry. It may well be that on his journeyings in North and South America the explorer took with him the wine of his native town, thus becoming one of the first of that long line of ambassadors of Sherry who have since spread its fame throughout the world.

Historical Descriptions

El Idrisi says of Jerez in his *Description of Spain*:

> It is three days' journey from Carmona to Xerez, an outlying town in the province of Sidonia.

From Seville to Xerez two full days' travel are necessary.

Xerez is a fortified town of medium size, surrounded by ramparts. The neighbouring country is of agreeable aspect, consisting as it does of vineyards, olive groves and orchards of fig trees. Wheat is grown, and all necessary foodstuffs can be procured at reasonable prices.

Rallón, a seventeenth-century historian, describes the town:†

Seen . . . from the south, it is situated on the crest of a hill, at the foot of which is the dry river bed in which at one time ran the waters of the Guadalete. [*This river, stretching some eighty miles from source to estuary, rises at the Peñón de San Cristóbal (St Christopher's Peak) near the town of Grazalema, which at an altitude of 5,600 feet is the highest point in the province. Rallón goes on to say that there are abundant fish in the river, including dace, barbel, eels, freshwater turtles and, most plentiful of all, shad.*] From the crest, where Jerez is situated, the town stretches towards north, east and west, spread over the plain in the form of an imperfect parallelogram, wider from east to west than from north to south. The four angles or corners of the town, as is the Moorish custom, face the four points of the compass, the disposition of the town and of the walls surrounding it being indisputably Moorish. At each of the four corners there is an octagonal *albarrana* tower, the walls are made of *argamasa [exceptionally strong Moorish mortar]*. At one time the town had no more than four gates or

---

* *The Odyssey of Cabeza de Vaca* (Appleton, 1933).
† *Historia de Xerez*, vol. V.

entrances, which still stand, each with its Alcázar [*fortified keep*], opening onto a courtyard which must be crossed in order to reach the second gate which gives access to the city. . . . These gateways are situated one on each side of the town, and there are in addition eight posterns which were opened to assist the movement of trade. . . . In the angle between east and south and within the city walls is situated the Alcázar Palace, which was at one time the Royal residence; it is square in shape and surrounded by its own imposing ramparts.

The area of the town was then about a hundred and eighty acres and the perimeter wall measured 4,800 *varas** (about four kilometres). Manuel de Bertemati was of the opinion that although the walls were Moorish they may possibly have been built on Roman foundations.

Two of the posterns giving access to the town were opened in 1500 to meet the needs of trade. They were called the *Puertas Nuevas* (New Gates); only one remains today. The other gateways and entrances were of various types—*postigos* (posterns), *arcos* (archways), *boquetes* (gaps) and *agujeros* (openings). Of these there remain today the Arco de Rastro near the fishmarket, the Agujero de Cuatro Juanes in what is now the main street, the Boquete de la Por-vera and a *boquete* in Calle Ancha, close to the *albarrana* tower already mentioned.

Jerez today covers about 500 hectares (1,250 acres), and though irregular in form is a clean and attractive town, thanks in part to the plentiful water-supply in what is essentially a dry district. The principal source of water since 1869 has been the springs of Tempul, which are also said to have supplied in Roman times the city of Cadiz, through an ancient aqueduct constructed and paid for by Lucius Cornelius Balbus ('the Conqueror') in 14 BC. Substantial remains of this remarkable structure can still be seen to this day, and parts of the present Jerez water-supply pipeline follow the route of the Old Roman aqueduct.

In the old part of the town the streets are narrow and tortuous, whereas in the modern sector they have been widened and paved to cope with modern traffic, which is particularly heavy as the main road from Cadiz to Madrid passes through the town.

A Century Ago

The picture a century ago was a very different one. By kind permission of C. Riddell Williams, an extract from a letter written by George Suter, British Vice-Consul in Jerez from 1869–87 and resident of the town since 1831, is reproduced here. Mr Suter witnessed the cholera epidemic in Jerez in 1834, in which year the city's first public cemetery was built. The letter reads:

The town was large and straggling, though with some good streets and several squares or open spaces. Hackney carriages there were none, and the place only boasted of three private vehicles, all of them of immense size and antiquated form. One of them, belonging to a marqués, was drawn by mules with rope

* The *vara* is the Castilian yard of about 83 cm. (33 ins.).

harness and when the noble owner wished to get either out or into his carriage, a three-legged stool had to be placed at the door by the footman in lieu of the normal steps. None of the streets were either drained, paved or lighted, so that in wet weather getting from one house to another was anything but an easy task, and I remember having seen stepping-stones in the chief street to enable people to cross it wihout having to wade knee-deep in mud or water. But if getting about was not an easy or pleasant matter in the daytime, much less so was it at night, though those whose business or pleasure obliged them to leave their houses after dark, managed somehow; if it was a family bound for the theatre or to a *tertulia* or evening party, it would be preceded by a servant carrying a lighted torch in one hand and a stout cudgel in the other. As to the young men, we had adopted a custom of having a small lantern with a piece of wax candle in it attached to the high-peaked hats then worn and a slight movement of the head would throw the light in any direction and reveal the secrets of dark corners or suspicious doorways.

Mention must be made here of the main square of Jerez, which today, as for many years past, is still the hub and centre of the town's activities—the Plaza del Arenal. It is believed that this name dates from about 1343, during the reign of Alfonso XI. This monarch died of the plague during the Siege of Gibraltar, then occupied by the Moors, and his entrails were brought to Jerez and interred in the Chapel of Santa María del Alcázar, his body being taken to Seville.

Manuel de Bertemati records that during one of the visits of Alfonso XI to Jerez two knights, Per Rodríguez de Avila and Rui Perez de Viedma, accused each other of treason and, in spite of the King's willingness to mediate in the dispute, refused to retract and challenged each other to mortal combat. An enclosure was set up for the pupose in the Plaza (then called the Campo de la Torrecilla, owing to its proximity to a small tower or fort near the eastern gate of the town), and although they fought on two successive days no conclusive result was reached; the King then went down into the arena and called a halt, pardoning and reinstating the two knights.

The balconies of the buildings surrounding the square used to serve as vantage-points for spectators at the bull-fights, jousts and tourneys held there and until comparatively recently the title deeds of the balconies were in many cases separate from those pertaining to the buildings themselves.

The Plaza del Arenal has borne many other names, reflecting the political changes in Spanish history—for example, Plaza de la Constitución at various times, Plaza de Fernando VII, de Isabel II, de Alfonso XII and de la República. Its official name is now Plaza de los Reyes Católicos (of the Catholic Monarchs), although everyone in Jerez still calls it by its original name, Plaza del Arenal.

Chapter 2
Sherry through the Ages

Bread and wine, though both are man-made products, have played a fundamental part in the history of mankind. No doubt it was both a cause and an effect of this that they were chosen by Our Lord for the institution of the Holy Sacrament. There are many references to wine in the Scriptures. The first to come to mind is when Noah, after the Flood, at the age of 601, sampled the wine from the vines he had planted, of which we are told that he partook with rather less than proper moderation. How that wine was made, what its quality was, and how much Noah drank are unknown; but evidently it was not Sherry, which cheers the spirit and sharpens the wit, for if it had been Ham would not have got away with mocking Noah as he did; in fact rather the reverse would have happened.

It is significant that Our Lord, at the start of his life on earth, should have performed his first miracle by changing water into wine, at the wedding feast of Cana. So much for the claim made by the detractors of wine that even when taken in moderation it is harmful to the spiritual and physical well-being of mankind. Throughout the Bible and the Apocrypha there are numerous further references to wine as, for example, in Psalm 104 v.15 ('wine that maketh glad the heart of man'), in the Books of Proverbs and Ecclesiasticus and in the First Epistle of St Paul to Timothy, in which Paul urges his disciple, who is frequently ill, not to drink water alone but to mix it with a little wine to preserve his health.

There are many references to 'wines from the East' in ancient history. These included Greek wines and, more especially, those of Falerno in the region of the Campania in southern Italy, which Horace mentions.* Other writers have also praised the Falernian wines, such as Strabo—who asserted that they reached their peak when they were ten years old—and Pliny the Younger.

* *Odes, ii, 3.*

It was England that first established the commercial importance of wine. André Simon has pointed out that there is no extant reference to any commerce in wines before the fifth century, although it is probable that the Romans, during their occupation of the British Isles, imported wine into the country.* It is believed that French wines were being imported into England by the ninth century, so that by the tenth they were producing appreciable revenue for the English exchequer. Those were certainly the 'good old days', in spite of the tax, for Mr Simon points out that wine was sold in the twelfth century at less than a halfpenny a gallon. The combination of low prices and low temperatures must have done much to increase the popularity of wine in England, and probably explains why the British have continued to occupy a leading position in the wine-import trade ever since. For political and geographical reasons French wines were no doubt the first to be imported into England; furthermore, on the marriage in the twelfth century of Eleanor of Aquitaine to Henry Plantagenet (afterwards Henry II), many of the Bordeaux vineyards passed to the English Crown as part of her dowry.

As far as Spain is concerned, no mention is made of her wines, although the vineyards had existed for centuries, until the time of the Roman colonization of the country. Then the wines of the Eastern seaboard were beginning to become well known and were compared with the best that Italy could produce. Special mention was made of the wines of Bætica (Andalusia), and it is probable that wine was known in this district as early as the time of the Phoenicians.

In his writings on the discoveries at Monte Testaceo in Rome, Bonsor mentions wine vessels which bore the mark of Andalusian potters, and according to Juan Moreno de Guerra this might possibly be confirmed by examination of the pottery shards found in large quantities in an olive-grove near Puerto Real, between Jerez and Cadiz. In Roman times Puerto Real was a centre for the production of amphorae for transport by sea, and abundant fragments have been found in the River San Pedro, which in ancient times was the shipping-point used by Jerez; Puerto Real was, in fact, the port of the Jerez district, of which it technically formed part until near the end of the sixteenth century when it became independent.

The Arab historian Abubenque Mohammed Rassis, writing during the second half of the tenth century, makes special mention of the importance of Jerez, which he calls *Xerez Saduña* or *Xerez Sidonia*. He refers to the active trade in gold and silver from the local mines as well as in oil, wine, cereals and other local produce, just as had previously been described by Aristotle. Similar references were also made by Strabo, and in the Books of Maccabees, the first two books of the Apocrypha, believed to have been written about 164 B.C.

Although the cultivation of some of the vineyards continued during the Moorish domination, the wine-producing industry undoubtedly suffered a considerable setback from the Moslem ban on alcohol. Nevertheless, it is equally certain that the trade did not completely disappear from Jerez, although the Arabs

* *The Blood of the Grape* (Duckworth, 1920).

preferred to use the vineyards for the production of raisins, an industry which continued to flourish long after Jerez was reoccupied by the Christians: there is a record giving the raisin export quota for 1642 as 2,320 hundredweight.

It is also certain that the Arabs, in spite of the Prophet's prohibition, were not total abstainers, as is shown by the Bacchic theme in much of Arabic-Andalusian poetry, a selection of which was translated by Emilio García Gómez in 1930. The Arab host used to send out invitations to his friends in verse. Abdul Aziz Abenal Cabtorna wrote: 'The day is damp with dew and the cheek of the earth is covered with a down of grass. Thy friend invites thee to partake of the enjoyment of the two pots now cooking on the hearth, which give forth an excellent aroma, and of a jug of wine in this most beautiful place. More could he offer should he so desire, but it is not seemly that too much pomp should be displayed for a friend.' The last Moorish ruler of Seville, Al Motamid the 'Poet King', was so fond of wine that he openly derided those who drank only water.

When the Moors were finally expelled from Jerez in 1264 a record was compiled giving details of the redistribution of its lands, and this document indicates that, in the parish precincts of San Mateo, San Salvador and San Lucas, there already existed many buildings called *bodegas*.* This is additional proof that the wine industry did not entirely disappear during the long Moorish occupation.

In 1265, according to Mesa Ginete, Alfonso X appointed delegates representing the bakers, vintners, cattle-breeders and other trades to undertake the collection of funds for the establishment of the Church of San Salvador.† This same monarch took steps to encourage the development of vine cultivation, and allotted by decree *six aranzadas*†† (about seven acres) to each of the forty councillors and knights of the fief of Jerez. This consisted half of established vineyards and half of land suitable for the planting of young vines. It is probable that the vineyards referred to in this decree were on the outskirts of the town, according to Diego Parada y Barreto.§ Referring to the diary of the military operations of Yussuf, who besieged Jerez in the reign of Sancho the Brave, he writes:

> The vineyards were near the town, between it and the Guadalete, because, according to the diary, on 30 May 1285. Yussuf moved his camp to this side of the river, between it and the town, setting it up *among the vineyards* and orchards, which shows that those vineyards were planted in what are nowadays called the *arenas*, around the area where most of the orchards and cultivated lands were, and indeed still are, to be found; so that these sandy soil vineyards can be considered the oldest in Jerez.

---

* *Libro del Repartimiento de Jerez.*
† *Historia de Xerez*, p.100.
†† The *aranzada* is the standard unit of measurement in the Jerez vineyards, equal to 1.17 acres (0.475 hectares). It originally represented the area that one yoke of oxen could plough in a full working day.
§*Notes on the history and present state of the cultivation of the vine and of the wine trade in Jerez* (1868).

In the church of San Lucas in Jerez the decorative Moorish-style motif in one of the arches on the left side depicts vine-leaves, instead of the more orthodox carvings of oak-leaves or thistles. This shows the economic importance attached to the vine in the locality at the time when this arch was built, about the middle of the fourteenth century. In 1402 Henry III issued a decree proscribing the uprooting of vines and olive trees, under penalty of heavy fines.

It seems quite possible that prior to the fourteenth century Sherry was chiefly a wine for local or regional consumption, and that such stocks as there were before that date were customarily housed in monasteries and convents. Agustín Muñoz mentions that the Carthusians, who came to Jerez in the fifteenth century, had their bodega at 8, Calle Naranjas.* It appears that the bodega was not a very large one, for it measured only twelve *varas* wide by thirty-nine long, that is to say a total overall area of about 335 square metres, so the stock of wine could not have been very great.

Early Exports

There is general agreement that the export of Jerez or Sherry wine, especially to the English market, began at a very early date, and some authorities maintain that there are authentic documents to show that Sherry was known in England during the reign of the Norman King Henry I (1100–35), although this seems highly improbable as at that time the Jerez district was under Arab rule. There can be little doubt, however, that England was the principal market for the early exports of Sherry, though the date is more likely to be during the first half of the fourteenth century, in the reign of Edward III, who, as André Simon records, banned the transfer of currency abroad in order to force French exporters to take English goods in exchange for their wines; this had the effect of driving away the French shippers, who then concentrated on the Flemish market.† As a result of discouraging these foreign traders, who had normally shipped the wines themselves, the English were ultimately forced to send their own ships to the south of France to collect the wine, which probably accounted in part for the rapid growth and development of the English merchant fleet. It seems likely, then, that Spanish wine was taken on board English ships when they put in at Spanish ports on their frequent voyages. This is in contrast to the trade between Portugal and England, which seems to have begun when Portuguese fishermen carried wine to England as barter for English goods.

There is a wealth of information available in Jerez dealing with early Sherry exports to the northern countries. Abundant documentary evidence exists in the Municipal Archives and in the College of Notaries Public. Although the latter college was founded in Jerez in 1320, its oldest documents date back only to 1411. The Minutes of the Jerez Town Council, however, are available from 1409, and extracts from these will be quoted from time to time in this chapter.

* *Las Calles de Jerez.*
† *The Blood of the Grape.*

The natural harbour of the Bay of Cadiz was either the mouth of the Guadalete at Puerto de Santa María or Matagorda, near Puerto Real, at the estuary of the River San Pedro (in fact, another mouth of the Guadalete), where Jerez had a fishing harbour. There was a flourishing pottery industry at near-by Argamasilla, which provided the wine vessels, jugs and amphorae so essential for the transport of the liquid wealth of the region, which includes not only wine and oil but also water from the many natural springs that still exist today.

Communication with the interior was ensured from Roman times by an ample causeway with magnificent bridges crossing rivers and sea-inlets at numerous points along the coastline between the 'island' of Cadiz and the Guadalete. This strip of coast was, in fact, given by the Arabs the name of *Alkanatir*, meaning 'the bridges'. Two fortresses stood guard over the area, one on the isthmus of Cadiz, a blend of church and castle, and the other, of the same origin, which was probably used as a Customs house or perhaps as a lighthouse, at a place called by the Christians Santa María.

During the fifteenth century the production of wine in Jerez began to reach substantial proportions. This may be attributed partly to a protective decree issued by Henry III of Castile, and partly also to the start of overseas trade.

Among the topics discussed at a meeting of the Jerez Town Council on 22 July 1427 were certain acts of piracy involving Spain and the Low Countries, from which it would appear that Spanish ships, manned by seamen from the northern province of Vizcaya, had been carrying on trade with Flanders. There are also references in the Council minutes for 1431–5 dealing with the export of wine. In this last year an agreement was reached to prohibit any further exports (then called 'sacas', literally 'drawings-off' or 'takings-away') owing to the serious shortage, and instead of any more wine's being exported for that year wine from other parts of Spain was allowed into the Jerez zone. A similar crisis arose in 1437, according to a record dated 5 April. In fact, in almost every year for which there are records there is a reference to alterations in price or to the general difficulties (or lack of them) affecting the sale of wine abroad.

The planting of vines in Jerez in what are called the *afuera* (outlying) vineyards of *albariza** soil probably began about this time, since it is known that in 1431 an agreement was reached fixing the boundaries between Jerez and Puerto de Santa María, in which reference is made to the albariza vineyards of the Balbaína district and the La Gallega vineyard, which marked the borderline between the two towns.

In August 1437 the Jerez Council was forced to destroy some beehives near the vineyards of the Carrascal district to avert possible damage to the grapes. It seems that much of the cultivated land of this region had originally been used for olive groves and was subsequently given over to vine plantation. Father Martín de Roa, SJ, to whose works I have previously referred, says: 'This region was famous for its wine, wheat, oil, honey, beeswax and other products which were sent to foreign

---

* For a discussion of the various vineyard soils of Jerez, see Part Two—Chapter 2.

lands. Although there is no excess of oil of good quality, the farmers are more disposed to plant vines, to maintain the considerable exports of sweet and full-bodied wines which meet with such ready acceptance abroad.'

In the Town Council records for 9 March 1468 there is another account of an act of piracy, this time committed by an English vessel, probably carrying off wine from this region, the plaintiff being a native of Jerez. Similar acts by the Portuguese are recorded on 20 June 1471.

Exports to England

It is believed by some that the regular export of Sherry to England did not begin until the reign of Henry VII (1485–1509), when ties between the two countries were temporarily strengthened by the marriage of his son Henry (later Henry VIII) to Katharine of Aragon, daughter of Ferdinand and Isabella of Spain. Bartolomé Gutiérrez's *History of Jerez* has an account of the role played by foreigners in the Jerez wine trade at that time. The author writes:

> On 13 September 1491 a public declaration was made by the local judges and deputies in Jerez to the effect that all persons, both Spanish and foreign, resident or non-resident, in the town, would be allowed to ship their *romania* wines, or any other product of their properties, free of tax providing they declared such products to be the produce of Jerez and swore this oath before the Official Notary, who would act as witness without charge.*

For reasons that are unknown, this *romania* wine, which was produced throughout the district, was not consumed locally but was always exported, and in fact when the *saca* was prohibited from time to time, the surplus had to be destroyed, with a consequent loss to the producers. There is a curious reference in the Ordinance of the Chief Magistrate of Jerez, the Marqués de Cádiz, dated 8 November 1482, which relates to the newly established town of Regla de Santa María, now called Chipiona. These regulations point out the Magistrate's knowledge of the present and future shipping arrangements from Chipiona, and his intention of ensuring that the wine shipped from there should be in good condition and not mixed or blended with musts of inferior-quality grapes, to the subsequent detriment of the export trade and its good name; and that this wine should therefore be prepared only from selected varieties which were, in order, Torrontés, Fergusano and Verde Agudillo, all especially suitable for the process used in the Jerez district. At the same time the Ordinance added that a fine of 5,000 *maravedis* would be imposed for any contravention of that order.

By the beginning of the sixteenth century there were already numerous English traders or agents in the district. When a new Mayor, Gonzalo Bernal de la Becerra, took office in Chipiona on 10 May 1519, he had to render homage to the son of the Duke of Arcos who was then 'Señor de la Villa', accompanied by a sponsor of noble birth, on this occasion 'the Englishman Juan Oste of this town [*Chipiona*] known to be and accepted as a *fijodalgo* [*old spelling of* hidalgo, "*noble*"]'. This

* *Historia de Xerez*, III, 286.

gives some idea of the social standing of Englishmen who came to the Jerez district as merchants and exporters.

An Agent's Preference

There is another intriguing reference to an English agent in the municipal records dated 6 September 1530, which deals with the petition of one Juan Esvique.

> [He] has for many years dwelt in the town and has bought both wine and oil, as well as dealing in other merchandise; and this town has benefited from his industry, because whereas he formerly traded in Sanlúcar, where he was in the service of the Duke [*of Medina Sidonia*], he formed the opinion that the wines of Jerez are better, and so decided to come and reside here and to induce all the people of England to purchase as much of these wines as they required, and this they have done.

The petition goes on to say that the recent decree prohibits anyone, regardless of nationality, from acting as another's agent for the purchase of wine, under strict penalty of a fine. Apparently Esvique had negotiated at some length with the authorities about this matter, pointing out the unreasonable expense incurred by 'rich English merchants' if they had to come abroad themselves on every occasion to conduct their business, and at the same time suing for the repeal of the Ordinance, since if a penalty were to be imposed for each transgression the cost of the wine would be too high and the export trade would accordingly suffer. Esvique (could this be a misreading of 'Esquire'?) goes on to say:

> I consider myself a native of this city and have many friends among the vintners here, and I have counselled them not to sell cheaply when they may be certain of obtaining higher prices: for butts worth five ducats I have offered five and a half and six ducats; and furthermore I have shown yet another civility towards them in that I have offered to supply anything they need for their vintages . . . These considerations ought to be taken into account and, if necessary, be inquired into further and investigated *in continenti*. I can bring proof of my statements, and I say that if merchants from Vizcaya, Burgos and Portugal can have their agents in this town to buy wine for them and to do business without themselves being present, and this is tolerated, then it is the more fair and just that I and those of my nation should be allowed to do so too, because the profit to this city therefrom is so much the greater. So far, the ships from my country have not arrived, but when they do all this will be clearly shown. The brokers from this city, motivated by passion and greed, have treated me ill and unfairly and have themselves provoked the Ordinances which Your Excellency has been pleased to enact. . . .

In consequence of acting for others Esvique was fined 6,000 *maravedis* and exiled for six months. He ends his appeal by observing how justified he would be in leaving the country and persuading his countrymen not to come to Jerez any more in view of the way in which they would be received.

Apart from the local consumption and exports, another important consumer of the wines of the Jerez district in the fifteenth century was the Spanish armed forces. Andrés Hidalgo Ortega says that in the Jerez Municipal Archives there is a letter written by King John II from Córdoba on 31 May 1431, in which he says that his troops are assembled and ready to move into the Plain of Granada, and that Jerez is to supply them with barley, bread and 2,300 *arrobas* of wine.* And a fortnight later the town had to supply the same quantity again. On another occasion 5,000 arrobas of wine were sent to the town of Loja, where the troops were stationed in 1482.†

Red vs. White

Here something should be said of the variety of Sherry that was probably made in Jerez about that time. According to Parada y Barreto, both red and white wines were produced, although the red was held in greater esteem, as is shown by a resolution passed by the Jerez Council on Wednesday 13 September 1410. Here: '. . . the Council decided to dispatch a substantial present to Don Alonso Núñez de Villavicencio, the Lord Mayor, who was with our forces in Antequera, and consequently ten arrobas of the best quality red wine were sent'.

There are also allusions at this time to the white wine of the region. Gutiérrez writes: 'At a meeting of the Town Council on 18 April 1456 it was noted that several Councillors neglected their duty and did not attend, and it was therefore resolved that a fine of one arroba of the best white wine should be imposed on each of the defaulters, and a further half-arroba for all subsequent absences.'

It is not clear if the Jerez *vino tinto* (of which later on, in the seventeenth century, no mention is made) was in fact a red wine as the term is understood today, or whether it owed its deeper colour to its age or perhaps had been heated or mulled. It may have been similar to the wine that Shakespeare called *sack*, though this in itself poses further problems which I shall have occasion to discuss.

It was, undoubtedly, during the sixteenth century that the taste for Sherry in England reached its apogee. The price rose from ten pence a gallon in 1533 to fifty-six pence in 1598, although import duties remained as low as thirteen pence a gallon until 1571.

Pedro de Medina gives a clear idea of the importance of the wine trade in Jerez at the middle of the sixteenth century.

This city is rich and has an abundance of all staple foodstuffs, such as bread, wine, meat, oil, fruit and vegetables. Here are produced nearly 60,000 butts of wine each year, of which more than 40,000 are exported, to the Low Countries and to England as well as to other parts. Half a league outside this town lies the River Guadalete, enabling sea-going vessels carrying bread, wine and oil to enter the inland waters from the estuary, six miles down the river. Also in the

* The *arroba* is primarily a measure of weight, representing roughly one basket of grapes (11.5 kilogrammes); hence its secondary meaning as a *liquid* measure of about 16 litres.
† *Efemérides Xerezanas.*

city there are more than 5,000 mares, and every year some 2,000 foals and horses are sold to many distant parts; they are of excellent stock, and special care is taken of the stallions to keep them in first-class condition, whilst the Town Council keeps a stud-book of them all.*

In 1566 the Duque de Medina Sidonia granted special privileges to the regular English buyers of wine from this district, although it is very likely that exports to both France and England tended to decrease towards the end of the sixteenth century owing to the hostile relations that developed between these countries and Spain.

In 1587 Sir Francis Drake, in command of an English fleet, attacked Cadiz and set fire to fifteen ships laden with merchandise and provisions (chiefly salt pork and wine) which had been equipped for the intended invasion of England by the Armada in 1588. Drake held the bay for three days, during which time he was able to load the wine which he had plundered from the Spanish ships; whereupon he set sail and anchored opposite Santa Catalina. According to historians the quantity of Sherry the English took on that occasion was about 3,000 butts.

An interesting reference is made to Drake's exploits in a book by Diego Parada y Barreto.

The celebrated seaman Drake, who played such an important role in the history of the British Navy and whose animosity towards Spain was so marked, made repeated raids on the Iberian coasts and shipping in the sixteenth century. Such was the fear he inspired that even today Spanish mothers threaten their wayward children by saying, '*Mira que viene el Draque*' ['*Look out, Drake is coming*']. The citizens of Jerez were often called upon to help in countering Drake's attacks on Cadiz, and it is of interest to record an incident that occurred when this celebrated seaman was himself in Jerez at an earlier date, because it may have a bearing on the origin of his hatred of Spain and his consequent celebrity.

Drake . . . was at first strongly attached to Spain, and established himself in business in Jerez, where he lived for some years and was apparently well content; but he quarrelled with a Jerezano called Melgarejo, who went so far as to strike him in public. This so infuriated Drake that he left the town, and from then onwards his open hostility towards Spain knew no bounds. Had this not happened, it is possible that Drake might not have left the country and his name would not have gone down in history.†

Fascinating as this story may be, there is no proof that it has any basis in fact.

Sherry for Soldiers

At that time the supply of wines to the Spanish armed forces also began to decline, although this was largely due to the end of the Reconquista, when the whole of

* *Grandezas y Cosas Memorables de España* (Seville, 1548).
† *Hombres ilustres de Jerez* (Jerez, 1875).

Spain was retaken from the Moors. Nevertheless Sherry seems to have played a necessary part in many military campaigns. In fact, Friar Esteban Rallón relates that in 1580, during the Portuguese War, not only did the town have to provide 6,000 *fanegas* (sacks) of wheat, 600 head of cattle, and so on, but also 'in wine alone 4,000 *botas* were taken'.* He adds that, because of the war, Philip II exacted great sacrifices from Jerez, and his Admiral, the Duque de Medina Sidonia, called for all the butts used for storing wine to be sent to him 'and not one to be left behind'. Friar Rallón comments:

> Never was there issued such an unreasonable and tyrannical order as this in all the history of the town, for at one stroke our people were left without the means of collecting and storing the wine of that year, and older wines that were ageing in their casks had to be transferred to earthenware jars and pitchers; some were unable even to do this, and their wealth was poured away at the whim of the authorities. There were many claims for compensation, and no few riots, in the town on this account, so that the Duke was forced to suspend the edict. By that time 4,000 butts had been requisitioned, and many honest families were ruined. It should be remembered that in those days the largest estates in Xerez were devoted to the wine trade, and since the wine was exported to many other countries it was necessary to make casks each year into which new wine was poured to replace the exports. On this occasion, due to the sudden requisitioning of the casks, timber attained a higher value than the wine itself, so the vintage was not collected and the damage caused could not be made good.†

After the discovery of the West Indies and the preparations that took place along the coast near Jerez for Columbus's second and third expeditions, it is probable that Sherry began to be exported to the Americas as well, although on account of shipping difficulties the quantity would scarcely compensate for the decline of exports to the countries nearer to hand in Europe.

Agustín de Horozco says that the wine production in the Jerez area was greater than that of any other place in the world, the vintage usually amounting to 50,000 butts, adding that the yield of the grape crop was often so abundant that not all of it could be used, owing to a lack of casks. . . . 'These wooden vessels are called *botas* and *pipas* and their cost is exorbitant, as such a great number have to be made each year, not only for the new wine but also for racking older wines, for the export from this Kingdom of those which are sent abroad, and for the Indies. Much wine is also sent to Germany and the northern and western districts where it is most highly esteemed.'††

No discussion of the sixteenth-century boom in the Sherry trade would be

---

* *Historia de Jerez* (1st ed.), III, 36. The *bota*, or shipping-butt, is the standard 30-arroba (500-litre) wooden cask used for transporting Sherry; traditionally the butts were loaded two to a cart and drawn by a single yoke of oxen.

† pp. 40–1.

†† *Historia de Cádiz* (Cadiz, 1598).

complete without Shakespeare's famous contribution: Falstaff's magnificent speech in praise of 'sack'.*

> A good sherris-sack hath a twofold operation in it. It ascends me into the brain; dries me there all the foolish and dull and crudy vapours which environ it; makes it apprehensive, quick, forgetive, full of nimble, fiery and delectable shapes; which, deliver'd o'er to the voice, the tongue, which is the birth, becomes excellent wit. The second property of your excellent sherris is, the warming of the blood; which, before cold and settled, left the liver white and pale, which is the badge of pusillanimity and cowardice; but the sherris warms it and makes it course from the inwards to the points extreme: it illumineth the face, which as a beacon, gives warning to all the rest of this little kingdom, man, to arm; and then the vital commoners and inland petty spirits muster me all to their captain, the heart, who, great and puff'd up with this retinue doth any deed of courage: and this valour comes of sherris. So that skill in the weapon is nothing without sack, for that sets it a-work; and learning, a mere hoard of gold kept by a devil, till sack commences it, and sets it in act and use. Hereof comes it, that Prince Harry is valiant; for the cold blood he did naturally inherit of his father, he hath, like lean, sterile, and bare land, manured, husbanded and till'd, with excellent endeavour of drinking good and good store of fertile sherris, that he is become very hot and valiant. If I had a thousand sons, the first humane principle I would teach them should be,—to forswear thin potations, and to addict themselves to sack.

Sherry also appears as the drink offered to the dying Le Fevre by the philanthropic and warm-hearted hero of Sterne's *Tristram Shandy*.

What was 'Sack'?

But what was Shakespeare's 'sack'? That it could be applied to wines other than Sherry is clear: a nineteenth-century authority wrote that the term had been applied to the sweet and dry wines of Jerez, Málaga and the Canary Islands, but that the first-named place was entitled to priority.†

Concerning the origin of the name itself, several theories have been advanced, although mostly without much relevance or conviction: for instance, that it is derived from the Japanese liquor *saki*, or is a corruption of the French *sec*, or is taken from the name of the wine-producing town of Xeque in Morocco or, finally, from the Spanish *saco* (sack, or bag), although the Spaniards do not even use this term to describe wine-skins, which they call *odre borracho*. At the risk of adding to the confusion I might add an observation of my own: that the name *Xera* which the Greeks gave to Jerez happens also to be the feminine of their adjective ξη΄ρος, meaning 'dry'.

The most rational of the traditional explanations is that the word may have its origins in the sporadic raids carried out by the English when they *sacked* the

* *2 King Henry the Fourth*, IV, iii.
† Thomas McMullen, *Wines* (New York, 1852).

coastal towns near Jerez, whence, in confirmation of their excellent taste, they never failed to take a supply of Sherry as loot.

Since the publication of the Spanish editions of this book fresh evidence has come forward, notably on the occasion of the visit to Jerez of Mr Warner Allen, the celebrated author of many books on wine. In my opinion, the real origin of the English word *sack* is now established as a corruption of the Spanish *saca*. This term, which had long had the general meaning of 'export', was also applied generically to wines other than Sherry imported into England,where Málaga and Canary wines were called 'Malaga Sack' and 'Canary Sack'. That the term was applied to the super-sweet Málaga wine automatically disposes of any theory connecting it with 'dry'.

By the middle of the seventeenth century Sherry enjoyed a wide popularity both in Europe and elsewhere. It appears that the white wines of Jerez may occasionally at that time have been shipped before their fermentation was complete. This, at least, is what one gathers from a very interesting document printed in 1648, 'Discurso demostrable en desengaño de las causas que dieron motivo a abrir la comunicación del Salado al río Guadalete' ('Report stating the real reason why it was necessary to join the Salado and Guadalete rivers'). It is not known if this had been a custom of the Sherry trade for any length of time, but we can assume that apart from these musts, or unfermented wines there was always a certain quantity of fully fermented clear wine shipped. In view of the time required in those days for transport by sea, it is highly probable that by the time they reached their destination all the wines were fully fermented and could be racked off their lees. This assumption is born out by Sir Edward Barry, who recalls that large quantities of wines used to be sent on their lees from the Canary Islands to England and Ireland.*

Transport Problems

The produce of Jerez used in those days to be taken to El Portal along a road which (in spite of the toll which was levied on each butt for its upkeep) must have been in a very bad state, and from there down the Guadalete to Puerto de Santa María. Owing to the permanent difficulties of transport the idea of connecting the Guadalete with the Guadalquivir by means of a canal, starting from the disused port of Alventos and, as it were, bringing the rivers nearer to Jerez, had already been contemplated in the time of Philip II (1556–98). This scheme made no progress, owing to the opposition of Seville, Sanlúcar and Puerto de Santa María. Later on, in 1648, in an attempt to stop the spread of an epidemic of bubonic plague which had been brought to Puerto de Santa María by the trade in silk and other goods from Murcia, the people of Jerez, in an effort to avoid shipping their produce through that port, built a canal connecting the Guadalete with the Salado or the River San Pedro, which was about six hundred metres distant from the

---

* *Observations Historical, Critical and Medical on the Wines of the Ancients and the Analogy between them and Modern Wines* (London, 1775).

Guadalete, at a place called El Granadillo. This canal, which gave rise to heated arguments, especially with Puerto de Santa María whose citizens wished to avoid at all costs the deviation of the Jerez trade from their port, remained open till 1666.

The 1648 'Discurso' advocates navigation on the Salado, which has only three bends and no sandbanks, whereas the Guadalete, as well as numerous bends, has eight sandbanks between El Portal and its mouth at Puerto de Santa María; moreover, transport down the Salado took only six hours as against eight days by the Guadalete.

The 'Discurso' continues:

This river has many shallows between El Portal and its mouth, which make it necessary repeatedly to unload the pipes of wine, these being the main cargo; and when, as in most cases, the wine has just been made, the *botas* or *pipas* (which are wooden casks made by coopers, with willow hoops, and some of them with some iron ones as well) cannot be properly bunged for fear of their bursting on account of the fermentation. They are, therefore, fitted with a pierced cork which can easily come off whilst loading or unloading and, as they are floated along the river, the water sometimes gets in with consequent damage to the wine, thus lowering its price in relation to that of wines from Sanlúcar or El Puerto by anything from 20 to 25 or 26 ducats, which means 20% or 22%. That this also causes a decrease in the Royal revenues from Xerez de la Frontera can be verified in the records, from which we learn that, whereas these revenues used to amount to 20 and 22 quentos, in recent years they have been no more than 13, 14 or at the most 15. The second drawback is the high cost and difficulty of navigation on the Guadalete. To get to the bay it is necessary to unload the casks at each of the shallows and wait for a high tide each time before loading them again and passing on to the next. Although the Bonete shallow has been removed, there remain eight more, without counting the bar at the mouth of the river; this means eight tides and hence eight days during which wages and freights have to be paid (of this there can be no doubt); and the higher the expenses and the longer the delays, the lower the price quoted for Jerez wines and consequently the smaller the Royal revenue.

The principal interest of all this is that it proves that Jerez was at a marked disadvantage, so far as exports were concerned, compared with Puerto de Santa María. Although this problem became less acute in later years there is no doubt that it was responsible for the setting-up of export houses in Puerto de Santa María for the shipping of Sherry.

History shows that Jerez has always been the indisputable centre of the Sherry trade, even though the speed and economy of shipping and the transport facilities at Puerto de Santa María did encourage Jerez firms to set up in business, or at least open branch offices, there. Some firms, too, for similar reasons, became established in Cadiz, though these were also motivated by the facilities offered there for chartering cargo vessels and fixing the rates of exchange, disregarding the fact that

Cadiz is at some considerable distance from the Jerez vineyards and hence from the centre of Sherry production.

Although it is not my intention here to minimize in any way the real importance of the combined efforts made by Cadiz and Puerto de Santa María in promoting the Sherry trade, it must be said that these circumstances have given rise to certain misconceptions about the true source of Sherry, which have from time to time appeared in foreign publications.

It is thus essential to place on record that *Jerez alone* is the true cradle of the Sherry trade, even though Puerto de Santa María, with its coastal position, and its vineyards contiguous with those of Jerez, does form part of the Sherry area and has from earliest times shipped wines under the names of *Jerez* and *Sherry*. Many authorities could be quoted in support of this: for example, George W. Johnson writes: 'Seven leagues from Cadiz is the town of Xerez de la Frontera, the birthplace of genuine Sherry.'* The total extent of vineyard soil in the Puerto de Santa María district has always been considerably less than in Jerez. In fact, Puerto had always been considered as an annexe so far as wine was concerned, as is shown by a court case that took place on 24 August 1508, in Jerez. It appears that two citizens of Puerto de Santa María, who also owned property in Jerez, had attempted to dodge payment of the eight *reales* tax levied on each butt of wine exported outside the Kingdom. The proceeds went to the construction of the new Collegiate Church (Templo de la Santa Insigne Colegial), which at the time was the main church of the diocese and whose task it was to administer the Sacraments to the workers in the vineyards and farms of its district.†

It is disappointing that information dealing with such aspects of the early Sherry trade as the yields of individual vintages, comparative costs and movements of exports during the fourteenth, fifteenth and sixteenth centuries should be so sparse and self-contradictory. In fact, no reliable statistical records were kept in those days, though one might well produce some from the numerous intermittent references in the minutes of the Town Council meetings. It is in these (the *Actas Capitulares*) that the vintages of 1479 and 1483 are recorded as being very lean, the latter year's crop having suffered severe damage from hailstorms. The musts of 1479, owing to the very low crop, reached the unheard-of price of 282 pesos, compared with 42 pesos in 1456, 46 in 1480 and 54 in 1483.††

Although there are some discrepancies, there are considerable sources available, both published and unpublished, concerning the volume of the vintage. It was reported, for example, that in 1598 large quantities of grapes were wasted owing to a shortage of casks and that the crop amounted in all to 50,000 butts, which is comparable to the figure given by Pedro de Medina, referred to earlier, for the mid sixteenth century. On the other hand the crop of 1560 was said to amount to only

* *The Grapevine, its Culture, Uses and History* (1847), I, 25.
†Mesa Ginete, *Historia de Jerez*, p. 146.
†† A peso has for many years now been an imaginary unit of value used solely in the Sherry district. It is equivalent to 3.75 pesetas.

8,000(?) butts and those of 1615 and 1617 to 10,000 and 6,000 respectively, the difference appearing excessive. It is, therefore, difficult to draw an effective comparison for those early years.

The statement made by Pedro de Medina in 1548–9 concerning exports from Jerez to England is corroborated by certain manuscripts saved from the fire in the Four Courts which are now kept in the Record Room in Dublin Castle under the heading of 'Repertory of Decrees'. On page 29, under the entry for 1 December 1555 (during the reigns of Charles V in Spain and Edward VI in England), it is stated that:

> Judgment was given that the accused, Francis Tyrling, merchant, of Antwerp in Flanders, or in his default, his guarantor, John Anwarp, jeweller, of Dublin, shall pay to the petitioner, Thomas Fitzsymons, merchant, of Dublin, three butts of good Sheries wine in accordance with the agreement existing between the plaintiff and the defendant Francis Tyrling or that in lieu thereof he should pay a fine of eight pounds per butt according to the price of the wine at that time, plus costs.

Similar documents exist, dated 1561, in which the name is written *Sherry*, just as it is today.

The records of exports before 1800 are incomplete and not too reliable, nor is there any indication of the basis on which they are calculated. Exports from Jerez in 1643 are given as 9,425 butts and in 1795 as 9,186 butts, whilst the total number of butts of Spanish wines exported to England during the years 1697–8–9 is given as 15,794, 15,702 and 23,402 butts respectively.

It can be estimated that more than three-quarters of this total represents Sherry exports. The figures show that the annual export averaged around 10,000 butts, of which some 8,000 would have been from Jerez. This, though not a vast quantity by modern standards, shows that the trade to England was as constant and stable then as it is today.*

The firm establishment of this trade with England had coincided with the accession to the Spanish throne of the Bourbon dynasty, which began with the reigns of Philip V, Ferdinand VI and Charles III. In that era (1700–88) it was estimated that nearly ninety per cent of the total exports of Sherry went to England. Exports of fully matured wines began at this time, although the shipping of young wines mentioned previously still continued. It is known that—for reasons which will be discussed shortly—there were then no large stocks of wine in Jerez as there are today, which seems to imply that most wines shipped were new, and explains why the Jerez bodegas, where the wine is stored today, are on the whole comparatively new buildings, although the Sherry trade itself is one of the oldest in existence.

The era of peace enjoyed by Spain after the reign of Philip V was undoubtedly beneficial to the national wine trade, which reached its peak during the eighteenth

---

* A poetic connection between Jerez and England is given in Part Five (1).

century. That this expansion did not come to Jerez until considerably later can largely be attributed to the establishment of the Gremio de la Vinatería (Guild of Vintners), whose statutes were approved by the Royal Council of Castile on 26 October 1733. The following table of Sherry exports for the first forty years of the Guild's existence tells its own story:

Exported	22,497 butts and	8	arrobas of musts			
and	60,125 ,,	,, 25	,,	,,	mature wine	
To home ports	86,884 ,,	,, 20	,,	,,		
To the Indies	1,115 ,,	,, 21	,,	,,	,,	,,
Total	170,623 butts and	14	arrobas			

If these figures are correct, they represent a yearly average of little more than 4,000 butts, hardly fifty per cent of the total exports of Spanish wine to England alone at that period. It will also be noted that far more clear wine than new was shipped, the very reverse of what had been the case in the previous century.

The Guild

The Guild's functions were numerous. It fixed the prices of wine, both for home consumption and for export (Ord. X); these included the cost of the cask, there being a reduction of from five to ten silver pesos if the wine was bought without cask. It fixed also the price of grapes (Ord. XI), the quota of butts to be shipped to Nueva España (i.e. Central America) (Ords. VIII and IX), maximum wages (Ord. XII) and standard cask capacities (Ord. XIV). Most far-reaching of all, the Guild exercised strict control over wine stocks, which were forbidden unless expressly authorized by a permit issued by the Guild (Ord. XIII).

The Guild also banned the introduction into the Jerez zone of wines from other regions of Spain. This however applied only to wines intended for local consumption: the entry of wines from other districts intended for subsequent export was permitted by Royal Decree of 23 September 1773. A week later one Antonio Mallol, merchant of Cadiz, complained to the authorities that the Customs house of Puerto de Santa María proposed to levy duty on 148 butts of wine from Catalonia in transit to another port. Since this wine was not meant for local consumption it was exempt from taxation, which could only be levied at its ultimate destination. In this way the citizens' rights of free trade were not infringed.

Normally, in those days, only the wines of the district were consumed locally, although similar musts and wines were brought in from neighbouring areas to be blended with those of Jerez for export. Similarly, Jerez musts could not be sent for local consumption either to Puerto de Santa María or to Sanlúcar, as these were production zones in their own right. It was naturally very difficult to enforce the Guild's regulations in the absence of any legislation limiting the right of each town to use the names of other districts when exporting wines which were in demand on foreign markets. This topic has always given rise to argument, as it still does today, and will be dealt with at greater length elsewhere.

Apart from these regulations there were many others covering every aspect of such subsidiary industries as the raisin trade, which has since become extinct.

The Guild offset its expenses with a levy on every butt stored in and dispatched from Jerez; it was also cited in 1816 as lessee on behalf of the Treasury of the right to collect taxes on sales from the growers and producers.

A document dating from about 1772–8 records the minutes of a meeting convened to study whether or not the Guild as it was then constituted should continue to function, and whether certain of its statutes (for example, that concerning the sizes of casks) should still be observed.

In view of the restrictive nature of so many regulations, and possibly because, with two exceptions, the governing body of the Guild consisted of persons not concerned with the wine trade, its influence declined steadily throughout the eighteenth century. Overseas buyers turned to other wine-producing areas where there was greater liberty than in Jerez, and the decline in the export business was such that there were only nine shippers in the true sense of the word left in Jerez by 1754. As has happened many times, unfortunately, in the history of the Sherry trade, it was forgotten that the export business was the true source of local prosperity, and that it was therefore necessary to protect and stimulate this side of the trade. It is thus probable that the Guild was directly responsible for bringing about its own dissolution in 1834. Undoubtedly, if more freedom had been allowed to the trade, and if the measures proposed by the Guild, instead of being restrictive, had aimed at uniting the interests of growers and shippers so as to encourage exports, the result would have been very different.

There is one legacy of the Guild of Vintners which plays its part in the trade today. In the middle of the eighteenth century the Guild adopted as its patron saint San Ginés de la Jara, whose feast-day is 25 August. The name of this saint was brought back into public prominence in Jerez in 1948, when it was decided to revive the *Fiesta de la Vendimia* (Vintage Festival), which in the heyday of the Guild had been an annual event. The central point is the blessing of the first grapes and musts which are pressed in the *lagar* set up specially in front of the Collegiate Church of Jerez. There is also a cavalcade of decorated carts alluding to various aspects of the Sherry trade, as well as to San Ginés de la Jara. Prominent features are the election of a Queen of the Vintage and her maids-of-honour, and literary and bodega competitions. In 1956 the shippers decided that the Vintage Festival should be dedicated to a different country every year and that the first nation to have this honour should be England.* It is now the custom that several young

---

* Subsequent festivals were dedicated as follows: 1957, Sweden; 1958, Ireland; 1959, Holland; 1960, West Germany; 1961, Belgium; 1962, Denmark; 1963, Norway; 1964, Scotland; 1965, Switzerland; 1966, Finland; 1967, Sherry District; 1968, Italy; 1969, France; 1970, Canada; 1971, United States; 1972, Spain; 1973, EEC; 1974, Japan; 1975, Florida (USA); 1976, Midwest (USA); 1977, Northeast (USA); 1978, California (USA); 1979, Andalusia (Spain); 1980, Austria; 1981, Mexico; 1982, Boston (USA); 1983, City of London; 1984, Amsterdam; 1985, Berlin, 1986, Oporto; 1988, Copenhagen; 1989, Cognac.

ladies of the country to which the Festival is dedicated attend the Vintage Festival in Jerez as maids-of-honour to the Queen.

In the notes of Miguel Herrero García of the Spanish National Book Institute, taken from the works of Friar Melchor de Huélamo (1607), the author expresses the belief that San Ginés lived during the reign of Alfonso II 'the Chaste' (792–842) and that he was born in France, being the nephew of Charlemagne and heir presumptive to the throne of France, where he was brought up. He came to Spain to visit the tomb of Santiago el Mayor at Compostela, and decided to become a hermit. Going against the wishes of his family, he pursued his ambition and embarked for Italy, but a violent storm off Cartagena forced him to disembark at Punta Roldan, off the Cabo de Palos near to the monastery of the Order of St Augustine. There and then he adopted the life of a hermit and spent the rest of his days in the Hermitage of Los Angeles, which was later occupied by the monks of the Franciscan Order. Just as many peasant communities in Spain have adopted as their Patron Saints those who have renounced the world and lived in solitude, so the vine-growers of the village of Yepes, in the province of Toledo, were the first to adopt San Ginés de la Jara as their patron, and were followed in the eighteenth century by the Vintners' Guild of Jerez.

The derivation of the suffix *de la jara* is intriguing, though not clear, since it is unlikely that the word has anything to do with the *jarra* (jug) used when racking wines. The more probable explanation is that the Saint was given this name because of the *jaras* (rock-roses) growing in the countryside where he chose to live.

Chapter 3
Growth of the Trade from 1800

In the two preceding chapters I have briefly outlined the more noteworthy events relating to the history of Jerez and the development of its wine trade up to the end of the eighteenth century. From 1800 onwards there is more accurate information available concerning the growth of the trade.

Tribute is due to all those past generations of Jerezanos whose foresight and initative have combined to make the wine so well known: it is largely due to their enterprise that there is probably no other town of comparable size whose name is more widely known than that of Jerez. Although much of this success is the result of the special characteristics of climate and soil found in the region, the personal effort expended by the people themselves has been another prime factor in the conquest of overseas markets.

An outstanding instance of this excellent public-relations work was that of Tomás de Geraldino, a citizen of Jerez and Spanish Ambassador to the Court of St James during the reign of Philip V, who was at all times tireless in his efforts to popularize Sherry throughout England. This is the way it has always been: whenever a Jerezano goes abroad he automatically becomes a public-relations man for Sherry. As a result of all this, whenever mention is made, either at home or abroad, of the wines of Spain, Sherry is the first to come to mind. King Alfonso XIII, who died in exile in 1941 with the name of Spain on his lips, was one of the most enthusiastic promoters of Sherry, and when he was in England as a young man succeeded in arousing interest in this wine in Court circles. Since then the Sherry trade has had many ups and downs, but on the whole has continued to flourish.

Nevertheless it is true to say that this interest and initiative on the part of individual firms might have had even better results if the propaganda had been collective. Co-operation and teamwork would undoubtedly have produced positive results, although such a combined effort is admittedly extremely difficult to organize and put into practice, owing to the great variety of wines that would have had to be included. Some of these have apparently little in common, and yet all bear the name of Sherry.

All the information available through the centuries points to the conclusion that Britain has always been and still is the leading market for the Sherry wines. The English were the first to call Sherry 'the best wine in the world', and it represented forty per cent of all the wine imported into England during the last century. A large number of English firms established businesses in Jerez in the early 1800s, as soon as the flow of trade became steady. Associations of wine-importers had already existed in England several centuries earlier, as is revealed by an interesting reference in the Minutes of the Jerez Council meeting of 3 September 1582, where there is a copy of a petition, written in Spanish, made by the British Consul, Mr Entington, which reads:

> I have this day received a letter from England, from the head of the Company comprising all the gentlemen who have dealings with the Spanish realm in the trade of wine, in which letter I am informed that all the merchants in England, Ireland and Brittany who deal in the wine of the City of Xerez are greatly aggrieved and disturbed by the fact that whereas the butts from Xerez used always to contain thirty arrobas of wine, this being so with the casks branded with the name of Xerez, they now find that some butts are short of two arrobas others of two and a half, and that for each butt which has its full measure there are four which do not. The said Company, and I on their behalf, being Consul of the said nation, do petition Your Worships to summon the persons in charge of this Guild and order that this state of affairs be remedied, as is seemly for the reputation of this town and the public good, in accordance with the traditions of dealings which hitherto have always been considered the most scrupulous and trustworthy in Spain. If Your Worships are pleased to command that the butts be examined you will find it to be as I say.

The document goes on to say that the difference could most likely be attributed to the fact that the casks from Cadiz, Puerto de Santa María and Sanlúcar, which had less capacity than was customary in Jerez, were actually being shipped as Jerez butts. After this was read it was agreed that an answer should be given regarding what was to be done.

Charles I had done much to encourage the importing of Sherry into England, particularly after his visit to Spain, when he declared it to be his favourite wine. A later British sovereign, George IV, was another devotee of Sherry and did much to make it fashionable during his reign (1820–30). It is said that he first tasted Sherry at a banquet given by the Lord Mayor of London, who had interests in the Sherry import business.

The Guild of Vintners had, as I have said, banned the storage of Sherry in bulk except in a very few special cases, on the grounds that it could lead to the monopolization of stocks by middlemen bent on making large profits at the producers' expense on the wines intended for export. This meant that many deals could be clinched only when the arrival of the ship in the Bay of Cadiz was confirmed, and this tedious arrangement was obviously a great impediment to trade in general. At that time the wine trade in Jerez consisted of the actual vineyard-owners or growers on the one hand and the shippers, who disposed of the wine for sale or export, on the other. The small-scale holding of stock which is nowadays such an important part of the business was then practised only by a few shippers and by such religious orders as the Dominicans (established in Jerez in the thirteenth century) and the Carthusians (in the fifteenth). In 1803 there is a reference in the diary of Juan de Trillo Borbón to a fire that broke out on 5 August in a bodega belonging to the Dominican monastery, which resulted in the loss of a considerable quantity of wine and casks.

Wholesalers Arrive

The occasional need of bodega-owners who did not own vineyards for musts of well known origin to add to their soleras gave rise to the establishment of the wholesaler, who came to form one more link in the chain between the grower and the bodega-owner or shipper. During the Sherry boom there always existed a guild of wholesalers, and if only they would return once more in greater numbers than at present it would cause a tremendous revival in the trade. Their disappearance is partly explained by the fact that many shippers were obliged to become growers as well in order to guarantee the replenishment of their soleras; on doing this they discovered that it was essential to keep stocks of wines as well.

As a result of this both growers and exporters found themselves obliged to construct suitable buildings for the storage and maturing of their wines.

> They are extremely spacious and well ventilated, divided by aisles and supported by very high stonework arches. No underground cellars are used for storing the wines, which reach maturity and perfection at ground level. There are bodegas with a capacity of two, three or even four thousand butts. . . . These pipes or butts are placed in rows, with lanes between the rows to allow free passage. Three butts of thirty arrobas each, one on top of another, take up a space of one vara in each row. The larger *toneletes* [puncheons], which hold sixty arrobas, occupy one and a quarter varas and the *toneles* [largest casks of all] which contain eighty to a hundred and twenty arrobas, need one and a half varas' space.*

Present-day calculations allow three square metres for each butt on the lowest tier: that is to say, in a bodega of three hundred square metres there is room for a hundred butts at ground level, after allowing for the space occupied by supporting columns and arches and for adequate space for access to the butts. As it is customary in Jerez to have three tiers of butts it may safely be said that every square metre of floor-space allows for the storing of one butt.

* Esteban Boutelou, *Memoria sobre el cultivo de la vid en Sanlúcar de Barrameda y en Jerez de la Frontera* (Madrid, 1807).

In a report compiled in 1796 Francisco Xavier Virués de Segovia y López de Spínola, attaché to the First Secretary of State in Madrid, wrote of the bodegas: 'The storehouses or bodegas containing wine belonging to the export firms of Haurie, Gordon, Beigbeder, Lacoste and Harkon have a total capacity of more than one and a half million arrobas of wine.' Writing of the same period Parada y Barreto says: 'The town of Jerez then began to be a general centre for the export of wine, and numerous foreign firms were established there, such as those of Haurie and Gordon, who were still in existence as Sherry shippers in 1868.' Again Adolfo de Castro writes: 'The firms of Haurie, Gordon, Beigbeder, Martínez and Cabeza y de Tixera have been well known for a long time.'*

The Oldest Firm

The two last-named bodegas were the original home of the well-known C. Z. firm, founded by Pedro Alonso Cabeza de Aranda y Zarco. The present owner is the firm of J. M. Rivero, who can pride themselves on possessing the oldest wine business in Jerez, since they are direct successors of Pedro A. Rivero, son-in-law of Francisco Antonio de la Tixera. There is documentary evidence that this firm paid taxes on its grapes and wine in 1653, and it still preserves very interesting archives, including references to various purchases of wine in 1700 and of grapes in 1717. Letters dated around 1728 show that the firm was then executing orders for Sherry.

Joaquín Portillo says of the bodegas:

The bodegas of Jerez are numerous and lavish. In November 1837 there were more than 518, the most notable being those of Don Patricio Garvey and Pemartín & Cía, also those called the Haurie Bodegas and others more recently erected by Don Pedro Domecq. The latter are greatly to the public benefit since the land involved, hitherto impassable, has now been made accessible. His Majesty King Ferdinand VII whilst on his way from Cadiz to Madrid in 1823 was pleased to honour the Haurie Bodegas with his presence, this establishment then being occupied by the aforementioned Domecq. At that time many gentlemen of substantial means returned from Latin America on account of the revolutions there, and within a very few years many fine new bodegas appeared. The creation of these new establishments and the need to secure adequate stocks had the effect of raising the price of wine beyond the growers' most extravagant expectations: in 1824 and 1825 the price of a butt of must reached ninety pesos or more. This was regarded as scandalous, and, since the conditions were freakish, the same level could not be maintained. The average peacetime price for a butt of export wine is 110–200 pesos, according to quality, which includes the value of the cask, taxes and all expenses up to the moment of shipping. The more mature wines are naturally in greater demand and more highly esteemed, and hence the old wines which bodega owners hold in reserve for blending with wines of less age and body cannot be bought for less than 1,000 pesos a butt.

* *Historia de Jerez de la Frontera* (1845).

Such old wines are like the nectar of the gods, and can be found only occasionally, on the table of the true connoisseur.*

At the beginning of the nineteenth century more stocks of wine were being accumulated and many fine bodegas were being built. The price of wine rose accordingly as more capital was invested, and new vineyards were consequently being planted all the time. This, in turn, brought about a surplus of grapes and a corresponding drop in prices, which in 1839 fell as low as eight to ten pesos per butt. The number of bodegas in Jerez rose from 440 in 1754 to 518 in 1837 and between 900 and 1,000 during the years 1855–68, which gives an idea of the wealth that the Sherry trade meant to the town.

Export figures from 1800, together with details about each vintage, are given in Part Five, Appendix B.

The First Railway

In 1827, a Mr Stephenson, possibly the famous inventor George or his son, visited Jerez. If this was indeed the man who built the 'Rocket' for the mining railway from Killingworth to Hetton in 1814, then it is fitting that his name should be connected with the establishment of the first railway in the Jerez area. The application for this line was made by Marcelino Calero Portocarrero on behalf of a group of financiers, and the concession requested was for a railway from Jerez to Puerto de Santa María, Rota and Sanlúcar de Barrameda, a total distance of fifty-two kilometres. The *camino de hierro* ('road of iron') as it was known in Spanish was to be called the 'Camino de Cristina' in honour of the reigning Queen. Two years later a Royal Decree dated 23 September 1829 granted the first railway concession in Spain to José Díez Imbrechts of Jerez, for a line from Jerez to El Portal on the Guadalete, a distance of some six kilometres, with exclusive right of exploitation for fifty years.

Unfortunately both these projects collapsed, probably due to lack of financial support, although the Camino de Cristina received the Royal Assent in 1830. As a result Spain did not become the fourth country to adopt the new invention, as she would have done had either scheme been carried out. In fact the first railway constructed in Spain was the line between Barcelona and Mataró, a distance of twenty-nine kilometres, which was inaugurated on 28 October 1848 and was closely followed by another from Madrid to Aranjuez, a distance of forty-nine kilometres, which started running in February 1851. In 1852 work began on the railway from Jerez to the Trocadero via Puerto de Santa María (twenty-eight kilometres), thanks to the enterprise of a group of Jerezanos. This was therefore the first railway in Andalusia and the third in the whole of Spain.

The Trocadero was an old makeshift dock where small wooden ships had put in for repairs, and was situated on the estuary of the San Pedro, between Puerto de Santa María and Puerto Real. Its name was probably derived from its function as an advance point where brokers gathered to *trocar* (barter) such merchandise as

* *Noches Jerezanas* (1839).

grain, cattle, wine and salt in exchange for other goods brought by ships entering the Bay of Cadiz, hence *Trocadero*, 'a place to barter or exchange goods'. These operations were subject to a tax of one per cent, the right to levy this tax having been granted by Ferdinand and Isabella to the Marqués de Cádiz in the fifteenth century, the entire proceeds going to the upkeep of the Suazo bridge near San Fernando.

Construction work on the railway continued until 22 June 1854, a memorable day for Jerez, as the inauguration ceremony took place in the presence of high ecclesiastical and civil dignitaries, including the Cardinal Archbishop of Seville and the Captain-General of Andalusia, the former giving the new enterprise his blessing. This railway solved the acute problem which had always handicapped Jerez in the transporting of wine. Previously everything had had to be sent to the Bay of Cadiz by mule or ox-drawn carts, so that this new mechanical means of transport was of paramount importance to Jerez, which could now compete with the coastal towns on equal terms.

In 1870 an urban railway system, which existed until 1969, was established in Jerez, and was bought by the Andalusian Company in 1890 from its owner, Federico Rivero O'Neale. (Now all public railways, rolling-stock and installations are State-owned.) This line links up the bodegas and shipping-points with the main-line system. With these two lines, and a special wharf (the Muelle de Comillas) in Cadiz for the shipment of Sherry, wine can now be sent by rail from the bodegas direct to the ships waiting alongside the wharf.

The Trocadero shipping-point has not been used since 1922; it was in a bad state of repair, and no effective storage-space or protection was afforded to the wines awaiting shipment, so that they were constantly exposed to the weather and to pilfering. It was therefore decided to abandon the Trocadero quay altogether and take advantage of the facilities offered at Cadiz, whilst at the same time an agreement was reached with the railway company to establish special transport rates.

The saving in time and shipping expenses brought to Jerez by the railway system was disastrously offset in 1854 by the appearance of oïdium* in the local vineyards. This disease had spread from the French vineyards, where it had appeared the previous year and where it had so greatly reduced the vintages that the French Government lowered the duty on imports of Spanish wines from seventy-five francs per hectolitre (which rate had been in force since 1816) to thirty centimes.

Expanding Exports

The Sherry export business continued to expand during this period, owing to the demand of foreign markets, and reached its highest level between 1867 and 1877, the average annual export in that decade being around 50,000 butts. The peak year was 1873, when 68,467 butts were shipped from Jerez and 30,443 from Puerto de

* See the notes on vine diseases in Part Two, Chapter 5.

Santa María. Including the quantity sent from Sanlúcar, total exports from the whole of the Jerez export district in 1873 exceeded 100,000 butts, a figure which has only in recent years been surpassed. At that time the price of musts was around 100 pesos; it reached its maximum of 237 pesos in 1863. This price was due to the exceptional prosperity of the business, which was however only temporary. The number of Sherry shippers at that time was large, very different from the nine firms which, according to Parada y Barreto, existed in 1754. It is curious to note that the import duties on Sherry into the United Kingdom in 1841 were 5s. 6d. per gallon. Since then they have increased periodically, reaching a record level in 1959 when the duty was £2.10s. per gallon (£270 per butt). There were two consecutive reductions of 12s. each time in 1960, bringing the duty to £1.6s. a gallon or £140 a butt, but this has since been increased.

Until 1874 the Sherry trade had been exclusively concerned with the shipping or transporting of wine in bulk, especially to England, where the client usually bottled the wine under his own name and brand. However, about that time some Sherry, mainly intended for the home market, began to be sold in bottles, a development which was only to be expected in view of the fact that Sherry is made in a very special way in comparison with the majority of other wines. This practice was soon extended to overseas markets, first the Latin American countries and then others.

The first firm in Jerez to establish a trade in bottled wines is believed to have been that of J. de Fuentes Parrilla, which was founded and started bottling wine between 1871 and 1873. Later, in 1890, this company was taken over by the firm of Diez Hermanos, which still trades under the original name. Also among the first houses to become known for bottled wines were those of Alejandro Santarelli and Gabriel Sánchez de Lamadrid.

This aspect of the trade is without doubt one of the most interesting, for it carries not only the names of Spain and Jerez but also those of the shippers direct to various overseas markets. This system of distribution is most appropriate for such a choice product as Sherry.

Over twenty years, the proportion of bottle exports to bulk shipments has increased dramatically:

	Bulk	Bottle
1970	90%	10%
1975	72.5%	27.5%
1980	59%	41%
1985	46%	54%
1989	28.5%	71.5%

It was envisaged that all Sherry would be shipped in bottle by 1993, under legislation passed in 1988.

Reasons for Decline

It is clear from the export statistics that about the turn of the century there was a considerable decline in the overseas trade. Some ascribed this to the high prices, which had increased in proportion to the expense of working the vineyards. Others put it down to growing competition from other sources, both foreign and Spanish, whose use of the name *Sherry* made it necessry for Jerez to produce a cheaper type of wine in order to compete effectively Others again felt that the decline was due entirely to adverse publicity, whilst still others blamed the shippers themselves for deliberately lowering the quality of the wines destined for export. All these considerations no doubt played their parts, but the real reasons were two: the lack of demand for Sherry in England (where substantial stocks were always available), either because Sherry had become unfashionable or because of the current activities of the anti-Sherry campaign; and the lack of protection afforded to these wines in those years, not only overseas but, incredibly, in Spain itself. It is obvious that protection of the name on the home market should necessarily precede any Government action to ensure that the name of Sherry is protected abroad, as has occurred in all foreign wine-producing regions which had the same problem as Jerez.

After the end of the 1914–18 war its star continued in the ascendant, and by 1948 Sherry had once again become fashionable.

After the dissolution of the Vintners Guild in 1773, no exact information is available concerning associations of growers, wholesalers or shippers in Jerez. In 1867 several commissions representing the growers, producers and exporters of Sherry met together to discuss the reduction of the import duties into the United Kingdom. On 27 June 1885 an *Asociación de Exportadores de Vinos* was formed; then on 1 August 1889 the *Asociación Gremial de Criadores Exportadores de Vinos* was established. These groups did good work in furthering the interests of the Sherry trade, which has always played such an important rôle not only in local economics but in the prestige of Spain itself, because it carries the name of Spain all over the world.

On 3 January 1931, three months before the Republic was established in Spain, the *Sindicato Oficial de Criadores Exportadores de Vinos* was formed on the basis of the then existing legislation. All exporters in the district were obliged to belong to the Sindicato, membership being necessary if a shipper was to qualify for remission of taxes on the spirits contained in the wines destined for export. The former Asociación Gremial continued to function simultaneously with the Sindicato Oficial and was instrumental in solving many of the labour conflicts and strikes which used to occur frequently at that time. The Asociación Gremial was dissolved on 8 March 1937, the Sindicato remaining as the sole official body. Later, the functions of the Sindicato and of other similar bodies which then existed were absorbed by the establishment in this district of a branch of the *Sindicato Nacional de la Vid, Cervezas y Bebidas*, a national organization embracing all alcoholic beverages which was established by law on 23 June 1941. This Sindicato has its local and provincial headquarters in Jerez.

Association Formed

In 1910, at a time when the Sherry trade was showing a steady decline of about 10 per cent annually, reaching its nadir of only 10,000 butts in that same year, the Sherry Shippers Association was formed in London. Its members are Sherry exporters who have an office and agents in the United Kingdom. The London Association, like its Jerez counterpart, carries out the praiseworthy task of protecting and furthering the interests of the Sherry business in England.*

Defining the Word

It is appropriate at this point to deal with the word *Sherry* itself. The British, who have always shown such a marked appreciation of Sherry, called it first 'Sherris' and later 'Sherry'. What, then, is the origin of this word, which in itself means nothing?

There is complete agreement among all authorities that Shakespeare and other English classical writers who mentioned 'Sherris' derived this word from the original name of the town of Jerez. The names of both the town and the wine undoubtedly stem in turn from the name of Sherish given to Jerez by the Arabs.

When an Englishman asks for a 'Sherry' or a Spaniard for a 'Jerez' he is ordering exactly the same wine as his ancestors have done under these names for several hundred years—or he was until comparatively recently, when imitations of Sherry began to appear on the market. It has been alleged that the name *Sherry* was not geographical but simply generic, indicative of a 'style' or 'type' of wine. But when encyclopædias, dictionaries and similar works of reference all clearly define Sherry as 'the wine produced in the district of Jerez', then it is absolute nonsense to permit such denominations as 'British Sherry', 'Australian Sherry', 'South African Sherry', or 'Californian Sherry'.

This leads us to the question of the 'Denominaciones de Origen', the control laws, a subject which concerns many wine regions in Spain, Jerez perhaps more than most, since Sherry is the wine which appears to be the most imitated. There is a common saying that 'imitation is the sincerest form of flattery', but this compliment can never compensate for the harm caused to the trade. It is interesting to note that, of all the wine countries, Portugal is perhaps best placed to protect the name of its best-known wine, because in England, which was for many years its main market, the names *Port, Porto* and *Oporto* have been protected by law since 1916, and a fine can be imposed for the improper use of these names for other wines.

Through the ages, the product of the vine has always been subject to imitations: it has been sufficient that a wine should sell well for other regions to start imitating it. On this subject André Simon says: 'To steal a rich man's money is wrong, even if the rich man never feels the loss; to steal his good name, to obtain money by falsely representing oneself as his relation is a much more despicable offence: it is both a theft and a lie.'†

* For list of members, see Part Five, Appendix F.
† *The Blood of the Grape.*

There is no doubt that this question should have been settled years ago, but it requires the co-operation of so many people that it is a very complex problem, particularly because, after a name has been misused for a long time, the users try to maintain that names which are really geographical have become generic.

A differentiation must be made between products which can be manufactured in any part of the world by a given method, simply taking the name of the first place where they were manufactured in that way, and others whose names do not refer to the way in which the product was obtained but are the geographical names of the places from which they are exported. In the first case, obviously, the product can be exactly the same although it comes from different localities; in the second case this is not so, because the finished product is influenced not only by the method of manufacture and the raw material but also by the nature of the soil on which it is produced, the grape-varieties planted and the climatic conditions of the district.

Very little or nothing was done about these questions before 1878, when the International Trade Mark Congress took place. As a consequence of the recommendations of the Congress, the countries which attended formed the International Convention for the Protection of Industrial Property. The first meeting took place in Paris in 1883, and several resolutions were tabled about the question of geographical names. The Rome Conference of 1886 also dealt with these matters, but the resolutions tabled there were not ratified by the countries which took part. These agreements were expanded by the resolutions passed at the Madrid Convention of 14 April 1891 which, referring to the prohibition of false certificates of origin of goods, states:

[Article 1] . . . all products which have a false certificate of origin issued by one of the contracting countries or of a place situated in one of these countries stated directly or indirectly to be the country or place of origin will have an embargo placed on them preventing their being imported into any of the countries mentioned. The embargo can also be effected in the country in which the false certificate of origin was drawn up, or in the one where the product with the false certificate of origin should have been introduced. . . . If the legislation of a country does not admit the embargo on the import of the goods this embargo will be substituted by other ways or means allowed by the law of the country for a similar case.

[Article 4] . . . the tribunals of each country will decide what are the names or appellations that due to their generic character are not included in the present agreement; *in spite of the above the regional appellations of origin of the products of the vine are not included in the exception established by this Article.*

The Articles of the Paris Convention of 1883 were revised by the Brussels Conference of 14 December 1900 and the Washington Convention of 1911, at which the Madrid Convention was discussed and ratified by: England and New Zealand; France, Algiers, Tunis and all the French colonies; Portugal, Madeira and the Azores; Spain; Italy; Belgium; Holland, the Dutch East Indies, Surinam and

Curaçao; Austria-Hungary; Switzerland; Brazil; Cuba; and Mexico. Later other countries adopted legislation which conforms to the agreements reached at the Washington Conference—the Argentine, Australia, Bolivia, Chile, Denmark, the Dominican Republic, Ecuador, Greece, Nicaragua, Panama, Paraguay, Peru, Rumania, Serbia and Sweden.

The Washington Convention ratified Article 4 of the Madrid Convention: that is, it confirmed the indisputable right of the products of the vine to display their names if these are geographical, thereby excluding the possibility that in any case whatsoever these names should be considered generic. The Madrid Convention was also ratified at the Hague in November 1925, and the above-mentioned Articles 1 and 4 were reaffirmed and strengthened. France, the premier wine country of the world, has also been the pioneer in getting countries together to arrive at international agreements, which should be binding on all markets; but up to the present, the legislation not being the same in all countries, results have not been entirely satisfactory.

Protecting 'Sherry'

Spain too has been considering for some time the question of control laws. During the dictatorship of that great Jerezano General Primo de Rivera, steps were taken to protect the name of Sherry, and on 28 March 1924 the municipality of Jerez was accorded by the Ministry or Works, Commerce and Industry the proprietorship of the mark *Jerez* in favour of all those growers, traders and shippers residing in Jerez, which concession was also registered in Berne according to a certificate issued on 5 September 1924. This concession was granted by the Ministry as the result of the verdict brought by the Spanish High Court in the lawsuit between Jerez and Puerto de Santa María—in which Cadiz also took Puerto de Santa María's side—referring to the use of the name *Jerez*. These legal arguments over the name were definitely settled later, when the 'Legislative Council for the Geographical Denomination of Jerez' was formed, and it was decided that Puerto de Santa María, Sanlúcar de Barrameda and the three Sherry firms established in Cadiz should have the right to ship Sherry. (Since then, these last companies have been liquidated, and at present there is no firm in Cadiz allowed to ship wines under the *Jerez-Xérès-Sherry* denomination.

On 8 September 1932 a Decree was promulgated by the Spanish Government, under the heading of 'Wine Statute', regulating the production and sale of wines in Spain.* This Decree became law on 26 May 1933.†

On the English market, protection has come slowly but surely. On 25 May 1925, in the London Police Court at Marylebone, at the instigation of the Sherry Shippers Association, a civil action was brought against the firm of Pipers, Ltd, for labelling and offering for sale a wine that had not come from Jerez but was being

---

* Official *Gazette*, 13 September 1932.
† *Gazette*, 4 June, 1933. The text of that part of the Decree (Section IV) relating to the Control Laws appears in Appendix D.

marketed under the name of Sherry. Eminent counsel took part in this interesting test case, and the judgment pronounced made it quite clear that Sherry is in no sense a generic term but describes the wine produced in one specific district of Spain. Therefore anyone who asks for 'Sherry' must be served with wine produced in the Jerez district. The defendants were fined twenty guineas with seventy-five guineas costs.

Similar verdicts have been given in a large number of other cases of a like nature, as can be verified by Press notices published in the London newspapers during 1925 and 1934, warning traders that fines had been imposed in several cases for misuse of the name *Sherry* to describe a wine not produced in the Jerez district of Spain. For example, the following notice appeared on 31 January 1934:

SHERRY: IMPORTANT WARNING TO WINE MERCHANTS
Merchants are warned against describing as *Sherry* any wine not being genuine Sherry produced in the neighbourhood of Jerez de la Frontera in Spain.

A trader in January 1934 was prosecuted in a Police Court for selling Australian wine under the description *Sherry* and under another description of which the word *Sherry* formed part, and on his pleading guilty the Magistrate imposed fines amounting to £8.8.0. with £10.10.0. costs.

The attention of the Sherry Shippers Association should be called to all cases in which the description Sherry is applied to a wine not produced in the Jerez district of Spain.

The Sherry Case

Despite these early successes, it was not until the famous case of 1967 that a real advance was made in the protection of the name of Sherry on the British market. I am greatly indebted to Mr R. W. M. Keeling for the following summary of the background, course and consequences of this case.

At the beginning of this century, a resourceful Greek who left his native country for England began to make 'wine' in England on a commercial scale in a novel and, as it soon proved, extremely successful way. Familiar, of course, with the traditional trade in unfermented musts which is still common in Greece (the musts being heavily treated to postpone fermentation), Mr Mitsotakis conceived the idea of abstracting part of the fluid content of the must, reducing it to the consistency of jam. It could then be conveniently packed and sent to England, where it could be rejuvenated with local water; then carefully selected yeasts would be introduced, and a palatable fermented product produced very cheaply.

Production by this method began in 1905. Where the drink was made to look and taste something like Sherry, it was called 'British Sherry'.

Even before 1905 traders in England, particularly in the north, had been making and selling a product called 'British Sherry'. Sometimes it was made from rhubarb, sometimes from raisins; it was often drunk by 'total abstainers', and it seems to have been a popular drink after funerals. But whether called 'British Sherry' or 'Sherry' or, as sometimes happened, 'British Sherry-type', and whether made by Mr Mitsotakis's method or by earlier and simpler means, the drink had little in common with the wine which is the subject of this book except colour and, in some cases, alcoholic strength.

The real Sherry merchants, sophisticated gentlemen carrying on a trade for sophisticated gentlemen, remained totally unaware of the home-made products drunk at the wakes in Yorkshire and Lancashire, of, if they were aware of them, considered they were not worth serious attention. The two trades remained poles apart.

Then several things happened all of which together began to constitute some kind of threat to the Spanish trade. First, after the First World War, the home-made product began to make effective use of mass advertising; second, the South Africans (who had sent so-called 'Cape Sherry' to Britain in the nineteenth century but whose vines had been ravaged by phylloxera) re-entered the British market with a product which was exhibited at the Wembley Exhibition of 1925. Australia produced 'Australian Sherry' for the same exhibition. It was the Indian summer of the Empire, and the popular slogan was *Buy British*. British and Empire wines quickly made progress; just before the 1935–45 war they were joined by Cyprus, which began making a local fortified wine and selling it as a cheap substitute for Sherry, 'Cyprus Sherry'. At the same time the start of the Spanish Civil War in 1936 began to make the Sherry trade difficult, and the outbreak of the Second World War reduced it to a trickle of its old self.

After the war, the quality of the British and Empire wines improved. South Africa copied increasingly closely the methods used in Jerez, and began to build up stocks of old wines. Australia, too, cultivated the famous *flor*, said to be indigenous only to Andalusia and the Jura. Cyprus and Britain both concentrated on producing, with modern machinery and advanced laboratory techniques, cheap, sweet, strong wines for the masses.

As the standard of living in Britain rose in the fifties and sixties, the demand for wine, once the privilege of the few, grew rapidly. The trade in British wines became huge. Much more British wine (though not all of it was 'British Sherry') was sold in 1965 than Sherry and Port put together.

But were these products Sherry? Some people seemed to think so. Advertisements began to appear showing girls in bright mantillas with trays of 'British Sherry'; television commercials, watched by millions, showed placards—*News for Sherry Lovers*—followed by pictures of 'British Sherry', and introduced popular film—and television—stars to drink cheap, sweet fortified wines and call them 'Sherry'. South Africa joined the 'Sherry' chorus—*Five reasons why you should drink South African Sherry*, screamed the powerful South African Wine Farmers Association in the British Press in 1963. *First, because it is real Sherry.*

But was it? Few merchants dared to use the word by itself on a label unless the wine came from Jerez, and those that did were successfully prosecuted by the Sherry Shippers Association, a group of English wine traders importing Sherry from Spain. But the advertisements grew more provocative; and some wine writers—a new, ever-growing group with much influence on public taste and habit—began to suggest that 'Sherry' was no more than a 'generic' term, denoting wine of a certain type made originally in Spain but now made anywhere.

Then, in 1967, the Spaniards themselves lighted a fuse which caused some major explosions in the English wine trade. A British company, supported by a powerful Spanish concern, began to import and sell in England a Spanish sparkling wine under the name 'Spanish Champagne'. For the French this was the last straw: they had seen 'Spanish Burgundy', 'Spanish Graves', 'Spanish Sauternes' and 'Spanish Chablis' littering the shelves of English wine merchants (labelled, it must be stressed, not by the Spanish producer but by the English importer and bottler), and 'Spanish Champagne' at last stirred them to action. After three years of legal battles, the French won an outright victory in the High Court, as a result of which 'Champagne' was defined as 'the wine of the Champagne district of France'. The goodwill in the word *Champagne*, said the Court, belonged exclusively to the Champenois. 'Spanish Champagne' blurred the distinction between Champagne and the sparkling wine of Spain, and appropriated to the Spanish wine part of the goodwill which properly belonged to France. It had to stop.

The Champagne case revived all the old arguments about the use of geographical wine names in England. Nowhere was the practice more chaotic than in the field of 'Sherry'; and the Spaniards decided to see how far they could use the Champagne case to secure a definition of Sherry and at least put a limit to the use of the word in the English market, the most important market for Sherry in the world.

They faced a vastly more difficult task than the French. 'British Sherry', 'South Arican Sherry', 'Australian Sherry' and 'Cyprus Sherry' stood against them in deeply entrenched positions, known by millions of Englishmen, many of whom had probably never heard of Jerez. (Ask an Englishman where Sherry comes from and you may get a curious reply. A wine-waiter in a first-class hotel in the north recently declared with great authority, 'Real Sherry comes only from Portugal.')

The case opened in the Chancery Division of the High Court of Justice in London on 9 February 1967, before Mr Justice Cross. The opposing sides were represented by the leading barristers of the day. Sir Milner Holland Q.C., led for Sherry; Guy Aldous, Q.C., for Vine Products. In twenty-nine days the court slowly filled with papers, wine-lists, show-cards, posters, books, maps and bottles. Witnesses were called from all over England and from all sections of the wine trade to say how the word *Sherry* was used. The use of the word in English literary texts was minutely examined: the Court heard with evident satisfaction what Falstaff thought of Sherry; how in 1619 an English poet used to enjoy 'a pleasant pynte of poetic Sherry'; and that in 1625 a gentleman from Tavistock fought three Spaniards with an English quarter-staff 'at Sherrys in Spaine'. For several hours a Professor of Arabic Studies from Madrid explained the etymology of the word Sherry with the aid of Moorish documents from the British Museum, and copies of twelfth-century Moorish maps from the Bodleian Library at Oxford. The President of the Consejo Regulador de la Denominación de Origen Jerez-Xérès-Sherry explained the limits of the Sherry district, and the system of control which, with some variations, had been in operation since 1933. Evidence was given as a result of research in Jerez and Madrid of the history and tradition of controlling the output of wine in the Sherry district during the eighteenth and nineteenth centuries. As a contrast to the methods used for making British wines, the Judge was told exactly how Sherry is made.

The Vine Products side of the case occupied even longer. They were concerned with a less romantic story, and, as the case developed, they concentrated largely proving long continuous use of 'British Sherry' and the other contested descriptions. Thousands of wine-lists were produced and analysed. Hundreds of labels were shown to witnesses who were able to identify and date them; and many witnesses were brought from the trade to say how they described Sherry and what they thought it meant.

From all this mass of words and papers, the Judge extracted two principles on which he based his judgement. First, he held that 'Sherry', used by itself, means Jerez. Second, he held that 'British Sherry', 'English Sherry', 'South African Sherry', 'Australian Sherry', 'Cyprus Sherry' and 'Empire Sherry' had been used for so long without objection that it was too late to stop them now. So the two should exist side by side. But this did not mean British Sherry could be described or advertised as 'Sherry'. If this seemed hard, said the Judge, there was no necessity for a man selling British wine to use the word *Sherry* at all. Evidence had been given that some millions of bottles had been sold by Vine Products under a brandname with no mention of the word *Sherry*.

Thus Sherry was defined in the way the Spaniards wanted, because it matched the way Englishmen had used it for four centuries. So also these other descriptions such as 'British Sherry', which Englishmen had used for so long, were permitted to continue as composite descriptions. But the gate had at last been shut. There would be no more girls in mantillas—except for the produce of Spain; and after the case was over, the Sherry Shippers of Jerez were able to persuade the Canadians to abandon their attempt to introduce 'Canadian Sherry' into the British market, on the ground that it was not Sherry and that there was no history of long use of that description for Canadian wine in Britain.

In this way—not perhaps an easy way for the trade to follow—the long process of English law did justice to the historical claims of both sides.

Sensibly, the two sides in the old dispute agreed to work together to try to make sure the judgment was properly observed. Jerez set up a monitoring organization in London which guided the trade along the path set by Mr Justice Cross. No further litigation was necessary: and, gradually, careless users of the word Sherry by itself to describe the imitation wines were eliminated.

In 1973 the United Kingdom became a member of the European Community and, as such, became bound by its complicated and detailed laws relating to wine. France, Italy and Germany, the wine-producing member states, had lists of protected wine names which other member states were bound to respect. So 'Spanish Sauternes' and 'Spanish Chablis' and all the other abuses of French wine names, disappeared from the shelves of English wine merchants. The wines were re-labelled with the names of their Spanish wine districts. Unfortunately for Jerez, this new regime did not apply to Spain because Spain remained outside the European Community. 'British Sherry', 'Cyprus Sherry', 'Australian Sherry', 'South Arican Sherry' all continued, within the limits set by the judgment in the sherry case. Then in 1986, Spain at last became a member of the EEC. The Treaty of Accession, as expected, provided for recognition and protection of Spain's quality wine names within the rules of the EEC wine regime. As a result, 'South African Sherry' and 'Australian Sherry' have vanished. But the Treaty also included a special provision for 'British Sherry', 'Irish Sherry' and 'Cyprus Sherry', which allowed those three descriptions to continue to be used within the United Kingdom and Ireland until 1995. Only then will 'Sherry' achieve the same recognition and legal protection as all the other great European wine names.

Finally, it is interesting to transcribe some paragraphs about the name of *Sherry* by André Simon, a great authority on wine questions and on international legislation affecting this trade. Mr Simon advocates that the wine of each region be given the name of its place of origin; any other system means misleading the public. In particular the existing fashion of applying names which are supposedly generic but in fact geographical to wines from other regions, whose own names are less well known or difficult to pronounce, as occurs with those of California, South Africa and Australia, is clearly a fraud which should be punished. Mr Simon says:

> Pedigree wines should always be sold under their legal denomination of origin, but it is to be taken into account that although the geographical name of origin should not be applied to a wine which is not the exclusive product of grapes of the corresponding district, not all of the wines produced in certain districts necessarily have the right to carry on the different world markets their name of origin.*

He explains that 'denomination of origin' applies not only to the place where the wine comes from, but also to the maturing and developing processes employed.

* *The Blood of the Grape*, p. 119.

Bordeaux and Cognac, Champagne and Burgundy, Port and Sherry are geographical names of origin which should never be used in a generic sense as simply representing certain classes of wine; the significance of these names is firstly geographical and should be applied exclusively to the wines of well-known European vineyards, the boundaries of which are fixed by long-standing international commercial practices and by national legislation in force.

In April 1905, in the *Australian Vigneron and Fruit Growers Journal*, Cuthbert Burgoyne, a member of a well-known Australian wine-shipping firm, referred to the imitation and misuse of European wine names by the Australians.

These [the European] wines have made their brands known with their original names, which other countries have tried to imitate afterwards; it is well known that he who imitates will never be a leader, and it is evident that Australian growers should adopt their special denominations for the wines which are better produced on their soil, instead of usurping the names of wines from other countries.

I think that this patriotic and logical statement, which has recently been echoed by distinguished personalities in the California wine industry, sufficiently shows how right we are in protecting abroad the name of our wine; any further argument on this subject would be superfluous.

Concessions and Quotas

The export trade to Britain was until 1941 completely free, but after that date the business was controlled by concessions and quotas granted to the British importers, calculated either on volume by litres or on value in pounds sterling, and based on the volume of imports in 1939. The Jerez wine trade at that time thus had to restrict itself to these quantities.

It is disheartening to find that exports abroad have declined in the last few years in relation to the domestic market. For example, between 1934 and 1945 the home market accounted for 245,362 butts as against the foreign consumption of 374,463 butts (52% more). Yet in the two years 1946 and 1947 these figures were reversed with Spain consuming 71,420 butts as against 60,036 butts on the foreign market. That means that export figures were 19% below sales in the Peninsula.

Of course, these regulations refer only to the wines which bear the name of Jerez-Xérès-Sherry, and not to table wines destined for local consumption, which are brought into the town in considerable quantities from other regions. Local consumption in the eighteenth century was about 1,500 butts each year and this rose rapidly to 10,000 butts with the constantly increasing trade. This is a huge quantity, considering the population of Jerez. The table wine consumed locally, some of which comes from neighbouring provinces, is an important source of income for the Town Council because the Royal Decree of 29 June 1883 which affects Jerez, Puerto and Sanlúcar stipulates that these towns may levy duty on wines imported for local consumption.

This chapter would be incomplete if no mention were made of the important subject of the demarcation of the zone of Jerez. In compliance with the regulations laid down in the Spanish Wine Statute, a Control Board for the use of the name *Jerez-Xérès-Sherry* was formed on 4 August 1934.

After detailed discussions this board proposed to the Ministry of Agriculture in the following November a scheme for defining the zone and drawing up the requisite regulations. The Ministry, having considered the reports of the Wine Institute, the Ministry of Industry and Commerce, and the Treasury, approved the proposed zones, with certain modifications, issuing the Ministerial Decree on 19 January 1935. Under this the Control Board was officially constituted, in accordance with the provisions of the Wine Statute. The laws promulgated by the Madrid Convention of 1891 had been rather slow to take effect, but it is interesting to note that the Sherry Control Board and zone of origin were the first of their kind to be approved in Spain.

On 24 May 1935 the board's powers were temporarily suspended by the Ministry of Agriculture, and until 1 November its authority was restricted to the granting or countersigning of certificates of origin. This was due to certain difficulties arising in other zones which also had to limit their areas of production. On 27 July 1935 the Ministry of Agriculture issued a decree re-establishing the board, and by the terms of the modified ruling of 21 April 1936 it continued in existence until its definitive constitution was officially approved on 20 October 1941.

This constitution is still in force, and governs the operations of the board. Apart from demarcating the maturing, production and export zones, as described above, it also defines (in Article 15) the special characteristics of Sherry.

Alcohol Limits

In order for any Jerez wine to be marketed under the name protected by this constitution, it must have a minimum of 15.5% alcohol by volume with the exception of very sweet wines (i.e. Pedro Ximenez) when the sum of the actual and the potential alcoholic strength must not be below 20%.

The same constitution also defines the principal aims of the Control Board.

1. To watch over the quality and to co-ordinate, direct and control the production and marketing of the wine Jerez-Xérès-Sherry.
2. To promote, when circumstances make it advisable, the replanting of vineyards, especially in the Jerez Superior area, contributing technical aid where possible.
3. To see that the stocks of soleras should be maintained and to guard against loss of quality, so as to supply the markets with the highest quality wines.
4. To organize collective publicity, especially abroad, for the Jerez-Xérès-Sherry wines.

* See Part Five (6).

5. To watch over both national and international markets so as to ensure that the name Jerez-Xérès-Sherry is respected; and to prevent or prosecute any imitations.
6. To issue certificates of origin and to supply guarantee seals.
7. To represent and defend everywhere the general interests of the name Jerez-Xérès-Sherry.

These regulations also deal with the composition of the board, the registration of vineyards and bodegas in its registers, the quotas which the growers and shippers are expected to pay, the wines which may pass from the production zone to the maturing and export zone, sanctions, legal proceedings and appeals, and so on.

Chapter 4

Virtues of Sherry

The Sherry trade has survived many vicissitudes during its long history, and attempts have been made on several occasions to dispute the excellence of Sherry, which, like everything worth while, has frequently been the object of keen controversy. Sherry has always had its enthusiasts, but from time to time, either for reasons of commercial competition or from other motives, it has also had its detractors—apart, that is, from those sworn enemies of all wines who campaign for universal prohibition on the ground that all forms of alcohol are toxic and obnoxious. The latter, of course, have been of little account since the unhappy outcome of the American experiment, which ended in the repeal of the Volstead Act thirteen years after it had been passed in 1920.

> *God, in His goodness, sent the grapes to cheer both*
>   *great and small;*
> *Little fools will drink too much and big fools none*
>   *at all.*

A campaign directed specifically against Sherry was particularly intense towards the end of the nineteenth century, when exports to the United Kingdom had increased substantially, and other wine-producing countries were consequently beginning to experience a steady decline in their own exports. Many books and pamphlets were published on wines in general in which references to Sherry were invariably couched in critical terms. The major allegations were: that the presence of gypsum (calcium sulphate) was undesirable; that fortification with alcohol was undesirable; and that Sherry was an important contributory cause of gout.

When dealing with the anti-Sherry movement I should also mention the defence put up by the Town Council of Jerez, the medical authorities and the shippers themselves against these allegations. One notable supporter was Francisco Revueltas Carrillo y Montel, a doctor and surgeon of Jerez, who played a leading part in the organization of medical congresses: the Andalusian Congress (1876); the Congress of Medical Science in Cadiz and Seville (1879); the International Medical Congress (1882); and the Congreso Vinícola, held in Madrid in June 1886, which as convened at a time when a trade agreement with Great Britain and the renewal of a treaty with Germany were both awaiting approval by the Cortes.

At the 1882 Seville Congress a very full report was prepared, at the instigation of Dr Revueltas. It was entitled 'A Vindication of Sherry, being a scientific proof of its excellent hygienic and therapeutic properties', and dealt with the various attacks launched against Sherry, with particular attention to what had been termed 'the unwarranted use of gypsum'. The condemnation of this practice is quoted in a passage of the above report dealing with the preparation of Sherry.

> Sherry is prepared with the addition of gypsum, which produces a twofold effect: it eliminates some of the potassium bitartrate (cream of tartar) which is naturally present in the wine and produces in its place a certain quantity of potassium sulphate.

The advisability or legality of this 'plastering' of Sherry was fiercely debated throughout the last century, and more than once was the main basis for bitter attacks, more often for commercial purposes than for any valid considerations of health. It was no new development: the same practice had been debated, for example, at a meeting of the Cortes of Castile at Córdoba on 31 March 1570, at which, it is recorded, this 'long-established practice' was defended by Diego Mexia and Cristóbal León.

In the Jerez vineyards grapes are generally sprinkled with gypsum* just before the pressing begins. This traditional practice was recommended by Columella, and also Pliny, who observed that the custom had originated in Africa, two thousand years before his time. Some authorities believe that the practice goes back to the days of Ancient Greece, when it was discovered that wines fermented in marble or alabaster vessels improved in quality and became clear and brilliant more rapidly. This, of course, is purely hypothetical. The use of gypsum in vinification is in no way exclusive to Jerez, and indeed it is used in larger proportions in other wine-producing areas. It is also an accepted practice in the brewing industry.

An allegation once made against Sherry was that spirit was added to the wine in considerable quantities. This gave rise to all kinds of fantastic reports, either through ignorance or as part of a malicious campaign. Dr Revueltas writes in his report:

> So far as the addition of spirit to Sherry is concerned, let us go back to 1860, when the British Government sent a certain Mr C. Bernard to Spain with the confidential mission of ascertaining the alcoholic strength of Sherry in its pure and natural state. Yet the very aura of secrecy that shrouded Mr Bernard's task probably prevented him from visiting a sufficient number of bodegas or

---

* Technical details on the use of gypsum, and arguments concerning it, will be found in Part Five (2).

vineyards and personally witnessing enough pressings to enable him to arrive at the whole truth. Among the samples that Mr Bernard presented as being absolutely and undoubtedly pure were two supplied by Don Francisco Romero Gil, a grower from Jerez, and a Mr Campbell, a Sherry shipper and British Vice-Consul in Puerto de Santa María. These samples registered 15.5° Gay Lussac and 16.75° Gay Lussac respectively. A third sample, a very old, unique Amontillado supplied by Mr Campbell, registered 20.25° Gay Lussac.

Later information compiled by the British Government and published in various Parliamentary papers makes it quite clear that there do exist absolutely pure and natural wines in Jerez which exceed the strength of the three samples quoted above.

In spite of this evidence, Drs Thudichum and Dupré, who are considered the leading authorities on such matters, refuse finally and categorically to consider as pure any wine which exceeds approximately 15% alcohol by volume, basing their argument on the ground that it is not possible for the grape sugar to continue fermenting and producing alcohol within a liquid which already contains that percentage of proof spirit.

Against the statement of these learned doctors—whose authority we do not dispute but who may well have made a mistake—we must set the following facts, which are publicly known and familiar to all who have anything to do with the vintages and bodegas of Andalusia. . . . When the best-quality musts of Jerez, especially those popularly called *gordos* [full-bodied], finish their first violent fermentation and are racked off for the first time, it is difficult to find a cask whose contents have a strength less than 15%, and very easy to find higher strengths. This is so well known in Jerez that the wine trade is astonished that anyone should doubt it. A few years ago, when it was rumoured that poor-quality wines of below 15% had been shipped to England from some port along the Andalusian coast, to profit from a lower import duty, it was generally thought that the wine had been diluted with water. . . . It is not true to say that alcoholic fermentation is always impossible within a liquid which already has a strength of 15%. This may be true for other liquids in other climates.

After the first fermentation, Sherry musts still continue to ferment, although less violently, for an indefinite number of years, provided they are stored in ample wooden casks. In wines of outstanding quality not only the alcoholic strength but also the bouquet and pungency increases with each successive fermentation. This too is common knowledge in Jerez.

Even when the slow fermentation has to all intents and purposes completely stopped, the alcoholic strength of Sherry continues to increase year by year whilst the wine is contained in casks. This is due either to chemical reactions or to physical changes such as osmosis or evaporation which have so far not been conclusively determined. Drs Thudichum and Dupré suspect that this is the case, in their work entitled *A Treatise on the Origin, Nature and Varieties of Wine* (p. 649). It is a known fact, moreover, that in any mixture of alcohol and water in contact with the air the water evaporates spontaneously in greater proportion than the alcohol and more so when the blend is in a porous container.

In short, it is common knowledge to all those familiar with the Jerez bodegas that some absolutely pure wines are to be found there with strengths in excess of 38° and even 40° Sikes [nearly 23%].

Dr Revueltas goes on to state that analysis shows that the average strength of a genuine Sherry varies between 13.75 to 17.75% of alcohol by volume. His conclusions are given in the following table:

Variety of Sherry	
Pale, Fino, very dry	15%–18%
Old Oloroso	18%–20%
Exceptionally old, very dark, stored in wooden casks for 40–60 years	20%–24%

This [concludes Dr Reveultas] is the true alcoholic strength of genuine Sherry. Whenever Sherry is left to mature by itself, without any interference, it lives and develops by the action of its constituent parts; and in the course of the series of changes and fermentation which this living liquid undergoes it acquires a higher concentration of these constituent parts and hence a higher alcoholic strength.

On this same subject, Francisco González y Álvarez observes that his own views on the alcoholic strength of Sherry were confirmed by a series of experiments which he personally carried out.* One of these was to put aside the pomace (that is the skins, pips and stalks of the grapes) from a volume of six carretadas of grapes. Four arrobas of water were then added to the pomace every day for four days, and by the fifth day, when there was already fairly active fermentation, the mass of grapeskin was once again trodden and then pressed mechanically, a further arroba of water being added at this point. From this, a total of thirty-two arrobas of liquid was obtained. At the end of fermentation it was found that the strength of the *yema* (the liquid produced from the original pressing of the six carretadas of grapes) had an alcoholic strength of 12.5%, whilst the strength of the thirty-two arrobas obtained from the pomace had a strength of 12%. It was therefore deduced that the average original strength of each carretada was at least 14.5%, and that the volume of liquid added should be regarded not as an addition but as a replacement. Señor González y Álvarez adds that this proof is convincing enough to show that wines have sufficient natural strength to ensure their development without further additions, the only drawback being that as yet no adequate machinery had been evolved to extract all the vinous content of the grape, whilst at the same time purging the pomace of impurities before fermentation. 'It is obvious,' he says, 'that this difficulty would be overcome by fermenting the musts and the pomace together, although it has been proved that such a

---

* *Apuntes sobre los vinos españoles.*

procedure also has the effect of carrying forward any inherent defect, which later impairs the quality of the wine.'

My grandfather, who prided himself on his scrupulous accuracy in such matters, also conducted experiments relating to the alcoholic strength of Sherry. On one occasion a butt of wine purchased from Sr Valdespino's vineyards was set aside and a tiny amount of alcohol—less than 1%, according to his notes—added to it. The strength of the wine was subsequently recorded over the years:

Years elapsed	Alcohol by volume
5	15.5%
10	17.0%
20	18.75%
25	20.5%

More recent research performed by Dr Rivera Valentín, former Director of the Málaga Municipal Laboratory, Dr Bascuñana, Professor of the Cadiz School of Commerce, and Germá Alsina, Director of the Jerez Analytical Laboratory, has shown that under optimum conditions absolutely natural must which is allowed to ferment naturally can achieve an alcoholic strength of 16% and sometimes 17% after violent fermentation, given an appropriate state of ripeness and a suitable average temperature. It is impossible to ensure these optimum conditions, which depend on circumstances beyond the grower's control; but it is a fact that Sherry as we know it requires a minimum strength of 15.5% of alcohol for its proper development, and if due either to unfavourable climatic conditions at the time of vintage or to incomplete fermentation these conditions have not come about naturally, then the wine *must* be fortified with pure spirit until the minimum limit is obtained.

The reason for this is obvious. Sherry, during its development, must be in continuous contact for several years with the oxygen in the air, as it is by the various chemical reactions that this naturally produces that the essential aldehydes and esters which give Sherry its characteristic aroma and bouquet are generated. It is therefore necessary that the conditions should be favourable for the yeast, which constitutes the flor of the wine, to develop properly, as it is this microscopic organism living on the surface of the wine which gives rise by oxidation to numerous aldehydes and to the free acids which develop the esters.

These yeast micro-organisms find the optimum conditions for reproduction in Fino types of wine with strengths between 15% and 16% alcohol, and prevent acetification. What would happen if the wine had an alcoholic strength of only 12% or 13%? Germá Alsina's reply to this question is: 'At these low strengths there would be an insufficient barrier to the formation and development of *micoderma aceti*. For example, if a 12% wine were allowed to become covered with a flor, it would inevitably be doomed to become vinegar.'

In such circumstances the maturing and development of Sherry, as it has been practised for generations, would be impossible. In order to preserve the wine it would be necessary to protect it from all contact with the air and to suspend its vitality with an antiseptic to avoid the danger of successive fermentations. Sherry would thus become just another table wine.

Distinguished œnologists, both in Spain and abroad, are still carefully studying this debatable question of the *flor* and its influence on the maturing of Sherry.

Another factor which may require Sherry to be fortified is mentioned by Dr Rivera Valentín, who points out that the process of fermentation is affected by purely local conditions; it frequently happens that wine matured in one locality, where fermentation stopped on its reaching an alcoholic strength of, say 10%, 12% or 14%, may, if transferred to another district where the climatic conditions are different, begin to re-ferment. This would at the very least bring about a marked variation in the clarity and sugar-content of the wine, and might occasionally produce fundamental alterations in its constitution. To avoid this it is necessary to increase the alcoholic strength by fortification.

I have already shown how the initial strength of a wine increases with age, and in this context Germá Alsina remarks: 'This phenomenon can be attributed to various causes, including the hygrometric state of the air in the district and the varied porosity of the casks for water and alcohol in the case of liquids of low alcoholic strengths.'

It is highly probable that the great alcoholic strength found in some old wines may in reality be lower than is indicated by the official laboratory measuring procedure. These very old wines contain a large proportion of volatile elements which on being brought into contact with the alcohol during distillation reduce the density of the liquid obtained and consequently increase the alcoholic strength as recorded by the hydrometer.

Although the proverb—in Spanish as in English—says that 'good wine needs no bush', it is not out of place to devote some space to the special qualities of Sherry.

Wine in general has been praised in every age. Pliny says: 'With wine man can maintain his strength, his blood and the warmth of his body.'* And Fagon, the celebrated doctor to Louis XIV of France once advised his exalted patient: 'Your Majesty should drink wine, because it not only aids digestion of all foods in the stomach but also, by being distributed with them thereafter to all parts of the body, is transformed into blood of excellent quality, without risk of any illness.' If this eminent doctor has this to say of wine in general, what is one to say of Sherry?

At the international medical conference at Seville in 1882 it was stated that Sherry contained thermogenetic elements and high nutritive properties, and that it was important as a therapeutic agent and the best suited of all alcoholic drinks to medical use.

A group of doctors belonging to the Medical Academy of Jerez published a treatise on Sherry in 1883, in which they laid stress on its beneficial effect on the system, stating that it stimulated the appetite, assisted the digestion and induced both mental and physical vigour. Its daily use was recommended, particularly

* *Natural History* (XXIII, ch. 10).

during periods of epidemic illness, as its tonic effect created a degree of immunity to such diseases; this had been shown to be true during the cholera epidemic of 1834. The doctors added that Sherry was a quick-acting nerve tonic and preferable to spirits as a therapeutic medium when the patient is run down, and also an antipyretic. They recommended 15–500 grammes a day, according to the condition of the patient. The doctors affirmed that, even when taken daily, Sherry does not cause gout or gallstones, as witness the fact that in that same year although Jerez had a population of nearly sixty thousand, the majority of whom were inveterate Sherry-drinkers (some, indeed, to excess), gout was virtually unknown. If Sherry were indeed a cause of gout, one would naturally expect to find a high proportion of sufferers in a district where more Sherry is undoubtedly drunk per capita than anywhere else in the world. The truth is, of course, that gout is brought about by the concerted action of an excess of protein-rich food, a sedentary life and a cold, damp climate. In this district people eat frugally, their meals consisting mainly of vegetable foods, and the climate is in general quite warm.

Invigorating Qualities

The physician Federico Rubio y Galli praised these wines for their invigorating and pyrogenetic qualities, which enable the human body to sustain the rigours of work without any harmful effect or weakening of the nervous and muscular systems.

The consensus of opinion is that a high-strength wine like Sherry—a *vino generoso* (full-bodied wine) as it is called in Spanish—supplies a much-felt need in colder climates where sunshine is at a premium. As a celebrated orator, Emilio Castelar, once said: 'Sherry carries in each golden drop the rays of the Andalusian sun.' Hence the name 'Bottled Sunshine' sometimes used by devotees in England.

At the XIVth International Medical Congress in Madrid, Dr Nicasio Mariscal summarized the medicinal properties of Sherry. 'It is an excellent nerve tonic and digestive stimulant; it is a generator of physical and mental energy; and is a pyrogenetic and a hypnotic. Sherry is classified medically as a respiratory, plastic and complete nourishment, containing, in addition to alcohol, sugar, fats and proteins, and essential oils and salts, principally chlorides, sulphates and phosphates.'

Dr Decref visited Jerez on 26 January 1929 and delivered a lecture on the nutritional and medical properties of wines in general. Speaking of wine spirit, as compared with other spirits, he referred to an experiment carried out by M. Laborde on three dogs, to each of which he administered fifty grammes of spirits mixed with an equal volume of water. To the first he gave wine spirits, to the second spirits made from sugar beet, and to the third grain spirits. The first lay down and went to sleep; it got up an hour and a half later, walked about, ate some food and appeared to be perfectly normal. The second did not wake up until the following day, and the third slept for forty-eight hours. In the case of the two latter dogs it was some considerable time before they returned to normal.

Dr Decref also cited the interesting conclusions reached by Lindner in relation to the effects of alcohol on animals and insects. He writes:

. . . those which are by nature liveliest and most wide awake are those which have discovered the use of alcohol; they show not the least sign of alcoholic degeneration. For example, the development of bees and wasps into highly organized communities has been achieved thanks to their use—moderate though it may be—of alcohol. But the most important of the groups of insects which feed on sugar, nectar and honey are the ants. The ant's crop contains ferments which multiply and thus produce constant alcoholic fermentations, to which the insects of course become accustomed. Yet ants are possessed of very high intelligence without any signs of degeneration.

On the subject of inebriation Dr Decref affirms:

Fine Sherries, thanks to the œnanthic acid which they contain, engender esters as they mature, and it is these esters which provide the bouquet so characteristic of Sherry, and so much appreciated the world over. Because of this, even though the alcoholic strength increases spontaneously, the wines become progressively less dangerously intoxicating. These esters themselves produce rapid intoxication with a small quantity of wine, but are eliminated equally quickly through the lungs and kidneys. Moreover, the intoxication which they produce is transitory, forestalling and preventing the state of drunkenness produced by spirits. This explains the absence of alcoholism among inveterate Sherry-drinkers and also why the people of Andalusia themselves classify the state of intoxication which these esters or vapours produce as *healthy inebriation*, in contrast to that produced by alcohol or hard liquor.

Dr Decref adds that, within Spain itself, alcoholism is much less frequent in the wine-producing provinces than in those favouring other alcoholic drinks.

As the derivation of the word *bodega* undoubtedly stems from the Greek *apotheca* it might be thought that it had something to do with a chemist's shop. But there is no chemistry in the Jerez business: everything in Sherry is the produce of the grape. In spite of this, however, Jerez has since the end of the last century been sending tonic and medicinal wines to various overseas markets. These are produced by the addition to genuine Sherries of quinine and other legally permitted medicinal substances, though there is no doubt that Sherry is best known and most appreciated in its normal, completely pure state. It would be futile to attempt to give a list of these tonic or apéritif wines, as many shippers have such specialities, differing greatly in type and style.

Sherry is highly suitable for blending for medicinal purposes. It appears in the pharmacopœia under the technical name of *Vinum Xericum*, and is preferred to spirits in the preparation of tonic and medicinal wines since it contains a high natural proportion of tartaric acid, which effectively dissolves the additional medicaments, in the same way as it would dissolve iron if this were added. Sherry is also frequently used to cover the unpleasant taste of certain medicines, either by mixing the two together or by drinking a glass of Sherry immediately after the dose.

In the field of what might be called household medicine, it would be a pity not to mention the nickname given to Sherry by the people of Andalusia, who, with their typical instinct for frankness, call it 'milk for the old people', or sometimes 'chicken broth'.

Sherry for Longevity

The longevity of the inhabitants of this privileged district is a byword, and can be at least partly attributed to a constant but moderate intake of Sherry; this healthy pastime is most popular among the old—hence the affectionate nickname quoted above. Everyone knows about the Andalusian archbishop who reached the ripe old age of 125, and drank half a bottle of Sherry at every meal . . . except on days when he felt out of sorts, when he would double his ration.

George C. Howell has published statistics on the consumption of Jerez vintners and cellar-managers, considered as a class apart.* He demonstrates that 10% of them are moderate drinkers or virtual teetotallers, whilst the remaining 90% are established enthusiasts. A study of the mortality rate for the same professions shows that 10% die before the age of seventy, whilst as many as 15% survive to be ninety or more.

In Jerez, the wines have always been considered as antidotes, especially against contagious diseases. In *The Times* of 25 January 1892 there appeared an article which mentioned that, during the plague which afflicted London in 1665, drastically reducing the population, there was eventually only one doctor left, a Dr Hodges, who, according to his published memoirs, attributed his survival to the daily consumption of a few glasses of 'sherris-sack', which provided him not only with protection against the disease but also with the optimism which he transmitted to his patients.

In spite of the large amount of Sherry that is drunk in Jerez, cirrhosis of the liver is almost unknown in the district. Dr Lancereaux has said that this illness is caused by overindulgence in alcohol, whilst other authorities attribute it to potassium sulphate in food and drinks. Here we have further proof that the plastering of Sherry has no ill effects on health. Moreover, Dr José Luis R. Badanelli, in a report confirming that cirrhosis is almost unknown in Jerez, shows that in the majority of cases treated over a large number of years by Jerez doctors the patients were mainly non-wine-drinkers, many being women.

One of the questions invariably asked by life-assurance companies in their proposal forms is whether the applicant is a habitual wine-drinker. There has been the occasional case of somebody not daring to admit this, thinking that it might discourage the company from accepting the proposal; but in Jerez such a denial would only arouse suspicion, since any Jerezano who does not drink probably suffers from some secret disease.

* *Beverages de Luxe* – 'Sherry'.

Nowadays medical science recognizes that moderate consumption of wine is anything but harmful; and research has even established the quantity of alcohol that an individual can take in relation to his weight, in twenty-four hours, without suffering any adverse effect.

The words of Dr Fermín Aranda of Jerez, a distinguished surgeon and a strong partisan of Sherry, sum up what has been said so far: 'Sherry is a powerful tonic because it contains alcohol (medically antipyretic), ether (stimulant), iron (fortifying tonic) and nitrogen. These added to the vitamins it contains make Sherry a tonic without rival in the world.'

At Any Hour

Apart from the tonic and medicinal properties of Sherry, it should also be pointed out that few other wines share its advantage of being equally agreeable at any hour of the day.

I have already said that every Jerezano, when he leaves home, becomes automatically an ambassador for Sherry, but it must be said that the best ambassador of all is Sherry itself, a worthy representative not only of its native town but of the whole of Spain. Antonio Frates Sureda defines Sherry thus: 'Genuine Sherry gives every Spaniard what he needs—good advice to the perplexed; joy to the sad; zest to the overcautious; knowledgeable confidence to the ignorant; it is a wine which quenches rancour, seals friendships and inspires patriotism, since its colour is a blending of the red and yellow of the Spanish flag.'

Professor José María de Ortega Morejón, a distinguished lawyer who was also a fine poet, was kind enough to dedicate to me the following verse:

> *Con tus vinos de Jerez*
> *Se truecan, más de una vez,*
> *Por misteriosa virtud,*
> *En gracia la embriaguez*
> *La enfermedad en salud,*
> *La usura en esplendidez,*
> *En reposo la inquietud,*
> *El miedo en intrepidez . . .*
> *Y ¡hasta en sol de juventud*
> *el hielo de la vejez!*

> A noble wine your Sherry,
> Which with wondrous stealth
> Changes drunkards dim to merry,
> Human ills to vigorous health
> And grasping greed to kinder wealth.
> With it, dark doubt to calm gives way,
> And puny fears to valour bright,
> It is the sun of youthful day
> Which melts the ice of age-cold night.

The saying 'A wine for every taste and season' is especially true of Sherry. In the vast range of different styles there is one to suit every palate and individual preference—except, of course, those of the confirmed wine-hater, of whom José Barrón once said, 'To banish wine is to refuse one of God's greatest gifts.'

Anyone who has drunk a glass of good Sherry will agree that it makes the world look a considerably brighter place; I say 'good' Sherry, despite the popular Jerez saying that there are only two classes of Sherry: good, and better. Sherry satisfies at least three out of the five senses by its aroma, its colour and its flavour – fulfilling the criteria of the Ancients who demanded *colore, nitore, odore et sapore*. As for the other two senses, one might add that since Sherry is—or should be – served chilled it is pleasing to the touch; and perhaps the custom of clinking glasses arose out of a subconscious desire to gratify the ear.

Not the least of the qualities of Sherry is that it appears on the market as fully matured wine. It is not usually drunk until it is five or six years old, until which time it has simply been developing naturally. This is a valuable reminder that, as yet, not everything is sacrificed to speed in this modern age. Speed for its own sake achieves little, and the slow, measured pace of tradition which controls the production of Sherry in no way implies inefficiency. George Suter relates in his memoirs that in the 1830s the mails bringing orders for Sherry from London took three weeks to reach Jerez whereas today they take two or three days; but are we any the better off for that?

Sherry, for good or ill, does not move with the times. It takes as long to develop today as it did centuries ago. This is encouraging to those interested in the trade: there will always be those who prefer Sherry as the apéritif *par excellence*, in spite of the cocktails and other exotic drinks which from time to time usurp its position. Sherry will always be held in high esteem by the true connoisseur of wine because it conforms to the most exacting standards: it is clean but full-bodied, so important in an apéritif; smooth without being sweet; warming without being fiery.

Sherry is like good music: there will always be a public for it however strong may become the occasional fashion for more strident sounds. There is sufficient range in the choice of Sherries to cater for the changing rhythm of taste and fashion. This is amply proved by experience in exports to Britain. At some periods the Olorosos have been the fashion; at others, the less full-bodied Finos. It would seem however that, in general terms, climate is the main influence in each consuming country, and for this reason it is likely that a large proportion of the Sherries exported to Great Britain will always be medium-bodied rather than completely dry since a cool climate requires an accent on sugar in the diet.

The Spanish people themselves ascribe many comforting and fortifying properties to Sherry. In Castile and the north it is traditional to provide a bottle of Sherry for a mother when she has just given birth to a child, and to any sick person during convalescence. Throughout Spain no wedding or christening party at any level of society is complete without a glass of wine to celebrate the occasion, and Sherry is usually the wine chosen.

I end this chapter with a brief summary of some of the other virtues peculiar to Sherry.

The various types of Sherry are not only excellent apéritifs but are appropriate also during and after meals; the addition of Sherry in cooking gives zest and flavour to many dishes; a bottle once opened and only partially consumed can be recorked and finished later; Sherry is a wine not merely for adults in general but also for children and old people. The enjoyment of Sherry is not marred by smoking as is the case with so many other wines. It is said that tobacco is conducive to an atmosphere of friendliness and intimacy, and a glass or two of Sherry at the same time will lend added warmth and geniality to any occasion; many a business deal has been clinched and many a friendship confirmed over a glass of Sherry, which comforts the sad, strengthens the weak and cheers up all who taste it.

Sherry indeed possesses all those qualities which are called for in wine according to the aphorism of the five *f*s of the Middle Ages of the famous school of medicine in Salerno, which is a fitting conclusion to this chapter:

> *Si bona vina cupis, quinque quaesiturus in illis: fortia,*
> *formosa, fragantia, frigida et frisca.*

Which translated into English means: 'If you want to enjoy good wines you should look for five qualities in them: they should be strong, clean, fine aroma, cool and mature.'

Unorthodox ways with Sherry are listed under Mixed Drinks, Part Five, Appendix G; and Sherry's culinary merits in Appendix H.

Part Two:
THE
VITICULTURE

Chapter 5

The Background

The vine has been known from ancient times, and there are many references to it in the Scriptures. It is acknowledged to be the most fruitful and valuable plant of all. It is appreciated, especially in the East, not only for its fruit but also for the shade it offers. This being so, we are lucky that Eve chose the humble apple with which to tempt Adam, and not the more succulent grape—otherwise all wine-lovers would be guilty of tasting the Forbidden Fruit, and total abstainers thus provided with at least one good argument. The Jews considered it the most noble of plants, and for this reason the prophets frequently took it as the symbol of the Hebrew nation. No other plant has received so much honour as the vine in the Scriptures, the greatest tribute it ever received being the words of Our Lord when he said, 'I am the true vine.'*

The grape vine is the genus *vitis* of the Ampelidaceæ family. There are eleven Asiatic species, twenty American and only one European, *Vitis vinifera*. Of this there are incalculable European subvarieties, many within Spain itself.

Although it is almost certain that the vine was brought to Europe from the East, where it grows wild, it is not possible to determine its exact place of origin, nor the date on which it was first introduced into Spain. Most authors follow the traditional view that the vine was originally Asiatic, probably Armenian or Persian, maintaining that this is why the wines produced on the southern shores of the Caspian Sea have always been considered extremely fine. From Persia the vine is supposed to have spread through Palestine and Asia Minor into Greece, and from there to have followed the Mediterranean coastline—a typical zone for vine cultivation—to the Spanish coasts, where it seems certain that it existed before the Roman occupation.

* John, xv, I.

Who first exploited the wild vine, whether Noah or some other Biblical character, is not known; but in any discussion of viticulture. Noah must find a place, for it is he who has always been considered to be the first *planter* of vines. The Armenians claim for their country the honour of being the 'home' of viticulture, since, they maintain, Noah planted the first vine in the southern part of the country about three miles from the walls of the city of Erivan, and just north of where the Ark came to rest on Mount Ararat and where Noah had lived with his family before the Flood, and subsequently became a husbandman. It is believed that the Phoenicians brought the vine to Europe, and specifically to the Iberian Peninsula, on their first voyages, and that later inhabitants continued to cultivate it there and in other European countries.

The vine has become established, and its grapes are pressed for wine, in the lower-lying regions of every temperate country in the world. The geographical zone best suited to vine cultivation is that lying between 30° and 50° north latitude. The European northerly limit can be represented as a line running from the Loire estuary (47°N) in the west up as far as the Hamburg area (52° N) and finally down again to Odessa, on the Black Sea (47° N).

Although the vine thrives in many places north of this line, the must produced usually lacks sufficient glucose or grape sugar, since the grapes do not ripen fully, except in a very few cases; the wine produced is usually acid and soon becomes vinegar on account of its low alcoholic strength.

An interesting pamphlet on this topic was issued by the 5th Marquess of Bute, who sent a copy to me in 1948. It consists of extracts from the records of the Cardiff Naturalists Society, published in 1928 under the title *Welsh Vineyards*. A description is given of the results of large-scale planting by Lord Bute's father on his properties of Castle Coch and Swan-bridge near Cardiff, both of which are in Glamorgan at a latitude of 51.5°N. The brochure does not stipulate what area was cultivated at Castle Coch, but does mention that five acres were planted at Swanbridge. Ancient records show that viticulture had been known in Britain since A.D92, and that in 1086 there had been vines in fourteen English counties. This tradition accounts for Lord Bute's expectation of success in his enterprise. In fact the extinction of viticulture in England is attributed to the ease with which, from 1152 onwards, French wines were obtained from the territories held by England in western France.

Yet in spite of all his efforts Lord Bute achieved no great success from the time that the vineyard was planted in 1875 until it was uprooted in 1920. The grape variety most favoured by him was the famous Gamay Noir, and he based his methods of plantation, pruning and cultivation on those followed in the northern French vineyards. The first wines produced were white, although red wines were also produced later by adding the skins of the grapes, together with the stems, to the must during the primary fermentation. In one year forty hogsheads were produced.

The Press devoted considerable space to Lord Bute's venture, although most of the comment was sceptical of the experiment.

Punch observed, 'If at any time wine is produced in Glamorgan four men will be needed to drink it: the victim, two others to hold him down and a fourth to force the wine down his throat.'

Nevertheless it has been reported that what wine did not turn acid was perfectly palatable, not unlike still Champagne, and that one year the whole crop was sold in London.

The same pamphlet also records that in forty-five years only seven harvests yielded fully mature grapes, and that even in those years the musts were deficient in glucose, so that it was necessary to add sugar and, in some cases, even alcohol.*

The mean annual temperature around Cardiff is about 9.5° C. (49° F.); although many other northerly wine-producing areas have a lower average than this, those areas all have more hours of sunshine and real heat in the summer months, even if their winters are more intensely cold. Thus the ultimate suitability of the grapes for successful wine-making depends on the number of hours of sunshine and heat they receive between the budding and the harvest, whereas low winter temperatures do not affect the vine since they do not coincide with its period of growth.

It has been observed that the most suitable altitude for vines varies from region to region. In Jerez the average altitude of the vineyards is roughly between a hundred and a hundred and fifty metres above sea-level. Although there are good vineyards facing in a variety of different directions, those on south-east-facing slopes generally give the best must, as they receive the maximum of sunshine whilst at the same time being protected from the frosts and cold winds.

Nature of Soil

In spite of the importance of climate and latitude, and the altitude and disposition of the vineyard site itelf, the most important influence on the ultimate quality of the wine—given that the appropriate variety is selected and that it is cultivated normally—is undoubtedly the nature of the soil. Each wine district has one particular soil which gives its best wine, and this again varies considerably from one region to another. This is apparent from the fact that some parts of the Jerez vineyards produce better wine than others, although the variety planted is the same.

It was calculated that after the First World War the area of the world devoted to vineyards was slightly over eight million hectares; this total remained approximately the same until 1940. It is now (1989) around 9 million hectares.

Average annual wine production for Spain is today over 21.5 million hectolitres. This vast quantity shows how important viticulture is to Spain. Almost every region of the country produces wine, but its importance from the national point of view depends less on the quantities produced than on the value its exports represent in international trade.

For this reason, although the production of the Jerez area cannot be compared

---

* There has been a dramatic change in English viticulture since the above comments were written. This is outlined in an addendum in Part Five (3).

in quantity with that of other regions, it represents a great asset, which should be protected by Government legislation. It is necessary to acknowledge that in a country like Spain, where the soil is so varied and where the viticulture and viniculture differ so much from region to region, there cannot be a single body of legislation for all the wine districts, but that it is necessary, due to the diverse circumstances which affect them, to make certain exceptions from the general legislation decreed for Spanish wines which, in the great majority, are '*vins ordinaires*'.

The average volume of exports of Spanish wines for the period 1919–35 was approximately 3,500,000 hectolitres, whilst imports of foreign wines into Spain were almost negligible. Between 1936 and 1945 came the Civil War and the Second World War, then the unsettled post-war period, all of which made it extremely difficult to form an accurate appraisal of Spanish wine exports. With the passing of time these matters have gradually returned to normal.

If, however, the statistics for 1919–35 are studied, it will be seen that the consumption of wine per capita (the population of Spain was then about twenty-five million) was about seventy litres each year. This figure varies greatly from country to country: in the USA, for example, the annual consumption of wine (excluding spirits) was two litres per capita in 1914, and fell to one litre after the repeal of the Volstead Act.

The average yield for the European vine between 1910 and 1920 was 15 hectolitres for every hectare under cultivation, and the same figure is obtained for Spain taking the total surface area of Spanish vineyards as being 1.35 million hectares. At first sight this average of 15 hectolitres would appear very slight for such an expanse of vineyard, especially when the majority of wine produced is ordinary table wine from vines which usually have a higher average yield than the quoted figure.

Moorish Wine

There is little historical information available about the development of the Jerez viticulture before the *Reconquista*, except for the casual references quoted previously. Nevertheless it seems certain that some wines were produced during the Moorish occupation, as may be inferred from Bertemati, who writes:

> The citizens of Jerez used to cultivate several varieties of vine and turn their fruit into delicious syrups and soothing wines: especially reds, consumption of which steadily increased since it was held to be permissible, even among the most devout, for the bellicose inhabitants to fortify their courage in this way for the wars they were continually fighting or preparing to fight. But the Caliph El Haken, a strict observer of the Koran, outraged at the waywardness of his Moslem people, finally forbade the sale of wine and ordered that two-thirds of the vines under cultivation should be uprooted and destroyed.

Nevertheless it is presumed that most of the vineyards were used, during the five centuries for which the Moors occupied Jerez, for the production of raisins, and due to this a large number of vines were allowed to survive, patiently awaiting the arrival of Alfonso the Wise to restore the Cross to the turrets of the Alcázar and the golden wine to the cups of the people of Jerez.

Dating from the time that Alfonso X was in Jerez there is an anecdote about a famous Jerezano, Diego Pérez de Vargas, like so many of his compatriots a farmer who, through the force of circumstances, had also become a warrior. The story has it that Diego was pruning his vines one day when the King happened to pass by, and the astonished farmer turned to see the monarch gathering up the pruned branches. When the King saw the look of astonishment on Diego's face, he said, 'For a pruner like you, an assistant like me.'

Although the story may be apocryphal there is historical proof that Alfonso, who was extremely popular for his lack of ceremony, contributed much to the development of prosperity of Jerez by encouraging viticulture. Even so, no real development is known to have taken place until the start of the fifteenth century; we know that all tilling was still done by hand, with the *azada*, a combination of spade and hoe. Mention is made of this by Benito de Cárdenas, a fifteenth-century notary, who commented in his diary: 'On Monday, 18 March, the Marqués de Cádiz sent his brother, together with the Mayor of Arcos, from Jerez to Sanlúcar, whence they brought back six horses, cattle and a great many labourers who had been tilling the vineyards.' It would appear that the particular task in hand in the vineyards would be the *golpe lleno*, which consists of thoroughly breaking up the soil for future cultivation, and is carried out at that time of year in both Sanlúcar and Jerez.

There is little doubt that vineyard cultivation must have increased considerably during the sixteenth century, for there is a record of a petition signed by many citizens of Jerez on 9 February 1541 expressing their concern at the lack of arable land on which to grow wheat, so much having been planted with olive trees and vineyards.

By 1615 the Jerez vineyards must have been very extensive, as there is a record stating that the population then included over four thousand vineyard workers. The daily wages are reported as: gatherers and weeders, three reales:* pruners and foremen four; tillers three and three-quarters to five according to the distance they had to travel to work from the town.

At that time the vineyard acreage in Jerez was constantly changing, since it is recorded that in 1754 the land under cultivation measured 9,112 aranzadas whilst in 1784 it was only 8,000. Figures for the nineteenth century show a steady increase: in 1818 there were 8,335 aranzadas; in 1839, 10,600; in 1851, 12,813; and in 1868, some 14,000. This was the time of great prosperity: the part-time labourer used to earn as much as ten pesetas a day, from which it can be seen just how flourishing the wine trade was. For those times it was a great deal of money, and it was a popular local saying that the workers wore patent-leather boots in the vineyards.

* One *real* was equal to one-quarter of a peseta.

In 1882 the land covered by vines reached a total of over 17,000 aranzadas, of which 12,000 were albariza and the remainder were the darker *barro* (clay) or *arena* (sandy soil). According to the collective allotment plan drawn up by Adolfo López-Cepero for the rural area of the Jerez Council at the end of the nineteenth century, the expanse of vineyards stretched to 18,927 aranzadas. This particular plan was drawn up just before the invasion of the phylloxera plague, of which more will be said later. In 1945 the total vineyard area in Jerez was 13,146 aranzadas in the Maturing and Shipping zone, which when combined with the area of vineyards in the free-production zone gives a total of 22,572 aranzadas.

In 1877 there were 321 owners of albariza with a total of 11,417 aranzadas, 207 owners of barro—in the region around Jerez known as the Cuartillos sector—with 1,827 aranzadas, and 452 owners of arenas with 2,899 aranzadas. As may be seen the average holding was much larger on the albariza than on the other two types.*

Unfortunately it has been almost impossible to compile an accurate record of prices of musts and wines for these times, as the records for many years are missing. It was recorded, however, that during the seventeenth century the prices were low in years of average crops, rising appreciably only when the crop was very small.

It is only at the start of the eighteenth century that the 'peso' appears as the unit of currency for wine transactions. Before 1709 (in which year high unemployment and torrential rainfall brought serious hardship to Jerez) prices were reckoned in maravedis per *azumbre* (one-eighth of an arroba).

A wine journal of the early eighteenth century records that the price of must in 1700 was 80 pesos, and that in 1728 there was no crop at all owing to frost. During the years 1733–73, when the Guild controlled Jerez, prices fluctuated between 24 and 40 pesos a butt. An exceptional year was 1788, when musts reached what was then a record price of 150 pesos, and even went as high as 240 for a brief period. The price per butt in the nineteenth century also varied considerably.

Once again, owing to the lack of detailed statistical records, there is no accurate information on the volume of crops from year to year, although it is certain that Jerez suffered its lean times as well as times of prosperity, as occurs in all agricultural enterprises. The price of one aranzada of vineyard in the nineteenth century, when production was quite high, was rated at 5,000 pesetas until about 1830, and again towards the end of the century, but in 1868 the price was double that figure. A far cry from the fifteenth century, as Joaquín Portillo writes when discussing the prices of vineyards in connection with the building of the Charterhouse in Jerez: '. . . a vineyard was bought which also had trees, olive groves and a pigeon loft, all of which cost 90 D maravedises, a price which for those times was extremely high considering that the normal price for [about one acre] of farmland was 30 D maravedises.' The Carthusian monks moved into this monastery on 13 February 1476, which, although at first the quarters consisted only of the original farm buildings, may still be taken as the date of the foundation

* The list of albariza vineyards and map will be found as a supplement in Part Five (4).

of the Charterhouse of Our Lady of Protection of Jerez.* The Carthusians remained there until 1835, when the religious orders were suppressed in Spain, and the last mass was celebrated there on 19 August of that same year.

The Town

The town of Jerez, whose present population (1990) is 186,182, is situated at 36° 41′ N., 6° 9′ W. Basically, the land to the north of Jerez belongs to the pliocene age and consists of sandy soil, which may also at times have a high limestone content. The soil to the east, south and west is of the eocene and miocene periods. The eocene soil consists of calicified limestone and clay, the miocene of various types of clay, gypsum and limestone.

Jerez lies some ten kilometres inland from the Bay of Cadiz, and the climate is generally temperate, although this cannot be said of the whole Region of Jerez which, extending over nearly 550 square miles is one of the largest in Spain and naturally contains various types of terrain, some of which is mountainous. Meteorological records show the following average rainfall and shade temperature (Centigrade).†

	Winter	Spring	Summer	Autumn	Yearly average
Average Maximum	16.0°	21.5°	30.8°	24.4°	23.2°
Seasonal mean	10.7°	15.6°	23.7°	18.5°	17.1°
Average Minimum	5.4°	9.7°	16.6°	12.6°	11.0°
Rainfall in mm.	241.4	179.9	24.0	201.3	646.6
Average daily evaporation in mm.	1,626	3,123	5,150	2,878	3,194
Prevailing winds	NW–NE	SW–SE	SW–SE	SW–N	

The average number of rainy days is about 75 per year, although this figure varies quite considerably: in 1936 there were 117 days of rain, giving a total rainfall of 1,311 mm. which was a record level. The previous year was a 'dry' record with 392 mm. In 1945 there were only 53 rainy days.

The best areas for vine cultivation are usually of Tertiary formation, overlaid at various points by large alluvial deposits. They form a varied landscape of hills cut by narrow valleys, and plains of varied structure. These clay and limestone areas are rich in minerals, of which carbonate of lime is the most common; others are aluminium, magnesium, iron, silica and gypsum.

The usual classification of the soil around Jerez divides it into three main types: *albariza*, found to the north-west and south-west of the town rural limits in the areas called *afueras* (outside), the nearest being five kilometres from the town;

* St Bruno (1035–1101), of the noble Hartenfaust family, founded the first Carthusian monastery, known today as the Grande Chartreuse, near Grenoble, on 24 June 1084.
† Figures supplied by Fernando Ivison y Sánchez-Romate, engineer at the meteorological office attached to the Agricultural and Experimental Research Centre in Jerez.

barro, a dark clay soil principally found to the south-east and *arena*, really a combination of sand and clay found in patches to the north and east, and also here and there in the south, the vines planted in this soil being usually the nearest to the town. There are also mixtures of these which make up other related subtypes; more will be said later of these hybrid soils.

The albariza (misleadingly called *afueras* because not *all* the outlying soil is albariza) is highly calcareous, compact and with a fine surface loam distinguished by its white (*albo*) colour, as its name denotes. The whiteness is due to the calcium carbonate which is its predominant constituent. It is mainly found on gentle slopes.

The Best Musts

The best musts are usually produced from this soil, especially those which are more *fino* in character and have a cleaner pungency on the nose. Undoubtedly it is to the albariza that Sherry owes its prestige and reputation, rather as the single small district of Vega de Vuelta Abajo was responsible for the fame of good Cuban cigars.

When calcareous soils are well tilled they absorb air and moisture, which causes them to swell, so that the level of the soil in the vineyard bordered by a road is generally higher than that of the road itself, and in many places prickly-pear hedges are used to keep the soil from spilling over into the lanes.

One of the greatest problems still to be solved is the proper maintenance of these lanes during the winter, as at present they become impassable on account of the slipper surface which the wet, limestone-rich loam produces when it rains, and the vineyards can only be reached in dry weather. It is this limestone which retains during the winter the moisture and freshness so essential to the roots of the vine. The yield from this soil is comparatively low, and the average quantity of wine produced per aranzada may be reckoned as six or seven butts throughout the productive life of the vine. There are however years, such as 1945, where even this figure is not reached; in that particular year, following three years of drought, the appropriate yield was only two butts per aranzada.

The best farmland in Jerez—the small area known as *el Rincón* (literally, 'the corner')—is in the same general region as the best vineyards, the farmers also being able to profit from those rich alluvial deposits of loam and Tertiary limestone which, when they occur on or near the surface, favour the cultivation of the vine.

The barro is a mainly clay soil with a lesser limestone content, found in the lowlands. These *bujeo* areas, as they are also called, are dark brown in colour and rich in decomposed organic matter carried from the near-by alluvial land. The barro gives a higher quantity of must per aranzada than the albariza, and this is usually fuller-bodied, although less clean. Barro land needs more tilling than the other types, as weeds thrive on the organic deposits in the soil, and large fissures form in the surface during the summer months. Very often these clay soils have a limestone substratum.

The arenas are usually reddish-yellow in colour, owing to the presence of iron oxide. They are basically formed of sand—though never actually loose sand—with a high content of aluminates and silica. Loose sand does not exist in the Jerez vineyards, and the subsoil where the roots of the vine reach is often composed of clay or limestone.

The yield of these soils is much higher than that of the albarizas, and on account of their looser textures they are also easier to work, but the musts produced are more coarse than in the first two types of soil.

The list below gives an idea of the limestone content of the various vineyard soils found around Jerez.* The limestone content of barro is usually less than 30%; sand and clay, in widely varying proportions, make up the rest of the composition. Sand is the largest component of the arena (over 70%), with clay coming second and limestone (never more than 10%) making up the rest. There are very few vineyards whose soil is entirely uniform, so that it is quite normal to find more than one of the types already described in a single vineyard, the effect of which may be seen in the differing colours of the leaves, as well as in the quality of the musts produced. There do exist other types of soil which vineyard owners classify separately. Amongst these are: *Tajón*, a very hard and compact albariza which contains an average of 80% calcium carbonate; *tosca*, another albariza with a lower calcium carbonate content, though never less than 40%; *lantejuela*, a friable type of albariza containing about 50% limestone and often mixed with barro; *barrejuela*, a chalky soil striated with reddish-yellow streaks of ochre and highly valued by viticulturists, again with a limestone content of about 50%; *lustrillo*, containing gypsum as well as a loam of sand and clay called in Spanish *margas calizas* and with a limestone content of between 30–50%; *villares* or *almaduras*, a good farm soil in which archaeological remains have frequently been found; and *pelirón*, a stony soil, patches of which sometimes occur in sandy areas.

The *pagos* of Jerez, the groups of vineyards of homogeneous soil number about 150. The majority of the vineyards are now (1990) albariza, Jerez Superior constituting over 70% of the surface under vines.

The most important areas of albariza in the official classifications of the nineteenth century were Macharnudo (1,500 aranzadas), Balbaína (1,200), Añina (1,000), Carrascal (700), Carrahola (350) and San Julián (300). Also highly rated amongst the albariza and barro districts were Corchuelo (300) and Montana (250). These districts are still highly renowned, for the excellent musts that they produce. The chief arena district, Montealegre, also produced fine musts, though these were not suitable for the Fino type of Sherry, as their development was very different from those of the albariza districts.

Nowadays, however, plantations have changed considerably, as some pre-phylloxera districts like Burujena, for example, have been replanted, and found to produce extraordinarily fine wines. From 'Nuestra Señora del Carmen', one of the vineyards on the high hills of that district, the dunes of the famous Doñana

---

* Information supplied by Gonzalo Fernández de Bobadilla of the Œnological and Viticultural Research Centre in Jerez.

National Park can easily be picked out. Among the foremost albariza districts today, apart from this one, are the first four mentioned above, which have traditionally been considered to produce outstanding musts. Taking them in order of delicacy, it was found that Balbaína and Añina were the best, closely followed by Macharnudo and lastly Carrascal, which produced fuller-bodied wines, possibly because it is farther from the sea than the others.

Most visitors to Jerez are surprised not to see any vineyards on the approach to the town; but most of them are situated well away from the railway line and the main Seville and Cadiz roads. The Carrascal district, for example, is some way west of the Seville and east of the Trebujena roads. The Macharnudo district lies between the roads connecting Jerez with Sanlúcar and Trebujena, both of which carry much less traffic than the main Seville road whilst the Balbaína and Añina districts lie to the south-west of the Jerez-Sanlúcar road. These last two districts are the nearest Jerez vineyards to the sea (the Bay of Cadiz) and mainly produce Fino Sherry.

The land along the Jerez-Seville road is not albariza but arena, and, in view of the exhorbitant cost of tilling vineyard soil, has been given over to other types of cultivation, as has also the Abiertas district which has been taken over by the Caulina agricultural co-operative.*

It is not certain what varieties of vines were planted in Jerez before the fifteenth century, although, as I have said, there was a reference in 1482 to three varieties of vine known as *Torrontés, Fergusano* and *Verde Agudillo*. It is certain that black grapes were cultivated, and even preferred to the white variety, as may be seen from a fifteenth-century reference: 'At the Municipal meeting of 1 October 1433 Diego González with Fernando López de Morales, a cleric of the parish of Xerez, stated that they had reached an agreement with reliable wine merchants fixing the price of a load of grapes at 20 maravedises for the white grape and 25 for the black . . .'

According to two authorities, Simón de Roxas Clemente and Esteban Boutelou, the number of varieties planted in Andalusia was extremely high, totalling about 250. The former mentions forty-three different varieties that were cultivated in Jerez in 1807, although this number has since diminished considerably. Nowadays the main varieties are: White Palomino (or *Common Listan,* the principal species), Albillo, Perruno, Cañocazo (*White Mollar*), Mantúo Castellano and Pedro Ximenez in the Albariza; Beba in the barro; and Palomino, Mantúo de Pila, Castellano and the Black Mollar in the arenas. I do not know the origin of these varieties, but some sources suggest that they probably originate from Castile.

The Palomino variety is known as *Horgazuela* in Puerto de Santa María whilst in Sanlúcar it is called *Listan* and in other wine-producing regions in Spain it goes under the name of *Jerez*. At a Paris viticultural exhibition (the Chaptal Collection in the Jardin du Luxembourg) in 1866 there appeared a vine (No. 1,054) under the

---

* Some historians consider that the name *Caulina* derives from the Caulino wine which Pliny praised so highly.

title of *Cheres,* and Thudichum and Dupré believed this to be the Palomino variety, because of its high glucose content. This vine is undoubtedly the best suited to the Jerez soil and climate, and produces the excellent wines which have made this region world famous. The same authorities also believed that the Albillo variety was the vine called *Albuelis* by Columella. Other authors maintain that the Albillo was the variety referred to by Columella as *Argitis minor.**

From the Rhine

The Pedro Ximenez is said to have been imported from the Rhine valley in the sixteenth century by Peter Siemens (Pedro Simón), a soldier in Charles V's army. The grape has a flavour very similar to that of the German Riesling, and some believe the original Pedro Ximenez was the Elbling or Weissalbe variety, which has been cultivated in the Rhine valley from time immemorial. The variety is thought to have originated in the Canary Islands, from where it passed to Madeira and thence was taken to the Rhine and Moselle regions.

It is interesting to note that the vine is *not* the most important determining factor in the quality of the wine; the soil and the climate are more influential. In a pamphlet entitled *Beverages de Luxe* I chanced to read an article entitled 'Sherry' by Geo. E. Howell, from which I quote a few lines:

> The ancient family of Sancho, long-time owners of the famous vineyard known as El Caribe, sent some of their best and most vigorous plants and vine-stocks to California, which when replanted and grafted gave extremely good wines, though never with the remotest similarity to those of Jerez. This experiment, and the replantation of the vineyards with American stocks which was carried out later in all Spanish vineyards, are conclusive proof that the flavour and bouquet are mainly influenced by the soil and climate of each district, and that these are what distinguishes one wine from another.

The experiment referred to was carried out in the first decade of the present century.

Another test consisted of sending Spanish vine stocks to the Rhine region, and exactly the same result was obtained as with those sent to America. Experiments have also been carried out to produce table wines in Jerez, as in other regions of Spain, but the results have not been altogether happy, probably on account of the soil and climate of this Andalusian region. It seems certain that if other Spanish varieties were planted in Jerez the result would be more like a Sherry than any table wine, whereas a Jerez vine planted in another region would produce a wine without any of the characteristics of Sherry.

All this shows that it is the soil and the climate which mainly influence the must, since the same variety of vine planted at different levels of one vineyard produces contrasting types of must, because the soil has a different structure and the percentage of calcium carbonate varies from one part to another. Thus the wines of Jerez cannot satisfactorily be imitated elsewhere, even though the same vines and

---

* Lucius Junius Moderatus Columella (*c.*3 BC–AD 54), a celebrated agriculturist and farmer of Cadiz.

the same methods of maturing and processing are used, because this will still not take into account the climate and soil.

The lifespan of the vine used always to be considered practically unlimited: according to Pliny the Romans calculated it at about seven hundred years. In France and Italy there exist vines claimed to be three or four hundred years old. Generally speaking, however, it was considered in the latter half of the nineteenth century (that is, before the phylloxera scourge) that the productive life of a normal vine was about fifty to seventy years. In Jerez there was until a few years back a vine said to be over three hundred years old, in a patio in the Calle Antona de Dios, on a site originally belonging to the Rivero bodegas but latterly taken over for use as a school by the Christian Brotherhood of the Buen Pastor (Good Shepherd). The height of the vine was over three metres, whilst its girth at ground level was some 155 cm.

Although it is generally true that the crop produced in years of heavy spring rainfall is abundant but of low strength, and vice versa in dry years, heat and humidity affect different varieties of vine in different ways. It has been noted, for example, that the Palomino, Pedro Ximenez and Mantúo Castellano produce a larger yield in dry years, whilst mantúo de Pila, Perruno and Beba give better results in years with heavy rainfall. Any rainfall during the summer months has a harmful effect on the vine. As a Spanish saying goes, 'Rain in June gives no bread, no wine, but lots of gloom.'

A Devastating Plague

In 1863 the phylloxera plague reached France from America, and in 1875 it broke out in the vineyards known as Lagar de la Indiana, belonging to Eugenio Molina and situated about twelve miles outside Málaga, which therefore had the unfortunate distinction of being the first in Spain to be attacked. It now seems fairly certain, from contemporary accounts, that the disease must have been carried to Málaga from the south of France by plants sent there for cultivation. Another region invaded at the same time was Ampurdán, in the north-east of Spain. Portugal had been hit seven years before.

The phylloxera was a dreadful catastrophe for Jerez, as for all wine-producing regions. Countless conferences were held to discuss means of combating the disease, and large rewards were offered for any effective remedy against the seemingly relentless advance of the scourge. A commission was sent to Málaga from Jerez in 1876 to investigate its effects, and each province was obliged by Royal Decree of 19 June 1879 to give three lectures on the subject of phylloxera. The Jerez lectures took place in July of the same year, and an International Congress was held in Saragossa in October 1880 at which various means of combating the plague were mooted. At all these conferences manifold remedies were proposed, mainly insecticides and schemes of isolating a certain zone for the study of the way the disease spread and of controlling the entry of goods which might propagate it. At one time it was thought that the high mountains that separated Málaga from Jerez would serve as a barrier against the advance of the insect, but this confidence was misplaced. It was also believed that the compact nature of the albariza would check the spreading of the disease, but this hope proved equally unfounded as the phylloxera went even faster over this kind of soil than over the other looser, sandy soils.

All was in vain. On 21 July 1894 the first symptoms appeared In Jerez. It was a black day for the town, whose only remedy was the same as that of the rest of the viticultural districts of Europe: that is to say, replanting the vineyards with American rootstock onto which local varieties could later be grafted. The reason why the American root is resistant to the insect is that it contains it endemically, which is why it was not allowed to be imported into Europe at the start of the invasion. In the worst-affected regions whole vineyards were uprooted, in the hope that the disease would not spread to the adjoining ones and so at least some of the fruit might be saved, rather than wait for the vines to produce no grapes.

The plague raged from Málaga through Morón to Lebrija, and thence to Jerez, where it is said to have been brought by itinerant vineyard workers. The first vineyards to be attacked were one in the northern part, called Ducha, which had albariza soil, and another called Torrox in the south, consisting of white barro; but in fact the disaster struck almost everywhere at once, especially in the albarizas. Within a few years every vineyard in Jerez was ruined.

It is remarkable that, in spite of the very high cost of replanting a vineyard from the time that the soil is got ready until it yields grapes in the fourth year, the vineyard wealth of this corner of Spain not only has not disappeared but is increasing. The quantity of fruit that a vine yields is astonishing. The famous vine at Hampton Court Palace once gave 2,500 bunches of grapes in one year, whilst in Hannover, Pennsylvania, it is recorded that a single vine stock produced 4,000 bunches in 1840.

The productive life of a vine grafted onto an American root-stock—that is, the period during which it yields a fair return—may be limited to twenty-five years, after which time it is better to let the soil lie fallow for the following fifteen to twenty years, as it has been found that the best results are obtained in virgin soil, maximum production being reached between the sixth and twelfth years after planting.

For several years past a good deal of research work has been carried out by official centres to ascertain which stocks are best adaptable to the Jerez vineyards, using hybrids of American roots and European species, with a view not only to obtaining a better yield but also to lengthening the life of the vine, as it has been seen that American roots, as well as having a shorter life-span, have less defence against excessive limestone content, which gives rise to chlorosis and destruction of the root and general decay of the vine.

Besides the phylloxera plague there have at various times been other diseases in the Jerez vineyards, which, fortunately, have been of short duration. At present the two cryptogams most frequent in the district are oïdium (*Uncinula necator*) in the rainy years, and peronospora or downy mildew (*Plasmopara viticola*), which generally occurs in May or June as a result of mists and rain. Oïdium, generally known in Jerez as *cenizo*, produces a more or less dark stain on the branch and a dust on the grape, the skin of which cracks and subsequently rots; in vineyards attacked by this disease one notices a marked smell of damp and mustiness. With downy mildew, the leaves get covered with straw-coloured stains on the upper surface and with a greyish dust underneath. Oïdium also attacks stalks and makes the grapes fall; and if the disease occurs prematurely they do not get completely ripe.

There are several remedies for oïdium, but the most efficient and economical one, once the disease has started, is dusting the vine with sulphur.

To prevent downy mildew, the vineyards are generally treated with what is called 'Bordeaux mixture', obtained by dissolving two kilos of sulphate of copper in a hundred litres of water and adding slaked lime; this solution is sprayed on the plants mechanically.

Another disease which sometimes occurs in the Jerez vineyards is chlorosis, which is caused by an excess of calcium in the soil and turns the leaves of the vines yellowish. This disease can be remedied in May by treating the vineyard with a solution of 3% of iron sulphate in water, adding two kilos of slaked lime and thirty grammes of linseed oil for every hundred litres of water (the linseed oil is added to the lime when it is being slaked, so that it adheres properly to the leaves). Another remedy is to apply a solution of iron sulphate to the soil surrounding the vine about fifteen centimetres from its base, making a hole, fifteen centimetres deep, with an iron rod so that the solution reaches the roots. The same effect can be achieved by making a small trench round the base of the plant, placing the ground iron sulphate (about two hundred grammes per vine) in a groove near the root and adding six to eight litres of water to carry it to the roots.

Hidalgo in his *Efemérides*, referring to the seventeenth century, mentions an insect called the *purgón*, which must be presumed to be the *pulgon de las viñas (Altica oleracea,* or vine grub), and writes: '. . . at the municipal meeting of 10 April 1600 (page 1609) Don Diego Caballero de los Olivos (24th Alderman) proposes that 'the *purgón* be excommunicated [*sic*] as it has produced such havoc in the vineyards' and it was decided to offer special prayers in Jerez . . .'

In 1640 there was another plague of *pulgón* in Jerez; more prayers were said, and it was attributed to this act of piety that the blight disappeared.

Chapter 6
The Vines

It is time to say something about the various tasks which have been carried out in the Sherry vineyards from time immemorial and are still carried out today. I shall describe these processes in detail, year by year, because I want to put on record every stage of these traditional methods of cultivation. I am very grateful to many of my colleagues whose expert knowledge of viticulture has greatly helped me in collecting this information.

First Year

Agosta: This process, so called because it is invariably carried out in the month of August, is the deep tilling or turning-over of the soil where the vineyard is to be planted. The main object is to destroy the weeds and break up the earth. It is done with a narrow hoe (*azuela*), by men working in groups of three, about a yard apart. The soil is broken up to a depth of some sixty centimetres.

The cost of this work today has become excessive and except in small vineyards, tractors and a deep plough are normally used.

Levelling: This has to take place after twenty or thirty centimetres of rain have fallen on the ploughed surface, which has generally happened by December or January. In the past the levelling was generally done by hand, usually backwards and from top to bottom of the slope, by groups of ten workmen under a foreman. The main object is to get the land perfectly level and smooth, so that the chain used to mark out the location of the plants should have no obstacles in its way.

Today this operation too is mechanized, being carried out by levelling-machines, which do it more efficiently and cheaply.

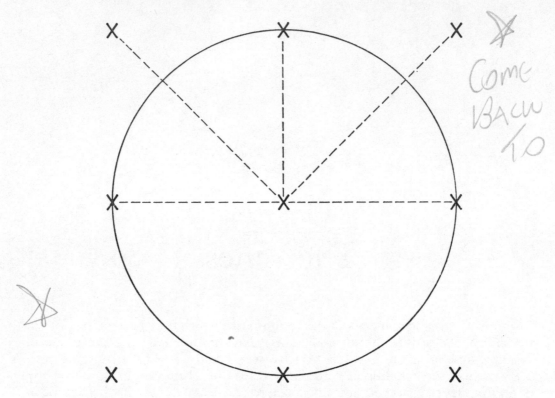

The *marco real* system of planting: not economical with space, but it has certain practical advantages.

Marking-out: It is difficult to give a hard and fast rule as regards the laying-out of the vineyard. It is generally necessary for a new plantation to follow the plan of existent adjacent vineyards rather than its own individual contours, as the tilling of the Jerez vineyards was in the past always done by hand labour except in isolated cases; but this question of which way the vineyards face is not of great importance. The marking is done with a special chain marked off to show the distance apart at which the vines are to be planted; at each mark the man carrying the end of the chain places a metal stake in the soil.

There are two systems used in the marking of vineyards, known as the *marco real* and the *tresbolillo*. The *marco real* is based on a square and the *tresbolillo* on an equilateral triangle. The latter system is at first sight the more rational as all the plants are equidistant from each other, which is not the case with the *marco real* (see comparative diagrams above).

In the *marco real* plantations there are four 'lanes', two at right-angles to the edges of the vineyards and two diagonal, but these latter are in effect useless as their width is only 70% of that of the other two. Although in *tresbolillo* plantations there are only three lanes (one at right-angles and two diagonal), the width of all three is equal, equivalent to 86% of the distance between the vines.

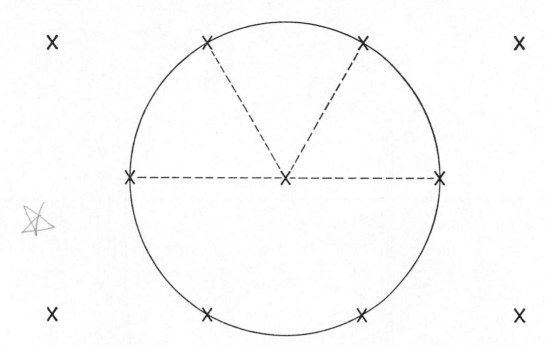

The *tresbolillo* system—always the same distance between any two adjacent vines, but less practical than the *marco real*.

This second system has the added advantage that more plants fit into the acreage – 231 vines for every 200 planted on the *marco real* system.

Although the *tresbolillo* is undoubtedly the more logical, as the vines are uniformly distributed throughout the plantation, there were until recently very few vineyards so planted because, as the work was always done by hand, it was not as practical as the rectangular system. Although an old farming adage in Spain says '*Retírate de mí que daré por tí y por mí* ('Get away from me and I will yield for both of us')—that is, the farther apart the vines are planted the more they will produce—practice has proved in Jerez that the ideal plantation for vineyards worked by hand is the *marco real* of 1½ × 1½ metres. This system not only keeps the moisture in the soil but also ensures that no soil is wasted, giving the plant all the room necessary for its normal development and maintenance. It is also easier for the men, who generally work in groups of ten along the oblique lanes, as they can reach across the whole width of a lane without having to move from one side to the other. The number of vines per *aranzada*, planted according to the *marco real* system as indicated above, is about two thousand.

Spreading the fertilizer: After the site is marked the fertilizer is distributed—one esparto-grass basket full (about twelve kilos) for each hole dug, which corresponds to two plants. This work is generally done by boys, and about a thousand baskets

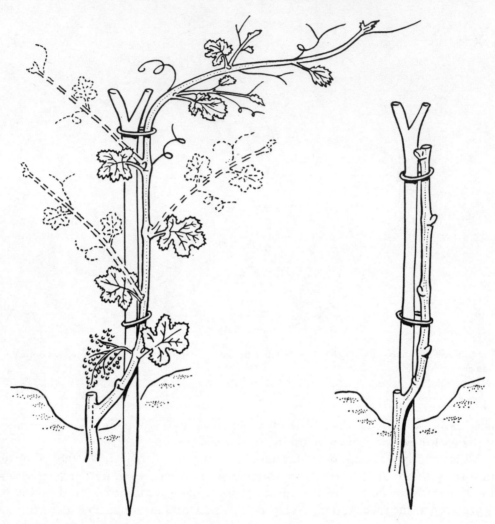

The young vine as it appears in the spring (*left*) and winter of its first year.

of fertilizer are used for every aranzada. Time was when these used to cost about one peseta each, including transport to the vineyards.

Selecting the stocks: Before deciding on the most appropriate variety it is necessary to obtain an analysis of the soil, as not all types offer the same resistance to calcium.*

Planting: Before planting, the roots are cut to between five and ten centimetres from the base, the new shoots being cut at ground level, leaving only the back bud, if it is long enough.

* For technical details, see supplement in Part Five (5).

Once the ground is thoroughly moist from the rain which generally falls before January, planting is started. This consists of opening a square hole between every two markings of the chain, with an *azada*. These holes are eighteen inches wide and go as deep as the *agosta* tilling.

The planting is done by groups of ten men under a foreman, who distributes the stakes, checks the size of the holes and sees that the rows are as straight as possible. To ensure this, for every two parallel rectangular holes, two are made transversely. The workman places the root, which should remain as nearly upright as possible, in the spot indicated by the iron stake. He packs the soil round the root and treads it down, then puts the heap of fertilizer left when the marking of the plantation was done into the hole, and covers it up. He repeats this procedure all through the vineyard.

Cavabién: This second tilling takes places in March, and is done with an azada by the same number of men. Its object is to till the land to a depth of about twenty centimetres and break up the hard surface of the soil so that the plant develops properly.

Golpe-lleno: The main object of this third tilling, carried out in May, is to rectify the *cavabién* and prevent the weeds growing and the soil hardening, thus facilitating the growing of the vine. Again, it is done by groups of ten men, and the digging and levelling are done at the same time; as, if they dug the whole vineyard first and then levelled it, they would have to work backwards and might damage the vines.

Bina: This fourth tilling is carried out in July, and is very important in the Jerez district as it serves not only to kill the weeds but, principally, to make the soil impervious to the heat of the sun and retain in the soil the moisture which is to supply the vine during the hot summer months. The process consists of cutting into the soil at an angle and then pressing it down with a hoe until it is compact, but without putting too much pressure on the plant.

Desgrama (weeding): This consists in going over the ground in August to kill the weeds which have survived the *agosta*, and is the final task of the first year.

Second Year

Deserpia: This is the first tilling of the agricultural year after the vintage, and when possible should take place once the grass has started growing after the first autumn rain. It is carried out, as usual, backwards and from top to bottom of the slope. Square holes are dug and the excavated soil built up into ledges round them. Apart from exposing the soil to the air, the principal object of this work is to absorb the rainfall, which otherwise would remain superficial and drain away, as most Jerez vineyards are located on gentle slopes or the sides of low hills. In low-lying districts, which generally have darker soil, it is preferable to bank up the soil instead of digging holes, because, although it costs a little more, this difference is

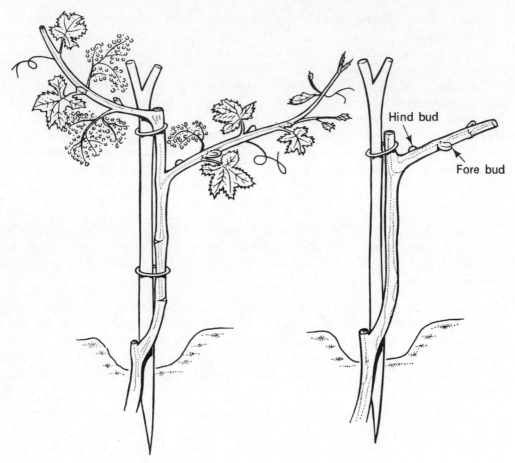

Second year—spring (*left*) and winter.

almost entirely cancelled out by the consequent saving of labour at the *cavabién* stage.

Desbraga: This is carried out with an *azuela* (narrow hoe) in December, and consists of digging a fifteen-centimetre trench round the young plant and cutting the surface roots, which prevents the new vine from getting too thick at ground level and produces a uniform thickness higher up to allow for grafting; at the same time the unwanted shoots of the previous year are pruned.

Cavabién: In late January the plants that have died are replaced, and then the *cavabién*, the second task of the agricultural year, takes place in the same way as the year before, in February instead of March.

Golpe-lleno: This third tilling is carried out as in the previous year, in April and May.

Bina: The fourth and last tilling is again done in July.

Grafting: In August the buds of the European variety are grafted onto the American rootstocks. About a fortnight beforehand some leaves are removed, to soften the stem and ensure that the bud graft will take; it is advisable to graft the stem on the eastward side to protect the subsequent year's buds against the strong and frequent east winds, which might easily fracture the shoot if the graft was done on the other side. The earth is removed at the base of the plant to the necessary depth; the stem is then cut to allow the insertion of the bud, which has to be joined up along its edges; if the vine is too thick the bud is placed a little to one side. The graft is tied with raffia and covered up with crumbled earth, which should be as fresh as possible, and the earth is heaped up round the new vine to a height of about forty centimetres. It is necessary, when selecting the plant to be grafted, to take only buds of healthy vines.

Third Year

Deserpia: This takes place in October as in the second year.

Desbraga: In December a trench is again dug round the vine, to see if the bud has taken; the stem is cut with pruning-shears one bud above where the graft took place. A cane is driven into the ground and the vine tied to it with three palm thongs, the last about forty centimetres above ground level. From May onwards each plant should be regularly inspected, as it is then that it will be budding.

'Shaping' the vine: In the Jerez district two systems are commonly employed to shape the vine, which is generally done in June. The first, called *de nieto*, consists of suppressing the buds below the level where the head of the vine is to be formed and severing the green branch two buds above that level, thus leaving two shoots which will be pruned in December. During the following year the upper of the two shoots is removed and the lower will bear the new growth, including the knob (*vara y pulgar*) which will finally become the vine stock. This system will produce grapes in the third year after planting. The other system, which appears preferable, is that called in Jerez *de virote*, which consists of leaving a shoot with no buds at a height above the head of the vine from which the branches have to grow. If this method is adopted the vine will not produce grapes till the fifth year.

The head of the vine should be about one foot above ground-level, but it should be longer or shorter according to the ground, if it is in the lowlands or should gain or lose height due to erosion or to the tilling of the soil. This low formation of the Jerez vines protects the soil in summer from the extreme heat and avoids excessive evaporation, which would be harmful.

In cases where the grafts do not take the stake is stuck into the ground at an angle, so that the workmen will know later—in February—that new wedge grafting has to be carried out, without having to check every vine again.

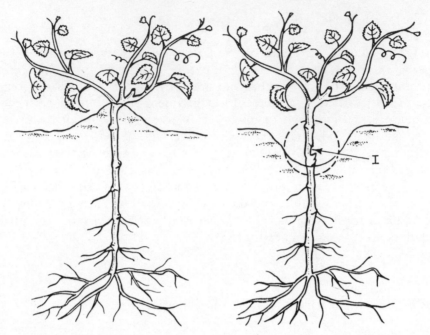

The vine in August (*left*); earth has been heaped round the plant earlier in the summer, and some leaves removed. This earth is now removed and the cuts made with a grafting-knife (*right*). The figure I indicates the area shown in greater detail below.

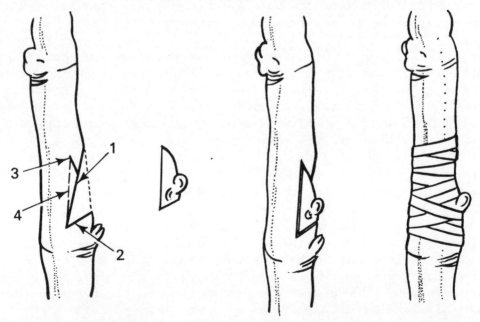

Close-up of the graft (*left*), showing how the cuts are made; in order: 1. Sharply angled downward cut; 2. Second downward cut at a flatter angle; 3. Short cut at a sharp upward angle; 4. Successive upward cuts to enlarge the 'groove'. The bud is inserted (*centre*) and the graft tied with raffia (*right*).

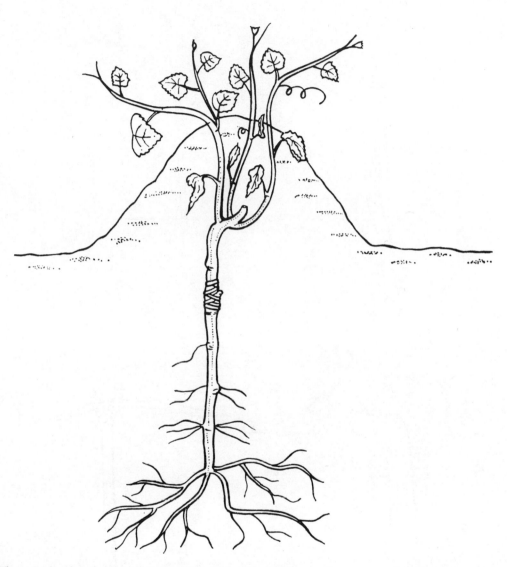

The completed graft: the vine is packed round with earth once again to protect the new graft against the cold.

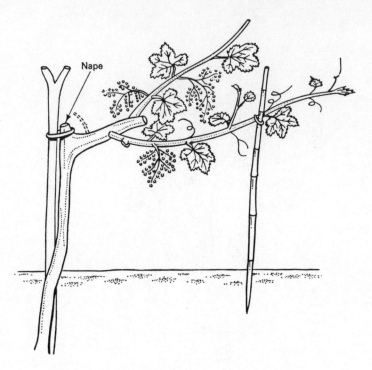

Third year—spring.

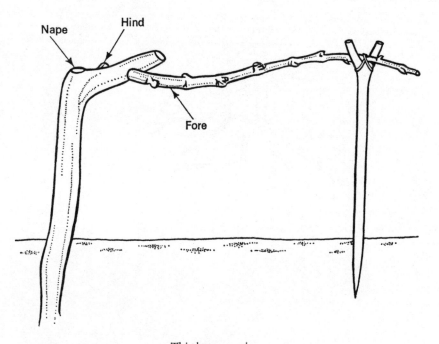

Third year—winter.

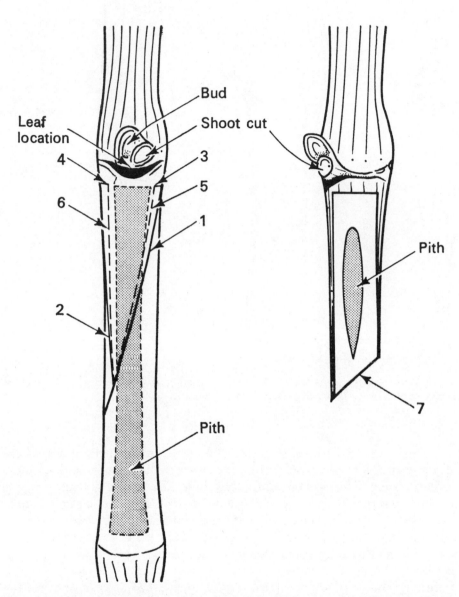

Making the wedge (*espiga*) for wedge-grafting. The pith must be exposed by the first cut, which is made on the side where the shoot (*nieto*) grows, below the bud. The cuts are, in order: 1. Angled downward cut right through the cane; 2. Less sharply angled cut, which must not expose the pith; 3. & 4. Very short horizontal cuts to make the 'shoulders' (*hombrillos*) of the wedge; 5. & 6. Finishing cuts. The view of the finished wedge (*right*) from the shoot side shows the bevel cut.(7).

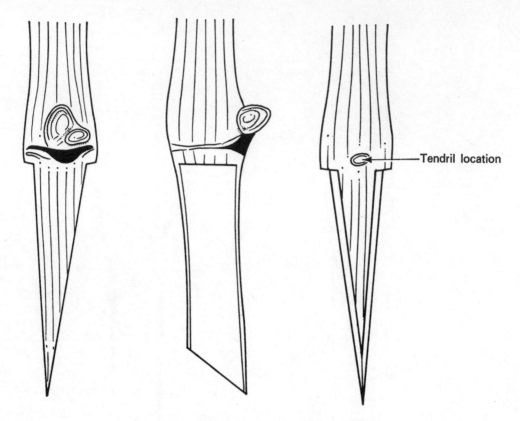

Three more views to show the shape of the finished wedge: (*left to right*) front, or bud side; lateral (i.e. the reverse of the view shown above); and rear, or tendril side.

In February the *espiga* (wedge grafting) is performed on the vines where the graft did not take. This involves cutting the stock with secateurs and selecting the most suitable stem. This is then split down the centre with a grafting-knife and a pointed stick inserted at an angle of about 13° or 15°. The two are lashed together with several strips of raffia, ensuring that the groove is well covered, to keep away the soil; then the top part of the stem is tied to the stake to prevent its moving when the soil is heaped up round it. Great care must be taken with all this if the graft is to succeed.

In February the *cavabién* is carried out, as in the second year, and in May the first inspection of the stakes is made as was mentioned before.

In April and May the *golpe-lleno* is done, as in the second year. In the same months the vines are treated with sulphur and copper sulphate to safeguard them against oïdium and mildew. In June the shoots of the American plant are removed and the buds inspected to see they are securely bound to the props. Sometimes it is necessary to go over the ground again, sprinkling sulphate of copper and sulphur. In July the *bina* is performed as in previous years.

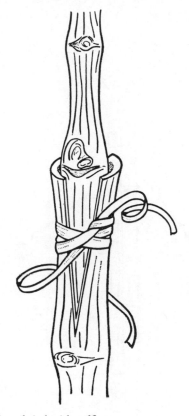

The wedge is inserted into the stock and tied with raffia.

Fourth and Subsequent Years

In the fourth year the vineyard should produce its first crop of grapes.

In October the stakes are collected and heaped in the vineyards by apprentices. These stakes, in Jerez, are in fact generally short canes, which is why cane-brakes are planted in many Jerez vineyards. In other districts oak or pine props are used.

In October the *deserpia* is carried out as before, and in November the *virote* pruning is done, which consists of cutting the branch at a height of forty centimetres from the ground, just below the bud above the one at the level of the formation of the vine (branch and knob).

If it is desired to obtain grapes in the fourth year the bud above the one reserved for the formation of the vine in the following year is left on the plant, and this will produce the first crop of any importance. Afterwards, during the fifth year, this bud is cut and the formation of the vine is achieved. From the two stems of the *virote* the upper branch is left on the vine and the lower one is cut, leaving two buds.

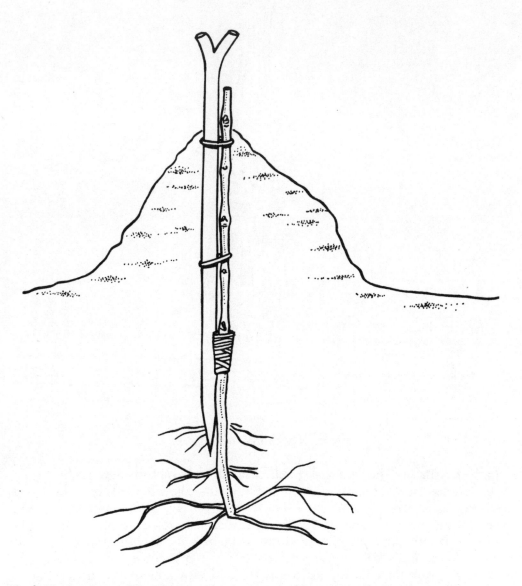

The finished wedge-graft in February—the vine is secured by a prop and covered over with earth.

Fourth year—spring.

During the fifth year, when the shoots start budding, it is necessary to remove the first if it is not parallel to the ground. This will cause the branch which grows later to develop horizontally, allowing the branch-and-knob system of the next year to start, and thus avoiding another year's delay before the definite formation of the vine is achieved; the upper bud should be on the opposite side of the stem to where the grafting bud was, so that the upper bud will be the knob which has to produce the second crop, and the lower one will start the branches of the future vine, that is the bud called '*de verde*' because it does not stop the sap circulation.

In the sixth year the upper part is removed, leaving only the *colodrillo* (head of the vine); in the lower part, in which two shoots have grown, one is left as the branch and the other one is the knob, so that they eventually grow from right to left and from left to right.

In the seventh year the cane is pruned, leaving two buds which go opposite ways. In the eighth year the long branch is pruned in the same way as the previous year, leaving the vine now with four stems, the cane and the spur, which are both to be left on the same side so that the year after they should work alternately, avoiding loss of strength.

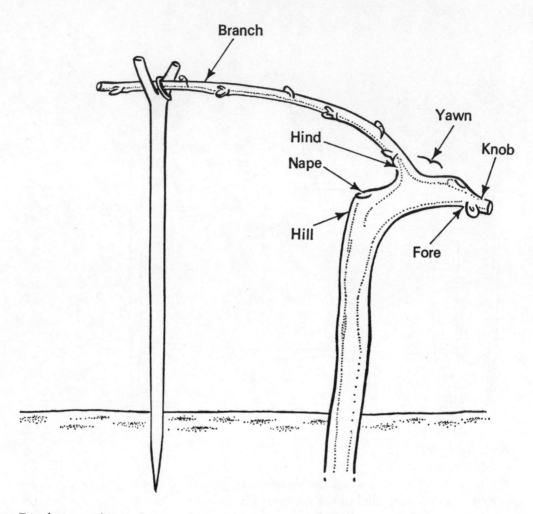

Fourth year—winter.

The branch differs from the knob in that it is left with seven buds, the knob having only four.

It is easy to understand the importance of pruning, in so far as it refers to the yield and the life of the vine, and there are many growers who consider that pruning influences not only the quantity of grapes that the vine will produce but also the quality of the must: the thinner the branch of the vine, they say, the more delicate the must obtained.

In November the canes pruned earlier in the year are collected up, to be burnt for charcoal—there is a saying in this part of the world that one aranzada of vineyard will produce as many sackfuls of charcoal as butts of must. These sacks weigh approximately fifteen kilos each.

In December the vines are dug round at ground level to remove the superficial roots.

In January palm thongs are made, to tie the vines, the branches are cut, and the ends sharpened to enable them to be driven into the ground as props. Once all this is ready the canes are distributed and the vines tied to them.

In February comes the *cavabién*, and in April and May the *golpe-lleno*, as in previous years. During this last month another pruning (the *castra* or *poda en berza*) is done. This work is of great importance in training the branches of the vine, removing the unnecessary buds and preparing it for the pruning to be done in the following year; it has a great influence on the life and production of the Jerez vines.

The copper-sulphate spraying is also carried out in May, two or three times if necessary, as is the sulphur treatment to prevent oïdium. The branches are tied to stakes to prevent the wind from splitting them. This operation contributes greatly not only to the wine and its development but also to the production of the subsequent year, because it keeps the branch from drying up, which would result in a weak shoot.

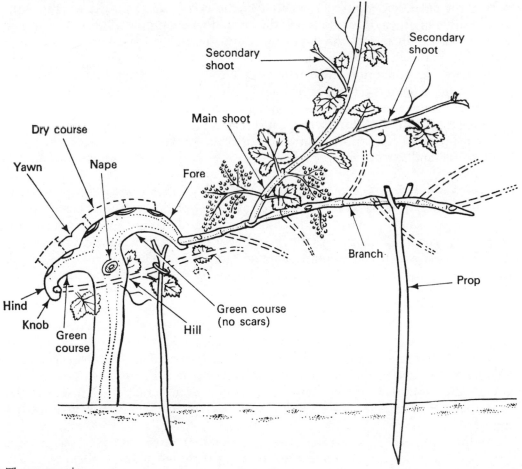

The mature vine.

In June the copper-sulphate and sulphur treatments are applied for the third time. In the vineyards planted with the Pedro Ximenez variety the sulphur has to be sprayed more thoroughly; if this is not done there is a definite danger of the grapes' not ripening properly and remaining quite small, which disease can reduce the crop by as much as one-half. In this same month of June the vines are also cleaned of the secondary shoots (*recastra*). This is a rectification of the previous pruning (*castra*) to prevent the growth of unnecessary knobs, which would give rise to bad formation of the vine head.

In July the *bina* is carried out as in previous years.

I have outlined above the different tasks carried out in the vineyards for the propagation of vines. In vineyards which are already producing normally, various additional stages are necessary.

The propping of the branches may be done twice: before flowering (end of May or beginning of June), lifting the branches which are drooping and near the soil, to avoid the shoots' touching the ground, which would result in the loss of a great part of the crop; and again in July, after the flowering, to avoid the weight of the grapes dragging them down to touch the ground where they would rot if it should rain; with the lifting of the branches warm air gets to the grapes, which is important in the Sherry vineyards.

Another procedure normally carried out in June is the *golpe y rajo* which comes after the *golpe-lleno* and before the *bina*. This superficial tilling is not always done, but gives quite good results, not only because the shoots develop better and produce more but also because pollination takes place more quickly and the shoot is less exposed to climatic fluctuations. With this complementary tilling the soil is kept softer and retains more moisture, so necessary in the subequent summer months.

Finally, the *rebina* (a repetition of the *bina*) is another very useful process. In August the soil develops cracks, sometimes as much as thirty centimetres deep and ten wide, especially in the lowland soils, and this tilling not only eradicates the weeds that generally grow after the *bina*, but at the same time assists the ripening of the grapes, which consequently contain more sugar. There is an adage in this part of the world which says, '*Quien rebina en Agosto, llena la bodega de mosto*' ('He who again tills the vineyard in August fills his bodega with must'.)

The various stages and methods of cultivation described above are the most usual ones in the Jerez vineyards, but it is impossible to lay down a hard and fast rule as to how many men and working days per aranzada each one requires. There is another adage in Spanish which says, '*A la tierra, no se le puede engañar*' ('You cannot deceive the land'), and that is very true. It must also be said that not all the additional work is indispensable in every case; the grower is the expert, and he must use his own judgement to decide what is necessary and what superfluous.

At different periods, as a result of social discontent, attempts have been made to impose fixed rules for the cultivation of vineyards, and to have them generally adopted, but in the long run such a ruling could only damage the Jerez viticulture, from the point of view not only of the owners of the land but also of the workmen, as when farming stops being remunerative it has to be given up altogether.

It is true that the Jerez vineyards have always been cultivated with an almost excessive care, unknown in other wine districts; tended, in fact, more as gardens than as farmland. As a result labour charges and other vineyard expenses in Jerez have reached a level which is bound to be an obstacle to the starting of new plantations, with adverse results for the whole Sherry district. The viticulturists in this region know that all the care they lavish on their vineyards is not excessive; that anything left undone would be reflected in the produce they hope to get. This care in cultivation has always been more characteristic of vine-growers than of other farmers: one recalls the words of the prophet Isaiah, who said: 'My wellbeloved had a vineyard in a very fruitful hill: and he made a trench about it, and gathered out the stones thereof, and planted it with the choicest vine, and built a tower in the midst of it, and also hewed out a winepress therein: and he looked that it should bring forth grapes . . . What could have been done more to my vineyard, that I have not done in it?'*

With the present methods of cultivation and the present wages it can be reckoned that the yearly expense per aranzada (1989) will never be less than some 160,000 pesetas, which is really exorbitant. Of course in vineyards which require any additional cultivation this figure will be even higher. To the above figures, which we might call theoretical, must be added the costs of defraying the expenses of the first four years after plantation, capital investments made during the vineyards's thirty years of useful life, management, workmen's insurance and compensation fund, subsidies, lighting, provisions and other more general expenses like transport, props, plant and tools: all this apart from the rent of the vineyard, land-tax and rates. Taking all these extras into account, it can fairly be said that the actual cost of the cultivation of one aranzada of vineyard in Jerez at present exceeds 200,000 pesetas per year.

Earlier Price-Fixing

In the eighteenth century the Guild used to fix the price of a *carretada*† of grapes, and for this purpose the Guild's deputies used to get together with experts nominated by the municipality. Referring to the year 1775, a report of one of these meetings states:

> It is reckoned that in that year the vineyards would produce one and a quarter carretadas of grapes. Asked what the cultivation and care of one aranzada would cost, including the living expenses of the owner responsible for the maintenance of the vineyard, they considered the matter carefully, taking into account the rates of which had been paid the workmen from 1 November 1774, and decided that the cost would be 321 reales and 23 maravedis, exclusive of tax, etcetera.

* Isaiah, v. 2–4.
† Literally, a cartload; in fact, the quantity of grapes necessary to produce one butt of must, approximately 690 kilos.

The meeting then resolved, in view of the said expenses and the yield of each aranzada, and taking into account that that year seventy-six basketfuls would go into each carretada, the amount of the crop and the value of the previous year's wine, that the price of each carretada of good grapes or butt of must should be eighteen pesos, for medium-quality grapes seventeen pesos, and for the inferior quality only fifteen.

In other years only fifty-five basketfuls went to each carretada.

It is interesting to compare this with the current cost of farming one aranzada as given above, although it should be borne in mind that these figures are not truly comparable, as the purchasing-power of currency now is very different from what it was then.

It should be said that there are generally other expenses, besides those which have been mentioned, arising out of other subsidiary activities which have not been taken into account. For example, unsuccessful vines—often amounting to fifteen per cent of the total—must be replaced; pruned branches have to be burnt, iron sulphate applied to the vines after pruning and the refuse of branches and roots removed from the vine collected (these last two tasks being undertaken by apprentices). Another expense is the digging of drainage ditches: the albariza vineyards are generally on slopes or in hollows, and ditches are necessary to drain off the rainwater, their number varying according to the size and location of the vineyards.

During the pruning of the vines, or just after, it is also advisable to clean off superfluous bark, to prevent parasites and fungus collecting underneath during the winter months, which would be very detrimental to the life and development of the plant. It is also necessary, though not every year, to fertilize the vineyards. The fertilizers considered best for vineyard use are organic manures, although nowadays these are not used enough, as there is generally a shortage, reflecting the dwindling numbers of horses and mules in Spain. When there are no organic fertilizers, a mineral fertilizer is used, a blend of superphosphates 18/20, potassium sulphate and ammonium sulphate in the ratio 12:9:4, 100 to 250 grammes of which is applied to each vine. It is said that the best mineral fertilizers for the vineyard are those composed of nitrogen, phosphoric acid and potash, but there can be no fixed rule because everything naturally depends on the soil; some growers consider that organic manures give a certain taint to the musts, while others maintain that the musts produced by mineral fertilizers are not so full-bodied and their alcoholic strength is generally not high enough.

For the distribution of these organic fertilizers, about 500 holes are dug per aranzada and a basketful of manure placed in each hole, which serves four vines. This is generally done every six years. To apply the mineral or nitrogen fertilizers, a hole or small trench is generally dug around the trunk of the vine, about fifteen centimetres from the stem and the same deep, the fertilizer placed in the hole and covered up and earth heaped round the vine afterwards. This mineral fertilizer is considered to remain effective for about three years.

Another extra expense occurs in very rainy or misty years, when three sprayings with copper sulphate are insufficient. A fourth spraying is more costly, due to the fact that the vines are by this time in full leaf, so that the workmen take more time to carry out the work.

One final vineyard expense, which comes when the grapes are ripe, is the paying of a watchman. He operates from a small hut on stilts,* which is generally placed by the vineyard-owner at a strategic point in the highest part of the vineyard. The reason for this can be found in the Spanish saying, '*Las niñas y las viñas son difíciles de guardar*' ('Girls and vineyards take a lot of watching').

* Called in Spanish a *bienteveo* ('I see you well').

Chapter 7

The Harvest

At last September arrives, and the season in which the miracle of the wedding feast at Cana is repeated, and the sweet juice of the grape transformed into wine. When the stem of the bunch of grapes takes on a dark hue, and the grapes themselves get soft and sweet, the vineyard-owner starts his vintage. The traditional date for the start of the vintage in Jerez is 8 September, the Feast of the Nativity of Our Lady, but, naturally, the exact date varies from year to year according to the state of ripeness of the grape. In other parts of Spain it is traditional for the vintage to begin on 21 September, the Feast of St Matthew. In Jerez, especially, the vintage cannot be started on a fixed date, nor can it be completed in a single picking, as it is necessary to go over the ground several times, choosing only the fruit which is completely ripe.

Naturally, the different varieties of grape are picked separately in each vineyard; though in fact the production of other classes of grape than the Palomino and Pedro Ximenez is insignificant.

The ordinary way of cutting the bunches of grapes off the vine is with a knife, and the workmen put the grapes into baskets made of olive branches, each holding 11½ kilos. (Some years ago they used to have, instead of baskets, open wooden panniers slung from a strap over their shoulders.) Sixty basketfuls make a carretada, the amount considered necessary to produce one butt of must. The workmen first remove any dry grapes, and then carry the baskets to the esplanade in front of the vineyard building. In the larger vineyards they are generally carried on mules provided with appropriate panniers, or, sometimes, in small carts. Each basketful is emptied onto a circular esparto-grass mat, and the grapes are generally left in the open for between twelve and twenty-four hours so that the moisture they may contain disappears. If they are left overnight they are covered with another esparto-grass mat to protect them from the dew. Next day, by which time they should be completely dry, each mat is carried to the *lagar* and emptied.

To start the vintage too early naturally affects the alcoholic strength of the wine. Sometimes, for fear of rain during the harvesting, there is a tendency in this region to start a little too early; but it is generally preferable to wait until the right time and, if it rains, to stop picking until the rain has ceased.

When the grapes are completely ripe the pips are easy to remove from the pulp and get darker in colour, as also does the stem of the bunch, which, at its base – that is, the part where it joined the branch—becomes the colour of dry wood or dark tobacco. This is when the grape attains its point of maximum yield, not only because it produces more juice but also because, as it contains more sugar, the must will have a higher alcoholic strength.

The vintage lasts for approximately a month, during which period the vineyard-owner has to pay more attention to his work than at any other time, for these few weeks will decide not only whether he will cover the expense he has put into the vineyard during the year, but also the ultimate success or failure of his capital investment.

Several factors influence the final result: the way that the vineyards have been cultivated; the rainfall and temperature during March and April, when the vines are budding, in May, when they are flowering, and during the fructification or ripening of the grapes in June, July and August; the weather during the vintage; and the care taken during the vintage operations—that is, the preparation, rinsing and cleansing of the lagar and casks.

While it is true that the yield from any piece of land mainly depends on providence, the viticulturist should never forget that the quality of the produce of his vineyard depends very largely on the care he lavishes on it. In years of heavy rain during the vintage there are owners who think that the grapes will rot in twenty-four hours and hasten the gathering and the pressing of the harvest, instead of temporarily stopping work. It should not be forgotten that, so long as the grapes are in good condition and not touching the ground, they will stay on the vine and not rot however much it rains. Rain does, however, mean that the harvesting has to be stopped, because it washes off the grape the bloom which, as will be explained later, is so necessary for the starting of the fermentation on which depends the quality of the wine produced.

Once the vintage is finished, especially in large vineyards, the public are generally allowed in to collect the grapes left on the vine.

After the grapes have been exposed to the sun, for a period varying according to the type of wine required, the pressing is started. In Jerez a good many vineyards now have mechanical presses with two or three cylinders, but it has always been said here that better-quality wine is obtained if it is pressed by treading, because the weight of a man is considered to exert the ideal pressure, whereas the machine is thought to break the stems so that the must produced contains too much tannin. This is undoubtedly a fallacy: mechanical presses nowadays can have the pressure regulated.

Till quite recently vineyards in Jerez were not mechanized, and the first machines introduced contaminated the must with iron, which is one of wine's worst enemies. That is why it has always been traditional in Jerez for all the plant and utensils used in the pressing of the grape which were in contact with the liquid to be made exclusively of wood. Iron should undoubtedly be avoided in all wine-presses as any iron content in wine would make it turbid. Nowadays, with modern machinery, all these inconveniences are avoided by machines made of stainless steel or covered with chromium or other substances not attacked or corroded by the acids in the juice of the grape.

The pressing, in general, till quite recently, was carried out by four treaders in each lagar. They generally wear shorts and short-sleeved shirts, and cowhide shoes with a combination of nails in the soles. It is customary for the treaders to start their work about midnight and work till mid-day next day; in this way they are able to rest during the hours when the heat is greatest. It is also said that this system is best for the fermentation, which should be as slow as possible.

The lagar is a sort of square trough on wooden supports about 80 cm. high. It is made entirely of wood, with a threaded iron bar, like a huge screw, in the middle, on which is a nut equipped with two levers. It measures generally between three and four metres square and the side walls are about sixty centimetres high and slope slightly outwards. Into the lagar, which has been perfectly cleaned and disinfected, is tipped one carretada of grapes. The workers, using wooden shovels, spread half this amount in a layer about twenty-five centimetres deep. It is at this time, or after the grapes have been trodden and before they are packed round the screw, that a handful or two of gypsum is sprinkled over them, sometimes with a scoop, the weight not to exceed 1½ kilos per carretada.

The Treaders

The treaders start stepping on the layer of grapes with a rhythmic motion, supporting themselves with their right hands on their shovels. They go from one side of the lagar to the other till they have pressed the first half of the grapes; these are then heaped on one side of the lagar so that the must will ooze out through the outlet into a tub, through the metal sieve where any stems, pips and skins which the must may at this stage contain are collected; the grapes are then trodden a second time. The process is then repeated with the second half of the load, and the remaining pulp is packed round the screw of the lagar, forming a sort of cylinder about 75 cm. in diameter and 1½ m. high. A shovel is used to round off the sides, and the lagar is swept with a small broom made of thyme twigs. The sprinkling of gypsum gives a more solid consistency to the heap. A strip of esparto-grass tape about 12 cm. wide and 25 m. long is wound round it, commencing at the base, where a small wooden channel is placed to allow the must to ooze out under the tape. This tape is fixed with a wooden peg at the bottom, and finished off at the top after the cylinder has been completed. On top of this heap come two dove-tailed pieces of wood called *marranos* (pigs), and on top of these two iron half-hoops; then the nut—called a *marrana* (sow) from the squealing noise it makes when tightened—with its two one-metre handles or levers. At first the levers are turned easily by two men, but by the end of this pressing it takes four, two pulling and two pushing. They have a tape round their wrists, fixed to the handle, so that they do not slip. Each *pie* is pressed two or even three times, the men unravelling the tape, undoing the cylinder and then building it up again around the screw. After the first pressing the pulp is put on a sort of grid to remove the stems, which would undoubtedly taint the must, due to the natural acids which they contain, if the pulp is subjected to too much pressure. This is the general custom: ideally, perhaps, the stems should be removed before the grapes are first trodden.

To the must from the first pressing is added that obtained from the treading, called *de yema*, and the result represents about eighty-five per cent of the total juice obtained from a carretada.

The must from the second pressing, which is not added to the previous one, is called *aguapié*, and represents about five per cent of the total. The juice of the third pressing, which is called in Jerez *espirriaque*, is not generally pressed in the larger vineyards, which have hydraulic presses where the pulp is put into special flat esparto-grass baskets and subjected to a high pressure. The juice thus obtained is called *prensas*. In small vineyards, where no hydraulic presses are available, they sometimes have a fourth pressing, called *estrujón*.

The *aguapié* was so called because it was formerly the custom to add ten or twelve litres of water before the second pressing, to dilute the increased tannin and acid content. Nowadays no water is ever added in this operation. The *espirriaque* is of inferior quality and is sometimes added to the *aguapié*. The *estrujón* is generally used for vinegar, or for low-strength wines which are later distilled. The product of these last pressings is approximately ten per cent of the total.

The must which comes out of the lagar goes through a sieve, as I have said, into a tub; then it is put into large jars with a scoop and funnelled into the casks. The funnels also have sieves, to ensure that no particle of the skins or pips contained in the must gets into the cask. A board called a *babero* (bib) is attached to the funnel, so that any overflow goes back into the tub.

Although the general rule is that one carretada produces one butt, in practice it usually happens that some must is left over in the tub after the butt has been filled, and this is put into a separate butt called a *gorrona*, which takes all the remains of the different pressings.

When the must has been in the butt for several hours violent fermentation sets in, and the liquid starts bubbling. The time taken to reach this state varies according to the air temperature, but it generally starts six or eight hours after pressing.

Transport from the vineyard to the bodegas is generally in carts—sometimes in lorries, when the vineyard roads permit—and the butts are fitted with a funnel or cane tube to avoid the must's overflowing with the froth of the fermentation, as this becomes more active during transport.

While on the subject of the transport from the Sherry vineyards to the bodegas in the town, I must point out how important it is for Jerez to have decent roads to the vineyards, to allow the easy and rapid transport of the must before the winter weather sets in. Any money spent on this would certainly be well invested, because, in view of the exorbitant price of spirits, it is understandable that one of the great aims of the vineyard owner is to have a normal fermentation so that the alcoholic strength of the new wine should be as high as possible.

Temperature during fermentation has a great influence on the quality of alcoholic strength of the wines. The great majority of vineyards have no decent bodegas to store the musts, which are generally left for several hours on the esplanades round the vineyard buildings, exposed to the sun and to great fluctuations of temperature. It would be preferable for the must, as soon as it has been pressed, to be transferred to the bodegas so that the violent fermentation can start there. Excessive temperatures during fermentation result, in the majority of cases, in the wine's not having the expected alcoholic strength.

Temperature variation influences the fermentation process in several adverse ways. First, it diminishes the potential of the yeast for the conversion of the glucose into alcohol. The maximum efficacy of the yeast is obtained at a specific optimum temperature. This depends on, among other factors, the variety to which the yeast belongs, but falls between certain limits which, in the case of Jerez, can be fixed at 17° and 35° Centigrade. Outside these limits the yeast is paralysed.* Secondly, the high temperatures also instigate the development of harmful germs which, besides consuming a certain amount of glucose and therefore reducing the alcoholic strength of the future wine, convert the glucose into other elements, for example acetic acid, which are harmful to the yeast, hindering its development, diminishing its effectiveness, and sometimes producing disagreeable aromas and tastes which spoil the wine. Thirdly, excessive temperature also increases evaporation, thus diminishing the alcoholic strength and the pungency of the wine.

As I have already said, each carretada should in normal years produce one butt of must. This varies, however, from year to year, and there are vintages where as much as ten per cent more grapes are needed. Naturally, the butts cannot be completely filled, as they would overflow when fermentation starts, so an ullage of, say, two arrobas is always allowed, leaving the butt with only twenty-eight.

A Vanished Industry

The ancient Jerez raisin industry no longer exists, and the grapes are used only for eating or for wine-making. Subsidiary industries for utilizing waste-products are non-existent in Jerez, because the quantity would not be sufficient to justify any industrial enterprise. The only by-product used is the charcoal referred to earlier. The residue of the stalks is spread over the narrow paths leading to the buildings, especially on the hilly stretches, to give a foothold on the slippery soil when it rains. As for the skins, it is not generally the custom here to make marc out of them, and they are usually fed to the pigs, as are the pips, which in other wine regions are used for making varnish. The lees resulting from the fermentation of must, which can be reckoned at two arrobas (that is, thirty-three litres) per butt,

---

* The Jerez musts generally contain between 210 and 230 grammes of sugar per litre; it can be said that each 17 grammes per litre of glucose produce 1 per cent of alcohol by volume in the resulting liquid.

are generally sold to the manufacturers of tartrates. I hope the day will come when the vineyard-owners will themselves be able to use all these by-products profitably, which would undoubtedly help to reduce the price of the must.

The must itself, which, once it is pressed, is transported to the bodegas in the town, I shall discuss in the next chapter, which deals with the ageing and maturing of wines, because, at the moment that fermentation sets in, the liquid has really become wine, marking the end of the work in the vineyards during one agricultural year and the beginning of the next year's cycle.

Modernization

Since 1948, viticulture in Jerez has undergone various changes in the course of modernizing the cultivation systems, although the traditional cycle described above remains unchanged. I have asked Cesar Pemán Medina, an eminent agricultural engineer who directs the cultivation of a large group of vineyards in Jerez, to give me a short resumé of these changes. Señor Pemán writes:

At the start, and during the period of transition, mules and horses were used for the deep ploughing of the land prior to planting; they also came to take part in the different stages of tilling during the winter, the ploughing of the actual vineyards, and cultivation of various sorts during the spring and summer.

The sprays used against vine diseases and pests, originally carried by the individual labourer, were also replaced, first by equipment harnessed to mules, later by cart sprayers and machines on high wheels which made it possible to spray several lines of vines at once. However, fully effective mechanization did not come until new plantations were planned with the distance between vines increased to 2.20 × 1.10 metres, allowing small tractors to work along the rows. A variety of implements and machines have since been introduced for tilling and spraying.

Even the vineyards still planted in the old way underwent a decisive change when small motor-driven ploughs and rotocultivators appeared on the market. All the traditional tasks in the Jerez vineyards today are carried out with even greater perfection by ploughs drawn by tractors, and the introduction of rotocultivators, either tractor-drawn or hand-propelled, allows ideal preparation of the land: after it has rained and the ground has been ploughed, these cultivators break up the earth and leave it perfectly loose. Even the hoeing around the base of the vine, which at first was more easily done by hand, is today carried out by machines, with the difference that the hollows made to collect the rain, instead of being around the vine, are made in the centre of the row by ridge-forming ploughs fitted to tractors. The result is very satisfactory, and the ingenious machinery is designed and made locally. Even planting is mechanized, the old way of digging holes having been superseded by the use of large augers fitted to a tractor, which bore the holes rapidly. All the tractors used in these vineyards are of the caterpillar type, as rubber tyres slip on the albariza. These caterpillar tractors have the added advantage that their weight is more evenly distributed and does not compress the soil too much. All tractors used are vineyard types—that is, narrow track, between 0.90 and 1.25 metres. The horsepower is between 22 and 39, most commonly 32. For vineyards which are narrowly planted there are rotocultivators of different types, their horse-power varying between 2 and 12; these small machines, which work without tyres, supported on their discs, are also used in wide-planted vineyards to till the land close to the vine. The smallest (2 to 5 h.p.) are numerous in most of the Jerez vineyards and work with wonderful efficiency, constantly 'combing' the soil near the trunk of the vine without ever touching it.

Another aspect of mechanization in the vineyards is the introduction of the numerous machines to assist with the spraying of the vines with fungicides and insecticides: these range from the power knapsack sprayer to Bell helicopters, which came into use several years ago in Jerez, where Spain's first experiments of vineyard-spraying with helicopters were carried out.

For vines planted in the old way there are machines that can be adapted to power cultivators or are self-propelled, and in line plantations various models attached to tractors are used, with accessories to enable them to cover several rows of vines at a time. At first all these machines used mechanical spraying systems, but more recently compression spraying has been introduced, with a low consumption of water, which is undoubtedly of great interest because of its efficiency.

As the new plantations in rows at 2.20 by 1.10 metres gave passage to mechanization, another factor appeared which has opened the door to the possibility of perfecting and completing the mechanization of the vineyards: the installation of trellises to hold and guide the vine, using wires on iron or concrete posts. This wiring is being adapted to the characteristics of Jerez's vines, soil and climate, but without introducing changes in the pruning, and so no modifications have been made that can affect the quality of the product.

Other machines are now being studied—for instance, deep fertilizers, vine-shoot crushers and others—and so it can be seen that Jerez viticultors have moved with the times, though always very careful not to influence the quality of the product.

New Development*

Since these notes were written twenty years ago, mechanization in the vineyards has evolved as follows:

The wiring which was initiated then has been generally adopted and, in consequence where tractors can be employed, hydraulic intervine ploughs have completely replaced the rotocultivators.

There is a tendency now to lift the formation of the vine and the wires some 20 to 25 centimetres, for more perfect spraying, and also keeping in mind possible future mechanical harvesting.

* These lines have been written by Señor Pamán for the 1990 edition, to bring it up to date.

The use of helicopters has been discontinued as more efficient spraying has been found necessary; this is carried out with technologically advanced machinery specific to the job.

All this has brought about the use of more powerful tractors, up to 55 hp, and consequently wider spread in the new plantations, up to 2.40 by 1.20 metres.

The vine shoot crushers are being replaced by mechanical rakes that collect the wood and carry it to the lanes to be burnt, eliminating the spread of insects and diseases.

A reference should also be made to the experimentation being carried out on a fair scale with a 'no cultivation' system, by which the soil is not tilled at all. The results after quite a number of years are surprising and indicate that the system can be applied in certain vineyards, depending on their age, the topography of the land and other circumstances.

After Phylloxera

As I have shown elsewhere, the production of the Jerez vineyards in the second half of the nineteenth century, before the phylloxera outbreak, was very high. Although much has been replanted since 1896, it is desirable that even more should be planted, so that Sherry stocks should be well provided with aged wines. Every Jerezano interested in the wine trade agrees that our efforts should be aimed at increasing plantation on the albariza soils; but it should be kept in mind that, as we have to fight against competition from other districts on the different markets, our principal task is to reduce the expenses of cultivation and production, because unless this is done our export trade is bound to fall, with a consequent loss to both the local and the national economies.

I am certain that the cost of cultivation per aranzada can be reduced, because, even in periods when wages were very high, and though all the necessary cultivation was given to the vineyards, the expense was still not in proportion to what it is today. I believe, too, that it would be possible to adopt a compromise method of cultivation, partly mechanical and partly manual, which would reduce costs; such a compromise has already been applied successfully in this district, but on a very small scale. Other systems of pruning might also be tried, different to the traditional methods, and if the experiments give good results they should be generally adopted: owners of local olive groves changed their system of pruning and increased production, and there is no reason why a similar experiment should not work in the vineyards, without impoverishing the vine. We should not forget that it is the duty of Jerez to increase production and make every effort to ensure that the great reputation of Sherry should not be lost.

Competitive Considerations

If it were possible for all Sherry to be expensive the problem would undoubtedly be quite different, but we have to take into account the competition from other wine regions that offer imitations at much lower prices—especially the very serious competition from countries like South Africa, Australia, California and Cyprus. If we are to succeed in the effective protection of the name, it is necessary that the genuine product should be universally available at a price which, while allowing a suitable profit to all those taking part in the production and the trade, should be accessible to every genuine wine-lover.

The wine trade, which for years has been protected by legislation in all wine-producing and -consuming countries, has gone through very difficult times since the war: the high costs of production, transport and Customs duties with which wine is burdened on all consuming markets, due to either purely economic or protectionist aims, apart from the restrictions that each country imposes on imports, have resulted in the wines being offered to the consumer at a very high price, and when this coincides, as at present, with an economic depression, it brings about a very considerable reduction in consumption.

It must also be taken into account that the cheaper the cost of production of the albariza wine the more easily and quickly we shall be able to replant all the land capable of producing this excellent Sherry.

I know, unfortunately, what it costs to plant a vineyard, and how expensive the cultivation of it is, but all the people of Jerez should try to the best of their ability to increase stocks of wine and, above all, to see that more vineyards are planted and, if possible, that the number of proprietors of small plots is increased. The viticultural associations, many of whose members are well aware of the problem, could surely suggest ways and means of fostering this development, having recourse, perhaps, to State subsidies, because the problem is one of national interest. It is also necessary to have the support of the sindicatos: the high cost of cultivation has often arisen from the impossibility of cultivating the vineyards according to their needs.

Although Esteban Boutelou, when he wrote about the viticulture of this region, considered it 'one of the most precious monuments of our agriculture', it must be accepted that times and circumstances change and that at present the Jerez vineyards produce more than before they were replanted, but this is mainly due to better cultivation and to complementary tilling and fertilizers which formerly were not used on the scale that they are today.

It is sad to think that, in an eminently agricultural district as large and rich as Jerez, the agricultural worker's occupation should always be despised, and that only those who cannot find work in commerce or industry should work on the land. The basis of prosperity in most countries is agriculture, and there is no reason to run away from the land. The present circumstances should not be taken as typical: they are abnormal, and, it is to be hoped, not permanent, as it is probable that, sooner or later, it will be possible to arrive at a more stable situation in Spanish agriculture.

So far as our viticulture is concerned, I believe that one of the causes of the lack of public enthusiasm for it is that little or no stimulus is given to the worker: there is no longer any possibility of a proper apprenticeship to the trade. It is to be recognized that there is no other field in which this occurs: even in bullfighting a man must start by being a *novillero*, which is more or less an apprentice, before he can become a full-blown matador.

The so-called 'apprentices' in the vineyards of today are not really apprentices at all, just young men who are paid less wages than the other workers for carrying out certain menial tasks, such as distributing fertilizers, painting the scars on the vines with iron sulphate after the pruning, collecting cut branches, and so on. They are not really *taught* to do this work; and if they carry out any other, more skilled tasks in the vineyard, whether they do them properly or not, they get the same wage as the skilled worker. I feel that Jerez should have agricultural colleges for the apprentices, as happens with other guilds—with even better reason, as viticulture means so much to the town. A census of workmen should also be taken, distinguishing between those who are skilled and those who are not, and this distinction should be recognized by an appropriate scale of wages, because when there is unemployment in industry every workman considers himself capable of being a vineyard worker.

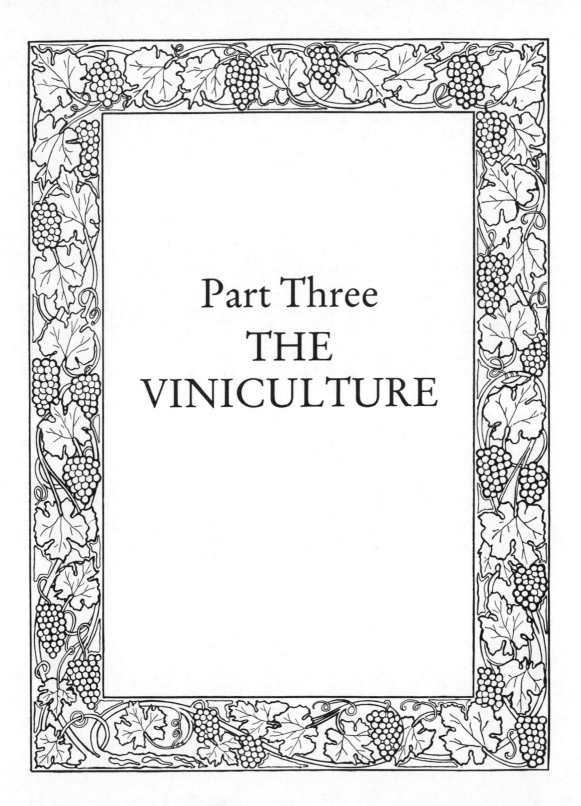

Part Three
THE VINICULTURE

Top: A view of the Carthusian Monastery of Jerez, by the river Guadalete.
Bottom: An early nineteenth-century view of Jerez.

Jerez de la Frontera, the Alcazar.

JEREZ DE LA FRONTERA

BODEGAS EN JEREZ DE LA FRONTERA

Top: Vineyards on sandy soil came right up to the bodegas.
Bottom: A nineteenth-century painting of the interior of a bodega.

BODEGA EN JEREZ DE LA FRONTERA

Leaving grapes to dry in the burning sun, the first stage in the transformation of grape-juice into wine.

Left: Vines shade a private bodega street that once led to the Cathedral.

SHERRY THROUGH THE AGES

Top: Some of the oldest butts in Jerez, well over 200 years old, which are made from cherry-wood.
Bottom: Untouched for over a century.

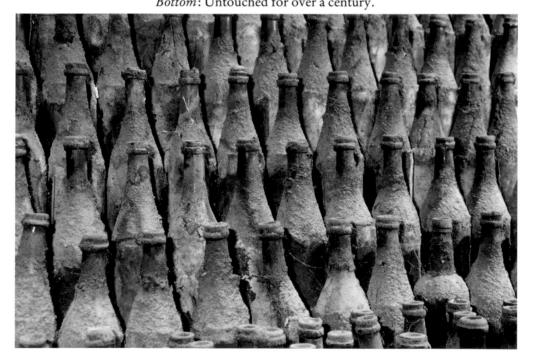

GROWTH OF THE TRADE FROM 1800

Right: Manuel Ma González Angel, founder of Gonzalez Byass. The author's grandfather.
Bottom left: Pedro N. González de Soto, 1st Marqués de Torresoto. The author's father.
Bottom right: Robert William Byass.

VIRTUES OF SHERRY

Enjoying Sherry.

THE BACKGROUND

Top: Two-stroke rotocultivators, one of the first modern solutions
to the tilling problem.
Bottom: 'Deserpia': banking the soil to avoid erosion.

Top: Completed 'deserpia' will collect and absorb all the rainfall.
Bottom: After pruning, vine canes are collected to make charcoal.

THE VINES

A bienteveo in a Jerez vineyard.

THE VINES

Top: Green lines of vines stretch across the landscape.
Bottom: The vines before the vintage are green and exuberant.

THE VINES

In the winter, after the pruning.

THE HARVEST

Top: Picking the grapes.
Bottom: Grapes drying in the sun.

THE HARVEST

Vineyard equipment: (1) azada; (2) azuela; (3) grafting-knife; (4) pruning-shears;
(5) picker's basket; (6) esparto-grass mat for drying grapes; (7) and (8) treading-shoe.

Top: Different varieties of Sherry.

Bottom: Four generations tasting together: the author in his ninety-third year shares wine knowledge with his son, grandson and great granddaughter.

THE SOLERA SYSTEM

Running a solera: the wine begins its slow maturing process through
the different age tiers.

Top: La Concha: an original nineteenth-century bodega.
Bottom: A bodega specially designed for the first phase in the Sherry's life: vinification.

THE BODEGAS

The sun's rays light up a dark cool bodega.

COOPERAGE

Raising a cask.

COOPERAGE

Softening the staves in readiness for driving.

BOTTLES AND CORKS

Top: A bottling line at Jerez.
Bottom: Stoppers from the cork oaks of Spain.

BOTTLES AND CORKS

Top: Finishing touches: labelling and packing.
Bottom: From an old album of labels.

Bodega, belfry and cathedral together: a view of Jerez.

Chapter 8

Styles of Sherry

As soon as the casks are filled with the freshly pressed must they are transported from the vineyards to the bodegas in the town.

The official definition of *must* given by the Spanish Wine Statute is 'the liquid that results from the treading or pressing of freshly gathered grapes before natural fermentation has begun'. It may be said therefore that the life-cycle of must as such in Jerez is extremely short, as the extreme heat at the time of the harvest produces the first violent fermentation about six or eight hours after pressing. Strictly speaking, as I have said, the liquid is *wine* from that time on.

The Statute quoted above defines wine as 'the liquid that results from the *total* or *partial* alcoholic fermentation of the juice of freshly gathered grapes, without the addition of any substance, and without any treatment other than those specified as permissible.' This legal definition is more or less repeated in the legislation of all other wine-producing countries, and in many others too, although not in England, where wine is considered as the fermented juice not only of grapes—whether or not they are freshly gathered—but also of any other fruit.

The grape has the highest sugar-content of all known fruit. The variety most used in Jerez is the Palomino; according to an analysis made at the Jerez Centre of Viticulture and Enology its most important characteristics are: Baumé density, 11.8;* sugar content, 232.3 grammes per litre; free acids expressed in tartaric acid, 3.82 grammes per litre; and tannin components, 0.141 grammes per litre.

The grapes, when first pressed, yield a sugary liquid completly free from alcohol, whose composition is approximately three parts of water to one of grape sugar (glucose and fructose) as well as various acids and salts which constitute a small percentage of the total weight. These salts are mainly carbonates, phosphates and sulphates of potassium, with calcium and magnesium salts in small quantities.

* For explanation of Baumé see Part Five (6)

It is interesting to compare the above analysis with another performed on must from grapes of the same cluster which has been exposed to the sun for twenty-four hours: Baumé density, 13.8; sugar content, 268.8 grammes per litre; free acids expressed in tartaric acid, 3 grammes per litre; and tannin components, 0.087 grammes per litre. This demonstrates effectively that, as the grape loses liquid on exposure to the sun, so it produces a must which is richer in sugars and which, on fermentation, will produce a wine of greater alcoholic strength. It is also worth noting that there is a reduction of acidity, owing to the various chemical processes which together constitute 'ripening'. It is reckoned that after the usual two days of exposure to sun the yield of the grapes undergoes a reduction of from ten to fifteen per cent.

Once the violent fermentation has ended—it generally lasts from three to seven days, depending on the air temperature—the sugary must first passes through a state similar in appearance to that of boiling, during which it rises in temperature, becoming even more turbid than when first pressed. Having given off gases, and deposited lees, the resulting liquid becomes less sweet and more alcoholic, and may now be called *wine*. But despite the official definitions—and the saying '*por San Andrés, el mosto vino es*' (by St Andrew's Day [30 November] the must is wine), it is customary in Jerez to call the wines *musts* until they have been racked off their lees, and even as late as the following vintage unless they have been previously fortified with alcohol.

Persian Origin?

Sir John Malcolm, in his accounts of Persia, writes about a belief common among the natives of that country that it was their King Jamshid who was the chance discoverer of fermentation. This monarch was especially fond of grapes, and had the idea of keeping them in earthenware jars so as to have a constant supply throughout the year. On one occasion, on sampling the contents of one of these jars, he found that the grapes were not sweet, so thinking that it would be dangerous to eat them he labelled the jar *Poison*. A short time afterwards a member of his harem, doubtless bored with her existence and no longer the favourite of her master, decided to put an end to it all by drinking this 'poison'. Instead of achieving her aim, however, she felt the effects of a pleasant dizziness which, far from killing her, encouraged her to have some more. The story has it that when the lady confided her secret to the king he was overjoyed at the news and joined her in finishing off the jar. It is not recorded, however, whether the lady regained her place in the King's affections as a result.

There is still a great deal to be learnt about fermentation, in spite of what has already been discovered of this fascinating and important phenomenon.

Fermentation consists of a series of chemical reactions: that is, the transformation of certain molecules of one substance or compound into molecules of another. These reactions are produced by micro-organisms called yeasts. In the fermentation of grape-juice, which is what we are concerned with here, the most important reaction is the transformation of one molecule of sugar into two of wine alcohol (ethyl alcohol), and two of carbon dioxide.*

An ideally sweet juice is not in itself sufficient to cause the reaction to take place: apart from the presence of the ferments, certain conditions of temperature and the presence of oxygen in sufficient quantitites are also essential.

The yeasts produce certain substances called enzymes which act as catalysts: that is to say, agents which, simply by their presence, make possible or accelerate the reaction or fermentation, without themselves taking any part in the process. In the case of wine, the catalyst is provided by the micro-organisms (dust) in the air which settle on the ripe grapes, waiting until they can grow and multiply in the medium they need—the must or sweet juice produced by the pressing of the grapes. The local name for this dust in the Sherry vineyards is *pruina*.

Pasteur, who rejected the theory of spontaneous generation, proved in his experiments that if the air were free of this contamination, and the grape-juice deprived of the bacteria which live in it, fermentation would not take place. In fact something like this does occur if it rains during the vintage. The must turns out to have less alcohol—not, as many people believe, because it contains less sugar, but because of incomplete fermentation caused by lack of yeast. The more one goes into these questions, the more difficult it is to believe that atheists exist. A lot has been discovered already of the workings of nature, and much more still remains undiscovered, but we must certainly acknowledge that the most valuable gift granted to man is the inquisitive intelligence which has enabled him to understand and even adapt to his own use many of the processes and laws of creation.

The must in which the yeast develops alters in composition as fermentation advances—that is, as the sugar in it is converted into alcohol. The development of the ferment slows down as the alcohol content increases, and finally stops altogether when violent fermentation ends.

The presence in the must of either excess sugar or alochol will also suspend fermentation; and there are other chemical substances, anti-fermentation agents such as sulphur dioxide, the addition of which will stop or retard fermentation.

The must, with its approximate composition of three parts of water to one of grape-sugar, turns after fermentation into a liquid composed of from eight and a half to nine parts of water to from one to one and a half of alcohol. This is only a rough proportion, and varies in different wines, depending on the conditions under which the must has fermented. The type of fermentation varies according to the catalyst involved, and, therefore, the quality of the wine obtained depends greatly on the way the fermentation took place and on the yeast which produced it.

The yeast previously referred to exists in the soil of the vineyards, in the air, in the casks, and indeed in everything that comes into contact with the must, so that there is no need for the addition of any yeast, as is the practice, for example, in the brewing of beer.

The yeasts needed to convert grape-sugar into ethyl alcohol belong to the genus *Saccharomyces*, and consist of minute cells or micro-organisms (the most impor-

---

* The chemical formula is given in Part Five (7).

tant of which is called *Saccharomyces ellipsoideus*), which live on the grape while it is still on the vine. Bearing this in mind, it is easy to understand the vine-grower's dread of rain during the vintage, for when the grapes get wet they sometimes lose part of the yeast needed for the fermentation, which may then develop badly due to possible secondary fermentations caused by pathogenic or harmful bacteria. The quality of the wine and its future development will depend on the quantity and type of the *Saccharomyces*, on the surrounding temperature and on the way in which fermentation has taken place. Hence perhaps the Spanish saying that Sherry is 'born and not made'; for most of the wine's life, apart from the initial period, the vintner is really only a spectator.

The ripeness of the grapes is naturally of great importance to the quality of the must: if there is little sugar the young wine will be weak and thin, and, correspondingly, a high sugar-content will make a wine of high alcoholic strength; although if the grapes are dried in the sun for long enough to concentrate their sugar-content—as happens for example in the making of wine from the Pedro Ximenez grape—the excess sugar acts as an anti-ferment, resulting in a sweet wine of low alcoholic strength.

A few days after the must's arrival in the bodega violent fermentation ends. This process is sometimes allowed to take place in the open, but it is preferable to keep the musts under cover both now and during the subsequent slow fermentation, which is also very important, since it is then that the wine is developing and acquiring the particular character which will distingush it in its future life. Even after the violent fermentation, when the wine has stopped 'boiling' and is almost dry on the palate, the casks are not tightly closed; instead, a cork or small tile is placed loosely over the bunghole, allowing air to reach the wine, while keeping the rain out should the casks be left in the open.

The reproduction of yeast-cells practically stops during the slow fermentation, due to the alcohol content of the liquid, but other biochemical processes take place which later on will give the young wines their individual characteristics. In Jerez, the slow fermentation is considered to end with the coming of winter, in December or January, the time taken by the musts to fall bright depending mainly on the temperatures during the months following the vintage: until it gets colder the fermented musts do not become clear. When this second fermentation is over, and the lees have settled at the bottom of the casks leaving the must clear, the process of racking-off can begin, but first each case must be marked according to its quality. I shall deal with this later; the time has now come to explain something about the different types of Sherry.

Different Sherry musts, although made from a single variety of grape, grown in the same soil, even in the same vineyard, and harvested and pressed the same day, may on fermentation produce completely different types of wine, even if the fermentation has taken place under identical conditions. This is undoubtedly caused not only by the yeasts in the must itself but also by micro-organisms existing in the vessels used, since there have been cases in which a must fermented in large vats produced wines of noticeably different qualities on being transferred to casks, although these were new.

Boutelou wrote:

The leading œnologists are of the opinion that the larger the amount of must fermented at one time, the better the result, as the elements of the wine are then more thoroughly blended and the fermentation is better. But in Jerez and Sanlúcar the musts are generally fermented in wooden butts or puncheons of thirty or sixty arrobas, never in the huge vats of six hundred, a thousand or more arrobas used in other wine districts in the Peninsula. Perhaps the wines would be better and more uniform, and could be drunk sooner, if they were stored in larger containers.*

Until recently, not enough experiments had been made to establish whether or not fermentation in large vats would give good results, and it was always thought that the ideal vessel for fermentation was in fact the butt of thirty arrobas, no more and no less. However, mainly owing to the scarcity of oak staves for the butts, it has been found necessary in recent years to resort to the construction of tanks, generally of reinforced concrete, and experience has shown that if the temperature of the fermenting liquid is carefully watched, and regulated when possible, excellent results can be obtained. When these tanks were first made they were usually lined with glass tiles to make cleaning easier, but it has been found in practice that the best thing is simply to plaster the walls with cement, and then to apply coats of tartaric acid. With the tiled tanks it sometimes happened that the acid in the must attacked the cement in the joints leaving interstices between the tiles and the walls where the liquid could enter and later set up acetic fermentations to the detriment of the next must to be fermented in the tank.†

As soon as the musts fall bright they are usually transferred to butts or other casks and then classified according to quality.

Special Techniques

The variety of chemical changes which occur in Sherry musts during the fermentation necessitated the development of the special techniques and processes used in the maturing of Sherry: the solera system, which has been used in Jerez from time immemorial, and the blending of one wine with another to achieve a desired quality or type and to conform to the requirements of the different markets. In one way this enormous variety is an advantage, in that it produces wines suitable for drinking on any occasion, but from the business point of view, as I have shown earlier, it has its drawbacks too.

Sherry, because of its high alcoholic strength, and the special characteristics which distinguish it from ordinary wines, is classified as a *vino generoso*, and is by nature dry, although sweet wines are also produced. This term *generoso*, from the

---

* *Memoría sobre el cultivo de la Vid en Sanlúcar de Barrameda y Xerez de la Frontera* (Madrid, 1807), p. 131.
† See Dr. Justo Casas's comments in Chapter 10.

Latin *of excellence* or, when applied to wine, of *breeding*, is given to all Sherries, whether sweet or dry. They are pedigree wines of distinction, select wines, which are not intended solely for drinking during meals but can be consumed at any time of the day. The Wine Statute of 1933 defines *vinos generosos*, dry or sweet, as 'special wines, with higher alcoholic strength than ordinary wines, aged or matured in their own particular fashion'. The wines of the Jerez district (apart from those made from the Pedro Ximenex and Muscatel grapes), being totally fermented, are completely dry, but in order to satisfy the demand it is necessary to blend them with other sweet wines from Jerez.

Unlike most other wine-producing districts, which in general offer one red and one white, one sweet and one dry, or one common and one fine wine, Jerez produces a profusion of both subtly and widely differing wines, from the palest topaz to the richest brown, from the absolutely dry to the sweetest dessert wine, and from a wine with fifteen per cent alcohol by volume to one which, through age, may have acquired as much as twenty-four per cent. This enormous variety springs not only from the wine itself but also from the particular methods used, and requirements of the Sherry trade, about which more will be said later.

It is often very difficult to draw a dividing line between some of the very similar types of Sherry, and say that a particular wine belongs to this or that class, so I shall confine myself to indicating the main groups into which the wines are generally divided.

From chemical analysis, it is almost impossible to distinguish one wine from another, and it is better to follow the advice of our ancestors, who maintained that wines can only be judged and appreciated by their taste, colour and bouquet. The colour presents no particular difficulties; the taste, though less easy to describe, can be compared with other tastes; but the bouquet or nose, *'la nariz del vino,* which is the most important quality, is the most difficult to define. To describe its effect one often has to resort to the use of adjectives which have nothing to do with smell but refer to size and shape, only appreciated by our other senses. New wine can be *verde* (unripe, perhaps due to being pressed before the grapes are ripe), or it can be *maduro* (ripe), *delgado* (thin) or *gordo* (stout), qualities which usually depend on its alcoholic strength; it can be *tierno* (tender) or *firme* (firm), depending on whether or not there is doubt about its future acidity; *crudo* (raw) or *cocido* (seasoned) refer to its development after the periodic appearance of the *flor*; *basto* (coarse) or *fino* (delicate) are qualities which depend on its greater or lesser content of aldehydes of different kinds due to successive oxidations. *Limpio* (clean) and *sucio* (dirty) are commonly heard words in the bodegas, and are used to describe the wine's smell; *blando* (soft) or *duro* (hard) according to its flexibility to follow a desired type. *Lleno* (full) or *vacío* (empty) according to its aroma; *punzante* (pungent) or *apagado* (dull) according to the volatile elements present to a greater or lesser extent; *mas* or *menos cuerpo* (fuller *or* lesser body) according to the wine's constitution; and so on.

Generally speaking, unblended Sherry cannot be finally classified until it is three or more years old, and is divided into two main groups: *Finos and Olorosos*. The

Finos are more pungent, dryer, with less strength and body than the Olorosos, which are usually darker. These two fundamental varieties are themselves divided into several sub-varieties, that is: *Finos (Palmas), Manzanillas* and *Amontillados* in the Fino variety; and *Palos Cortados, Olorosos* and *Rayas* in the Oloroso. Apart from these there are the *Abocados* (medium-sweet), and the sweeter wines, *Pedro Ximenez* and *Moscatel*.

I shall try to define and explain as concisely as possible the different varieties and their most important characteristics, but the reader must bear in mind that it is far easier to appreciate wine than to describe it.

Fino is of a pale straw colour, like topaz; it is light and very dry, though not acid. Its alcoholic content ranges between 15.5° and 17° Gay Lussac. Its bouquet is fresh, delicate and fragrant, from the *flor* which develops on its surface. Certain Fino Sherries notable for the delicacy of their aroma used to be referred to locally as 'Palmas' (one, two, three or four), the number of 'palmas' denoting their age. The popularity of these sherries only became general about the end of the last century, and at first they were drunk mainly in Spain and other warm countries, but they have since gained popularity abroad and continue to do so.

Manzanilla is a wine belonging to the Fino group, produced in Sanlúcar de Barrameda. (Although the vine-growing areas of Jerez and Sanlúcar are not contiguous, their rural districts are: many Sanlúcar owners have vineyards in Jerez, and vice versa.) The sea air in Sanlúcar has a decisive effect on the wine, making it even lighter than Jerez Fino and endowing it with a delicate and highly individual aroma. It is completely dry, and leaves a clean but faintly bitter aftertaste on the tongue, without being 'full' like the Jerez Fino. Jerez musts taken to mature in Sanlúcar usually become Manzanillas, and in the same way a Sanlúcar must brought to Jerez takes on the characteristics of a Jerez wine. Manzanilla is a very pale straw colour, although when aged it turns the deeper amber of an Amontillado. Its alcoholic strength is 15.5% to 16.5%, and in old wines may reach 20%, when it is called *Manzanilla Pasada*.

Amontillado originates from a Fino, and therefore belongs to this class. If a Fino is not drawn off periodically it usually becomes an Amontillado, which, like the Fino, is very dry and extremely clean on the nose and palate, with the same pungent aroma, though nuttier and fuller-bodied; in general it is a deeper shade of amber in colour and with age becomes darker still. This is brought about by changes in the biological, chemical and physical processes which take place when the normal system for Fino development is not followed. The Amontillado is generally higher in alcoholic content (17–18%); with great age it may reach 20% and, exceptionally, as much as 24%. The earliest known reference to Amontillado is said to date from 1796, and it is a wine much appreciated by connoisseurs.

Oloroso, as the name indicates, has a strong bouquet, but only if this is clean should the name be used. The Olorosos' aroma is less pungent than those of the Finos and Amontillados, and they have more body or vinosity on the palate, called *gordura* (fatness) in the bodega jargon. Although they are dry there is a vestige of sweetness on the palate, whereas the Amontillados leave a completely dry aftertaste. Their alcohol content is usually 18% to 20%, and increases with age, sometimes up to 24%. The colour is deeper than that of the Amontillados, approaching dark gold and becoming darker still with age. The most common colour is between gold and brown.

Palos Cortados are usually applied to a particular kind of Oloroso, which is fairly rare and is not produced in every vintage. These wines are very clean on the nose, in which they resemble Amontillados, but their taste is full bodied like that of the Olorosos. This variety comes between Amontillado and Oloroso, and, as with the Palmas, is graded (one to four Palos Cortados) according to the degree of vinosity. In colour and in alcohol-content it is the same as an Oloroso.

Rayas: This essentially jerezano wine belongs to the Oloroso group, but, being a rather coarser variety, does not have the delicate and clean aroma of an Oloroso. When this aroma is a little finer, but still not enough so for the wines actually to be called Olorosos, they are given the name *Raya Oloroso*. The Rayas and the Rayas Olorosos are both usually full-bodied, with a rich colour and a minimum of 18% alcohol, rather full in taste and sometimes retaining a trace of glucose, perhaps as a result of incomplete fermentation. Their colour is golden.

It occurs to me that the tastes of the Fino, Amontillado and Oloroso might be compared to those of an almond, a hazel-nut and a walnut respectively, although it is in fact impossible to define very clearly differences of taste and aroma among wines, and however much one writes on the subject the fact remains that only with practice can one learn to distinguish them.

In general, the different wines can be placed in one or other of the groups or types mentioned above the characteristics of which vary according to the constituents of the wine. The spirituosity can be said to depend on the alcohol content, and the vinosity, or body, on the tartar.

Dr Druitt, describing the different classes of wine in an article, drew an apt comparison.*

When a tailor wants to make a suit for a customer he takes the measurements and cuts the suit accordingly. This seemed too easy a procedure for the philosophical tailors of Latupa, who went about it in a more scientific way. They took the customer's altitude with a sextant, his width with a geodesic goniometer, drew up his trigonometrical formula, calculated by logarithms the appropriate sines and tangents, and turned out a suit that was . . . a complete disaster.

It is much the same with wine. There is no substitute for our senses, and to know if a wine is good there is no better method than to try it: a bottle drunk with a meal will soon tell you whether or not it is to your taste. . . . In spite of this seemingly obvious and foolproof method there are chemists, like the tailors

---

* 'Filosofía del vino en Latupa.'

A few British importers have listed *almacenista* Sherries, as if they were a distinct style. *Almacenista* simply means a stockholder, who matures wine and sells to shippers.

of Latupa, who pass the time calculating the constitutents of a wine to four places of decimals, and will only recommend it for its alcohol-content, or its acid-content, or whatever. . . . A good wine may well contain certain elements in a determined proportion, but this is not to say that another wine with the same elements in the same proportion will necessarily be as good.

This does not mean, of course, that the analysis of different varieties of wines shows no noticeable difference, but simply that an analysis is not a sound enough base on which to form an opinion of the quality of a wine. In a lecture delivered in Jerez Lucio Bascuñana compared the analyses of three varieties, Palma, Cortado and Raya. I reproduce them here, as being of some interest:

	Palma	*Cortado*	*Raya*
Alcoholic strength	15.73%	18.66%	18.70%
Dry residue at 100°	1.6498	2.5571	2.8060
Ashes	0.4847	0.5489	0.4907
Organic components	1.1901	2.1219	2.3152
Total acidity in SO_4H_2	0.2741	0.3651	0.3430

These figures give an idea of the difference in composition between some of our kinds of wine, but in actual practice the eyes, palate, and, above all, nose of the connoisseur are the only factors of any real use in making a judgement.

As well as those already given there are a few other names used in Jerez. *Vino de Pasto* is a slightly sweet wine; *Amoroso* is a suave and velvety Oloroso, also somewhat sweet. *Old East India* was a well known name in England, generally given to full-bodied and sweet old Olorosos. It owes its name to the practice followed many years ago by certain shippers of sending their wines as ballast on long round-trips by sailing-ship, as it was thought that a couple of crossings of the equator improved their quality. The real reason for the improvement, however, was the oxygenation which the motion of the ship caused in the incompletely filled casks. This old custom was perhaps the origin of the saying 'Mareado el buen vino de Jerez, si valía cinco, vale diez' (Sea-travelled Sherry, if it was worth five, is now worth ten). Although this custom has long fallen into disuse, it is still occasionally revived at a buyer's request. It was known in Pliny's time, since he mentions that: 'It also happens that wine which travels by sea is felt to double in vigour from the rocking it undergoes.'[*] Cervantes was probably referring to these wines when he wrote: 'They went with her to the inn, where the tables were again heaped up with food and their souls filled with gladness and mirth as their cups were filled with noble wine, which when sent by sea . . . improves to such a degree that there is no nectar to equal it.'[†]

Mention must also be made of the *dulce* and *color* wines, which are used in the Sherry industry to sweeten or colour other wines.

[*] XIV, xviii.
[†] *Persiles y Segismunda*, I. xv.

Pedro Ximenez is the best sweet wine used in Jerez. The grapes are picked very ripe and sun-dried for ten, fifteen and sometimes even twenty days before being pressed. Their sugar content is thus greatly increased, and as a result their fermentation is only partial, resulting in a sweet wine of low alcoholic strength. While the grapes are being dried they are covered at night with esparto matting as protection from the damp. The Cañocazo grape is usually mixed with the Pedro Ximenez, the two going very well together. The sugar content of a good Pedro Ximenez is usually from 22° to 25° Baumé, or approximately 400 grammes per litre. As might be supposed, these wines are very expensive to produce, because of the small quantity of must obtained from the dried grapes. The wine is, of course, extremely sweet, dense and dark in colour, with a noticeable flavour of raisins, and is much appreciated as a dessert wine, especially by women.

Moscatel wine is produced in the same way, though with a shorter drying period, from the Muscatel grape, but it is not so sweet as the Pedro Ximenez and has the characteristic Muscatel aroma caused by certain essential oils found near the outer part of the pip. Like Pedro Ximenez, Moscatel is very popular as a dessert wine. There is a slightly larger variety of Muscatel grape grown in the sandy vineyards of Chipiona, but its product has neither the delicacy nor the fruitiness of the smaller Jerez variety.

The name given to these sweet wines in the Wine Statute is *mosto apagado* ('quenched' must), a reference to their fermentation's having been prevented otherwise than by the addition of alcohol. The term, however, is used differently in Jerez, to mean wines that have had their fermentation deliberately stopped in order to obtain, as economically as possible, a sweet wine for addition to certain common dry wines. This is done by putting the still unfermented must into casks containing a quantity of alcohol, thus preventing fermentation and causing the wine obtained to retain all the sugar in the grape. The amount of alcohol usually employed is from fifteen to eighteen litres per hectolitre of must, and as it is advisable for the alcohol to be free from acidity alcohol made from wine residue should not be used.

These sweet wines whch are made naturally from the sweetest varieties of grape, are usually lighter in colour than those made from sun-dried grapes and have a density of about 8° or 9° Baumé, that is 130 or 150 grammes of sugar per litre of wine. Their alcoholic strength depends, of course, on the amount of alcohol used: as a general rule it is 15%, whereas wines made from sun-dried grapes register only 8% to 12%. The legal name given by the Wine Statute to the common sweet wines is *mistelas*, defined as 'wines made by adding alcohol to the unfermented must in sufficient quantity to prevent or check the fermentation without the addition of any other substance'.

No fixed rule can be given for the colour of sweet wines, as their tone changes with age, becoming deeper as they mature. When they are young they are a dark golden colour, and as they mature they become the darkest of all Sherries.

From the mixture of dry wines with sweet we get the wine called in Jerez *Abocado*, that is, a medium-sweet wine with a density of between 2° and 5° Baumé.

Amoroso is an Abocado.

Outside the Sherry district, between Villamartín and Prado del Rey, near the Tower of Pajarete, some very sweet wines used to be made which were called after the vineyards which produced them, although the name *Pajarete* or *Paxarete* has also been given to the blend of must or wine with arrope or sancocho, a syrup prepared from grape-juice. In certain markets—especially the USA—*Pajarete* means a sweet, rich-coloured Sherry used by the Americans some years ago to give their whiskey flavour and colour, for which reason it was called 'blending Sherry'.

Color called in Jerez *Color de Macetilla*, is a blend composed approximately of one part of unfermented must to two parts of grape syrup, the proportions varying according to the respective densities of the two ingredients. The blend ferments slowly, and when it is aged in casks a highly aromatic *vino de color* is obtained. In Rota, near Jerez, they make some highly esteemed *vinos de macetilla* by adding – especially to a Palamino must—twelve jars of *arrope* per butt. This is generally done on the third day after pressing, when violent fermentation is in full swing, and in this way a homogenous blend is obtained. *Color* wine, like other wines, deposits lees, and towards the New Year it is generally ready to be racked off.

Once it is fermented, the Baumé degree of the Color is about 11° or 12° and the alcoholic strength is abut 8% or 9%. If the arrope is blended with fully fermented must the blend is generally called *Color Remendado*, which is of inferior quality to the Macetilla Color.

The arrope is prepared in Jerez by reducing the must to one-fifth of its original volume, hence the name *arrope al quinto*. This is done by heating the must in large cauldrons over direct heat. *Sancocho* is obtained in exactly the same way, except that it is reduced only to one-third of its original volume. Arrope has a Baumé strength of 36° to 40°, Sancocho of 32° to 33°. Sancocho is slightly less dark and sweeter than Arrope.

These liquids are believed to have been produced by the Moslems. Since they were forbidden to touch any fermented drink, the unfermented grape-juice was concentrated so that the law remained unbroken.

Another wine peculiar to the production zone of Jerez is *Tintilla de Rota*, which is also made in Rota, though never in any great quantity; production is now dying out altogether. It is made from very ripe grapes of a special kind called Tinta, grown in the sandy soils of Rota, and especially in the vineyard of Tehigo. The grapes are sun-dried for many days until the Baumé reading has exceeded 20°, and then the biggest stems are removed and the grapes put into tubs, which are not completely filled, and covered with esparto mats, limiting their contact with the air and impeding complete fermentation. The tubs are stirred periodically for about a month, and due to the incomplete fermentation the wine keeps its characteristic bitter-sweet taste. Then the pulp is pressed in the lagar and fifty litres of alcohol are added to each butt, the consequent loss of density being sometimes made up by the addition of some arrope (which should be made from the same grapes), leaving the wine with 20° Baumé and 10% alcohol. The wine has, as might be supposed, an unmistakeable dark colour with a violet tinge, rather like blackcurrant juice, and quite unlike the colour of any other wine obtained in these parts.

The specific gravity of the wines described above ranges from just below unity in the dry wines to just over unity in the medium-sweet, *mistelas*, and *color* wines. The specifc gravity may be exceeded by as much as 20% for wines made from sun-dried grapes.

The Two Other Corners of the Triangle

The vineyards of Puerto de Santa María border on the Jerez vineyards and the different wines produced are, with slight differences, analagous to those produced in Jerez.

Although the trade in wines from Sanlúcar de Barrameda has long been flourishing within Spain, it is only since the beginning of the last century that exports have reached any sizeable proportions. There can, however, be no doubt that trade relations between Sanlúcar and other countries, principally England, have existed since a much earlier date. There is still in Sanlúcar the Church of St George, an ancient hospital and confraternity, founded by the English residents in Sanlúcar and ceded in 1591 to a brotherhood of Irish monks. These monks enjoyed the privilege of levying a tax on the merchandise shipped by English boats which called in at Bonanza or Sanlúcar, a privilege granted by the Emperor Charles I of Spain and later confirmed by Henry VIII of England.

The consumption of these lighter wines, like the Sanlúcar Manzanilla, that are so ideally suited for the Spanish climate has been increasing steadily over the past hundred years, not only in Spain but also in foreign markets where one might have expected other stronger or fuller-bodied wines to have been preferred, yet there is now a noted universal tendency for pale, dry wines, among which the Sanlúcar Manzanilla and the Finos are outstanding in popularity, to be preferred to other varieties.

Chapter 9
The Solera System

Every wine-producer, grower or shipper has his own methods of classification before the wine is racked off the lees. The Jerez system is to allocate each wine to one of three or four categories. The *catador* (taster), after examining the appearance, bouquet, and sometimes taste of the wine in each cask, classifies it according to its merits by marking the cask with a piece of chalk. The symbol used is the *raya* (oblique stroke, /). *Una Raya* (/) is awarded to those wines which have a clean nose and a reasonable body; *Raya y Punto* (/.) to those with a lower density or body; *Dos Rayas* (//) to those which are not altogether clean on the nose or may have some minor defect; and *Tres Rayas* (///) to those which are slightly acid or very thin or not clean on the nose—these are considered unfit to drink and used in the distillation of wine spirits, whence their name *mostos de quema* ('musts for burning').

Some producers, while keeping to the same basic system, mark the wines slightly differently. The markings consist of one, two or three *rayas* and a grid (#), which denotes *mostos de quema* and alludes to the grid of a hearth.

Those musts which have suffered acetic fermentation are set aside for vinegar and placed in a fifth category marked V^e (*vinagre*).*

To classify the musts it is necessary to take a sample from each cask, and then mark the cask according to the rules already described. Generally it is enough just to smell the sample, so long as the wine is bright; only in borderline cases is it actually essential to taste it.

The instrument used in Jerez for taking samples of wine from the casks is called a *venencia*, believed to derive from *avenencia* ('agreement' or 'bargain'), since the instrument has always been used in the buying and selling of wines for taking

---

* See Part Five (8) for chemical details of *vinagre*

samples from each of the casks that makeup the lot to be sold. The rod or shaft is usually made of whalebone, whilst the cup is made of stainless steel or, preferably, silver. At the top end of the shaft there is a hook which serves not only to hang up the venencia when it is not in use but also to prevent it from falling into the cask should it be dropped. Some venencias have the front edge of the cup bevelled to avoid its catching on the bung stave on withdrawal.

Sometimes, especially in Sanlúcar, the venencia is carved out of cane, the stem and cup all being in one piece and the bottom of the cup being one of the knots in the cane shoot. The cup of the Sanlúcar venencia is usually smaller in diameter than the metal ones, which makes it easier for the sample taken to be bright and free of the flor developing on the surface. Perhaps the Sanlúcar custom of ordering a *caña* instead of a *copa* of Manzanilla originates from the cane venencias.

It has always been thought in this part of the world that the venencia was invented in Jerez, or possibly in Sanlúcar, to draw wine out of the casks through the bung-hole without disturbing the flor: this would account for the use by the Sanlúcar cellarmen of the cane venencia, as the lighter-bodied Sanlúcar wines have a thicker film of flor. But in Warner Allen's *The History of Wine* an illustration appeared showing a Greek vase of 490 B.C., on which a cellarman holds a venencia of exactly the same shape as the Sherry venencias of today.

Writing about venencias reminds me of the anecdote about a Jerez bodega-owner who wanted to take a combined sample from all the butts of a certain lot of fine old wine to give to one of his agents to sell. However, being very careful and prudent where money was concerned, he wished to avoid the expense of hiring a man just to cart a heavy jar around. He therefore enlisted the aid of a bricklayer whom he met by chance outside the bodega, and who was known for his fondness for Sherry. The owner promptly invited the man to taste some of his excellent solera wines, an offer which was as promptly accepted. Giving his victim the jar, he then clambered up the rows of butts and proceeded to hand down from the second tier twenty or twenty-five samples of wine, naturally supposing that each was being tipped into the jar. The bricklayer, however, drank each glass as it was handed to him, until finally, on handing back the empty glass, he said politely, 'No more for me, thanks, Don José.' The furious and incredulous owner, seeing his economy measure gone so drastically wrong, demanded of the bricklayer why he thought he was carrying the sample jar. Full of innocent surprise, the bricklayer replied, 'But, Don José, that's exactly what I've been wondering.'

When the musts have fallen bright and been racked off the lees into clean casks fumigated with sulphur, some time between January and March, the wine is fortified with alcohol. The amount of alcohol put into the butt which is to receive the young wine varies from twelve litres to a maximum of thirty-six. In Jerez, and above all in Sanlúcar, the musts are usually fortified not with pure alcohol but with a half-and-half blend of wine and alcohol called *miteado*. If non-wine alcohol is used the wine loses strength, probably because this particular type does not combine well with wines and hence evaporates.

The butts normally have an opening in the front or head called a *falsete*, from which the wine may be drawn off through a mahogany or olivewood tube called a *canuto*. When the wine has fallen below the *falsete* the butt is tipped gently forward to allow the flow to continue without any of the sediment or lees being disturbed. This operation is called *picar la bota*. In this way the wine continues to be drawn out clear; as soon as the flow becomes turbid it is shut off, and the liquid lees which remain are put into tubs. These are subsequently emptied into casks, and allowed to stand for a few days, until the sediment has settled and more clear wine can be decanted. The amount left in the cask when it is restored to its horizontal position is usually about twenty per cent of the original volume—that is, approximately six arrobas out of a thirty-arroba butt. The total loss of liquid from must to wine may be broken down as: loss in fermentation and saturation of wood, 1 per cent; evaporation from fermentation to racking-off, 1.5 per cent; lees, 7.5 per cent—total, 10 per cent.

After a cask has had its lees removed the usual practice is to clean it with poor-quality or *quema* musts, since these may later be mixed with the thicker lees and subsequently distilled to produce the low-strength spirit called Holanda, which has a high ether content.* When the lees are not used for distillation they are dried and used in the manufacture of Cream of Tartar, their value naturally depending upon their tartaric content.

Sometimes there is a second *deslío*, or racking-off, in July or August: the wines are separated from the *cabezuela*, as this second deposit of sediment is called, and then either put into the *criaderas* (nurseries) or left in casks but not blended with other wines. Wines thus left are said to be *sobre tabla* (on the wood). Before this is done it is usual for the wines to be reclassified; they have naturally been stirred up, so it is necessary to wait for them to fall bright again before passing judgement on their quality.

Although at their first racking the musts were fortified to bring their strength up to about 15 per cent or 15.5 per cent, it is the old-established practice in Jerez to refortify those which show no tendency to become Finos. This means leaving them for three or four years without racking them off for second sedimentation, at the end of which period of time it is possible to classify accurately the quality of the wine in each cask. Throughout this time the taster has taken care to examine the wines in each cask from time to time, so that he can form an opinion of the type which the wine may become, until the moment when it is possible to say that a particular wine is a Fino or an Oloroso.

As time passes, the characteristics of each wine become more pronounced although a mild secondary fermentation continues for the whole of the wine's life, becoming gradually weaker as it ages. It is these secondary fermentations that really give Sherries their unmistakable characteristics, stimulating the development of the esters that distinguish one wine from another.

Later, when these wines have been fortified and come to be classified, those belonging to the Fino class are marked with one or more *palmas* according to their

---

* See Part Four, Chapter 13 for a full discussion of Holanda and other spirits distilled in Jerez.

degree of delicacy. Those which show no tendency to become Finos but are full-bodied and vinous are marked with one *raya*, whilst those which have already developed a certain body and are also clean on the nose are marked with a *raya* cut by one or more horizontal strokes ($\neq$), ($\neq$), the number of cross-strokes referring to strength and delicacy—hence the name *Palo Cortado*. There are some Olorosos which, being full-bodied, leave a softness on the palate which some people mistake for sweetness—in fact a well-fermented and balanced unblended Sherry is not sweet and this particular taste is due to the glycerine which is a natural constituent of the wine. This class of wine used to be marked with a distinguishing hook at the foot of the raya, a mark which old wine-producers called *pata de gallina* ('hen's foot', which it resembles).

When selecting wines to add to the Raya, Cortado and Palma soleras, some bodegas add another oblique line to the previous marks for special wines, thus making the *tijera* (scissors), *tijera cortada* (crossed scissors) and *tijera gancha* (scissors and hook) which correspond to the raya, cortado and palma respectively.

It is natural that on a second tasting the wines may be reappraised, and hence the original marking may be altered. The experienced taster, who is scrupulously fair, will put a wine into a lower category if he is at all doubtful about the aroma or palate of the sample. In this way he avoids any risk of lowering the standards of the better wines, whilst at the same time possibly improving those of the inferior ones.

Nature's Way

An early method of maturing Sherry, and one well suited to the wine, was the *añada* (vintage) system, because the most influential factors in Sherry production are ageing and periods of rest: in other words, letting nature take its course. At the start of the last century all musts used to be treated in exactly the same way: after they had first been racked off the lees a *jarra* (a wine jar of about eleven litres) of *aguardiente* (crude spirits) would be added to the wine. Later, after the must had been racked off the *cabezuelas*, an equal measure of the same spirit was added, together with two jars of *color* wine and three or four of Pedro Ximenez.

However, it is impossible to maintain uniformity of quality in the wine by the añada system, and so Jerez has reverted to the solera system.

The solera system has existed in Jerez alongside the añada system from time immemorial, and is now being adopted in other wine-producing regions. It should be noted that a solera is not merely a matured wine of dark colour, as many believe it to be, but a *method of development* used for all types of wine particularly indispensable in the production of Fino Sherries. In some wine-producing parts of Spain, the word is used to describe a wine which is simply not young, but this is not really a correct definition.

It is not known when the solera system was first used in Jerez, nor who was the first to devise it and put it into practice, although it has been suggested that the system began in Sanlúcar. As I have said, it aims at producing a uniform wine, both in age and character, whether it be Fino, Amontillado, Oloroso, Cortado or

Raya. Each shipper or bodega-owner usually has several soleras for each category, depending upon the specific needs of each business.

A solera consists of a number of casks stacked in tiers, or 'scales'. To give an idea of how the system works, we may take as an example a solera of six scales, the first consisting of forty or fifty butts. The wine from this scale is the one ready to be sold. The scale above has an equal number of butts of wine about a year younger, and so on, until the sixth and last scale where the wine will be about five years younger than that of the first. The wines of the different scales are always of the same kind, being, wherever possible, from the same source. The first scale is generally called 'the Solera'; the remainder are sometimes called *criaderas* or, in some bodegas, *2nd, 3rd, etcetera, solera scales*. The number of scales for Fino wines has to be larger than for the fuller-bodied Amontillados and Olorosos, because these vary much less from one year to another than the Finos.

In a well managed solera each scale has an average age, and the wine drawn from the first scale at any time would be approximately the same age as that taken out the following year. The date of foundation of the solera, shown on the labels of bottled wines by some producers, should not be confused with the age of the actual wine. The wine of the first scale will undoubtedly have some proportion from the year when the Solera was founded, but this will be infinitesimal; with a solera wine one can never assert that it comes from any one particular year.

The primary object of this process of maturation, which is a perpetual cycle, is to obtain a wine that does not vary in quality from one year to another, or is at least as similar as possible to the first scale. When wine is drawn off from the first scale, it is made up of equal quantities from each of the casks. These are then replenished from the second scale, this in turn is topped up from the third, and so on up the scales, till the last—provided that the number of casks in each scale is the same—will be minus the quantity taken from the first. This process is called in bodega jargon 'running the scales'. Wine, of course, changes as it matures and varies in quality from year to year, usually acquiring more strength, body and colour, so that the effect of the solera system is to compensate for the change produced by age, refreshing or rejuvenating the older wine by blending it with a younger one. It is, therefore, necessary that periodical drawings should be made to maintain uniformity; these are generally carried out several times a year. There is an old Spanish saying, '*El trigo en la pala y el vino en la jarra*' ('for the wheat a scoop and for the wine a jar'), which in practice has proved good advice. Its significance is that it is better to spread out the replenishing process (a jarful at a time, in fact) than to make good the entire ullage at one time. The reason for this is that the extensive aeration produced has an extremely favourable effect on the maturing process, and has contributed in no small measure to the success of the solera system.

The wine is siphoned from the casks into the jars, then poured into the butts of the next scale through a wedge-shaped tin-plate funnel called a *canoa* and curved, perforated tubes called *rociadores*, which are introduced into the butts. These distribute the new wine evenly, ensuring that it is thoroughly mixed with the old, and also serve to diffuse the pressure and prevent a violent jet which would stir up the sediment. Some rociadores have a special type of sheath at the end which forces the incoming flow of wine upwards, thus further safeguarding the sediment on the bottom of the cask against any interference. An alternative device is to fit in the bottom end of the funnel a cork (known as an *estrella*, or star) with perpendicular grooves round its edge through which the wine slowly passes. In Sanlúcar, instead of a rociador a cloth sock or sleeve called a *garceta* is used, which slows down the flow and diffuses the wine even more thoroughly. It has the same shape as the ordinary rociador, and is provided with a hook to prevent its falling into the butt.

The siphons used in this operation are filled by sucking air into them from one end, an operation known as 'calling' the wine in bodega jargon. The wine often catches the operator unawares by reaching the top of the siphon while he is still sucking air through it. (If this happens when spirit is being siphoned, the result, in extreme cases, can be asphyxiation. The remedy is to give the victim a glass of very sweet wine, say Pedro Ximenez or Moscatel, to counteract the burning effect of the alcohol, absorbing and diluting it and thereby avoiding the risk of damaging the tissues or lining of the throat and digestive tract.)

As I mentioned at the beginning of this chapter, wine may be regarded as a living organism, conceived as a sugary juice obtained from grapes and born with the first violent fermentation. Its infancy is the secondary slow fermentation, during which its character is formed. If we extend the analogy, this third stage corresponds to the nursery stage of a child. Consequently, it is the conditions during this period which largely determine what the child will be when it grows up. The scales of the solera may be compared with the various classes of a school, the youngest children starting in the lowest form and moving up the scale until finally they enter the highest. This promotion continues until university graduation is reached, with mature men properly equipped to follow their vocation; just as the mature wines that emerge from the first scale of the solera are responsible for carrying the name and reputation of Jerez to the consumer markets of the world.

Seasonal Activity

The word *solera* derives from *suelo* (floor), and, strictly, refers to the foundation or 'mother' of the wine, the deposit which settles at the bottom of the cask. This consists of the spores of the yeast which constitute the flor and which rise twice a year to the surface to reproduce and subsequently fall to the bottom of the butt.* The most active seasons for this flor are April and May, August and September. These times appear to coincide with the budding of the shoot and the fructification of the vines respectively. However, apart from these two peak periods the majority of Fino wines have a constant film of flor, sometimes thin and tenuous, at others more dense. It appears that a flor similar to that found on the Finos of Jerez

---

* This sediment continues to increase each year, and experience has shown that in soleras that have been established for a long period it is sometimes advisable to draw off the wine from the sedimentation and clean the butt, since otherwise the wine is exposed to infection.

also develops on the vins jaunes from the French district of Arbois, in the Jura; also, it is said, in Armenia, although I have no proof of this.

For a long time it was believed that the Jerez flor was formed by *mycoderma vini*, but after considerable research by œnologists, much of it performed in the Jerez Centre of Viticulture and Œnology, it was shown that it was caused by the same yeasts that bring about the fermentation of the musts. The Jerez flor, therefore, should not be confused with those ferments which in other regions constitute a common and dangerous infection to the wines.

Gonzalo Fernández de Bobadilla, who has done a great deal of research on the development of the Sherry flor, describes it as a combination of micro-organisms living on the surface of the wine, constituting what is technically called a film. Several white spots are visible when this film begins to form and these become much larger blotches of irregular shape, very similar to small flowers floating around on the wine, hence the name *flor*. These blotches constantly increase in size, blossoming outwards until the edges gradually unite to form a continuous white film over the surface of the wine. Later on this becomes thicker, and the flor comes to look like a layer of frothy cream. Being a living micro-organism the flor feeds on the constituent elements of the wine itself, absorbing them and thus changing its essential composition. It would be inappropriate at this stage to give details of the complex reactions which occur here, but if a Fino were compared with an Oloroso it would be easy to appreciate the differences in colour, aroma and taste. The fundamental reasons for these differences are that the Fino, during its maturing and ageing, has the flor developing on its surface, whilst the Oloroso after a certain stage in its development has no flor owing to the addition of alcohol.

Requirements for the Flor

The same authority points out certain requirements for the flor to develop in optimum conditions. The main ones are that the wine should have a large surface area in contact with the surrounding air, together with a constant average temperature of between 15° and 20°C., whilst the alcoholic strength ought to remain within the limits 15 per cent to 15.5 per cent. This means that less alcohol must be added to those wines which at the first racking-off show a natural tendency to become Finos, if it is intended that they should develop flor and thus remain in the Fino category. The total sulphur dioxide content should not exceed 0.018 per cent, nor should the tannin exceed 0.01 per cent, since this would coarsen the wine. Finally, an excess of iron can also affect the development of the flor.

The suggestion has been made that the flor can be compared to measles in children (except, of course, that the flor is recurrent), since both flourish most virulently when the organisms on which they live are at their weakest. Also, just as the human body is stronger once it has shaken off an illness, so also does the flor in certain cases set right some of the defects which may be present in the wine.

This micro-organism, which is first white in colour and later becomes a dull grey, is not artificially cultivated. It appears naturally in the springtime, and the cellarman has to do no more than promote its growth by leaving the butts on ullage, and loosely bunged. In this way the yeast, which is an aerobic plant, has the necessary air so vital to its development. For this reason wooden bungs are used, which, being loose, allow contact with the air while preventing any dirt from entering the wine.

In Olorosos, above all in the Palo Cortado type, some people perceive another, darker flor, almost imperceptible, which gives this type of wine a characteristic bouquet. Others however, assert that this aroma is produced by the direct oxidation of the alcohol which is converted to give aldehydes, acids and esters. For over half a century scientists and œnologists, have been working on the changes that take place in Sherry, and although such research lies outside the scope of this book it is hoped that the day will soon arrive when it will be possible to give concrete explanations of these and other interesting phenomena.

All this explains why the butts are kept in ullage and loosely bunged. These bodega butts, which generaly have a capacity of 600 litres, never contain more than 500, especially in the case of Fino wines, as the experience of centuries has proved that an ullage of about one-sixth of the full capacity of the cask gives the optimum surface-volume ratio for the development of this type of Sherry. It is a fact that Sherry keeps extremely well on ullage, even when in bottle, and one of the main reasons is probably that it is matured in full contact with the air. Experience has proved that Sherry is very stable, although the causes are really not very clear.

The last scale of the solera whch may be left with only about one-fifth of its capacity—that is, a hundred litres—is the one which receives, in the spring, the wine from the previous vintage, and in April or May it starts developing flor for the first time.

The first scale is normally kept at ground level. The second and third scales, and sometimes even the fourth, are stacked on top of the first, though three is the advisable limit, as the extra weight of a fourth scale can cause damage to the butts in the first. Subsequent scales are stacked elsewhere, in the same manner. It is traditional to arrange the first scale on special wooden beams (*palos de escalera*), which in turn rest on strong sleepers (*espolines*), placed exactly beneath the centre of each butt. In several bodegas in Jerez, and in the majority in Sanlúcar, scantlings or *bajetes de canto* shaped to the form of the butt are used instead of this system. These are made of a combination of rock and seashells, on top of which is placed a sheet of cork to protect the butt from damp.

Although the difference is very often imperceptible, it is generally agreed that wines stored at a low level develop more delicately and with finer breed, on account of the lower temperature, whereas those on the second and third scales sometimes become somewhat coarser since the temperature is rather higher. For this reason Fino wines are matured in cool and damp bodegas, in the lowest tier possible. Conversely, Olorosos develop better and acquire more body if they are placed on the third or even the fourth tier of the bodega.

The great skill of the shipper or bodega-owner lies in maintaining constant quality within each solera, so that from year to year the wine does not change at all, either for better or for worse. Thus the main responsibility of the Jerez bodega-owner is to check the strength of the wines, since some gain during the time they remain in cask, whilst others lose. Apart from this the ullage to be left in the casks must be calculated, since some wines develop with more delicacy than others. The manager or owner must also know how many times he will have to draw off the wine throughout the year without draining the solera—that is, making excessive withdrawals which would lessen the quality of the wine. The best time to draw the wine, especially for the Fino type, is when the flor is quiescent—that is, from October to February, and in the high summer.

Solera management is complex and it requires time to understand it thoroughly; the basic requirement being to have stocks in proportion to the expected withdrawals. Exports usually rise to a peak in the last quarter of the year, and gradually decline throughout the remaining months, when these fortified wines are least consumed, not only in Spain, where the heat of the summer months naturally encourages people to drink lighter and more refreshing drinks, but also in the majority of other countries.

Because the casks are loosely stoppered with corks or wooden bungs, the loss from evaporation is considerable, since in Jerez the casks are not completely filled, not even to *tocadedos* ('finger-depth'), as they say in bodega jargon. The loss varies from place to place and from season to season, and it is also influenced by the condition of the bodega where the butts are stored. The evaporation, naturally, increases in proportion to the surface area of the wine in contact with the air; so that the fuller the cask the less the evaporation. There is at least one compensation for this: the greater the loss from evaporation, the greater the increase in maturity of the wine. As a general rule it is calculated that the average annual loss through evaporation is as much as five per cent of each butt. If the butts are stored under cover and with a normal ullage of twenty per cent the figure may be slightly less; if they are left out in the open air it will probably exceed six per cent. It is estimated that it would take about seventy years for a butt of Sherry to evaporate completely.

Economic Factors

Apart from loss by evaporation, one must take into account the interest on the capital tied up whilst the wines are developing. The problem thus resolves itself into a triple economic question: the first and positive factor is the increased value of the wine due to its improvement in quality, whilst the second and third factors are both negative and correspond to the losses through evaporation and the accumulated interest on the capital invested. The positive factor outweighs the sum of the two negative ones during the first few years of the wine's development, but beyond a certain point it begins to diminish in importance, while the negative influences remain constant. From a theoretical and economic aspect it would be interesting to plot the graph of the increased value of the wine against the loss through evaporation and interest on the capital. It would be seen that on the wine's reaching a certain age—exactly what age it would be very interesting to know—the losses would exceed the increase in value, so that in time it would be economically unsound to continue ageing the wine.

There has been some debate on the question of fortifying Sherry. The fact of the matter is that when it is racked off the lees it is fortified with wine spirit of a strength of 95 per cent. The reasons for this are discussed more fully elsewhere in this book. The spirit is added in greater or lesser quantities, according to the type and class to which the wines are destined. This addition of spirit also acts in some wines as an antiseptic, preventing the possible development of *mycoderma aceti*. However, although many authors have maintained that no naturally fermented and unfortified wine can exceed 15 per cent by volume, since this percentage actually stops fermentation, the strength of Jerez wines does increase noticeably with evaporation and age, either because of the slow secondary fermentations, or possibly because of the process of osmosis, which causes part of the water-content to evaporate through the pores of the cask and so increases the percentage of alcohol (though it would appear at first sight that the reverse should happen). It is uncertain whether the same process occurs in other climates: it is said that it does not occur in England, and besides it is well known that the conditions of the casks and the surrounding atmosphere of warehouses where alcoholic liquids are stored sometimes cause their strength to increase, sometimes to diminish. Of Port, for example, it is said that its strength increases whilst the wines remain in the district or vineyards of the Douro, but diminishes after a certain time in the Port lodges of Vila Nova de Gaia, where the climate is more humid.

The wines which are drawn from the bodega casks undergo the process of fining or clarification in wooden or concrete vats lined with plate glass. This is important, since one of the qualities most sought after in wine is brightness, and the golden rays of the varied kinds of Sherry—when they are bright—give much pleasure to the eye. Undoubtedly a turbid wine cannot please, even if it is of the same quality, as much as one which is 'candle-bright'.* For this reason an essential feature of all bodegas is the sample-room, where the taster, away from the turmoil of ordinary business, can judge the quality and shades of his wines. These sample-rooms should preferably face north.

There are several ways of clarifying wines. Some use organic clarifiers, such as albumen or gelatine; others are mineral, the principal one being the famous 'Tierra de Lebrija'. The custom in Jerez is to use the white of an egg well beaten with a whisk of thyme. The number of egg-whites used per butt can be anything from four to twenty according to the type of wine. When thoroughly beaten they are mixed in a jar with seven or eight litres of the wine to be clarified, and then poured into the butt and stirred up well with a mixing-rod called an *apaleador*. In this way the albumen is thoroughly mixed with the contents of the butt, so that it precipitates part of the tannin contents of the wine in the form of albumen

---

* So called because it is a tradition throughout the world's wine cellars to examine clarified wines – which includes wines decanted before serving—by holding up a candle behind them.

tannates, which draw with them all foreign substances which the liquid might contain in suspension.

To complete the clarification a quantity of duly prepared Spanish earth is added to the cask after a few days. This is a smectic clay with an extremely fine grain. About a kilo is used for each 500-litre butt. It is first pulverized, the water being added in an earthenware pan until it is covered, then left to settle for about six hours, after which the water is drained off. The paste obtained is then worked over with an two-handed roller on a board to flatten it out and break up any lumps which may still be present. It is then placed in an open ten- or twelve-litre earthenware pan and approximately eight litres of the wine to be treated are gradually added. This is then mixed to a thick, turgid liquid which is poured into the butt, the whole contents being well stirred. The earth produces a colloidal suspension in the wine which, on coagulation, absorbs and precipitates all foreign substances contained in the wine. Its action is entirely a physical one; it acts as a sort of mobile filter which passes through the wine and leaves it absolutely bright by the time it settles at the bottom of the cask at the end of several days.

Potassium bitartrate, a natural constituent of wine, is one of the greatest enemies of brightness, especially after the wine has been some time in bottle. This compound is deposited in small crystals when the wine is exposed to low temperatures.

This explains why Sherry, especially the Fino variety, sometimes has a deposit of sediment: this is a natural phenomenon and in no way affects the quality of the wine. It is only its appearance that is spoiled, and then only when it has been a long time in bottle or has been subjected to violent changes of temperature.

The greater the temperature variations, the more cloudy or dull the wine becomes. This is particularly noticeable in wines exported to Scandinavia, the United States and Canada, since the decrease in the air temperature reduces the solubility of potassium bitartrate, causing it to be crystallized and precipitated as a sediment, whilst also affecting the wine's stability.

As a general rule it is accepted that Sherry, especially Fino, does not improve in bottle; at best it may be said to tolerate the bottle, as it may vary in colour and flavour; true, there are connoisseurs who prefer what the English call 'bottle flavour'. Nevertheless, the fuller-bodied wines—such as the Olorosos and sweet Sherries—may be kept indefinitely in a well corked bottle in a cool place, and may even mellow.

In all wines a deposit may be thrown after the wine has been in bottle for some time. This does not surprise anyone with other wines so it should not in the case of Sherry. In many cases, unattractive appearance in a Sherry is caused by lack of care in opening and serving it, a ritual act that merits the reverence it sometimes receives.

Another point worth mentioning is the temperature at which the wine should be served. Two wines of equal sweetness and the same alcoholic strength served at different temperatures will make different impressions on the palate, the colder one in general appearing drier. It is not possible to give a fixed rule about the temperatures at which Sherry should be served, since nothing definite can be written on the subject of individual taste. However, it is safe to assert that Sherry should be served chilled, but never ice-cold, since this would cause the wine to lose part of its fragrance. Almost certainly the optimum temperature is that of the casks stored in the bodegas, which remain closely related to the air temperature throughout the year.

Disease Resistance

Although Sherry, on account of its high alcoholic strength, is generally less prone to diseases and disorders than other wines, it cannot be said to be entirely invulnerable.

The four diseases or defects occasionally found in new Sherry, any of which is always considered adequate reason to reject the wine even after its sale has been negotiated, are: *nube* (scud); *peste* (taint); *ácido* or *picado* (acetification); and *hilo* (oiliness).*

Apart from the turbidity caused by the presence of potassium bitartrate, to which I have already referred, there are other similar conditions produced by *quiebras* (casse): they are *casse cuprica, casse oxidasica* and, most important, *casse ferrica*, whch is produced by an excess of iron in the wine.

Nube may be simply described as a bacteriological infection which generally affects wines deficient in acidity. It frequently occurs in Finos and also in the musts produced in years of drought. Nube may be detected by swirling the wine round in a glass: if the condition is present, a thin, whitish, smoky effect spreads through the liquid. The only means of eliminating the trouble is to treat the wine with a disinfectant, such as sulphur dioxide, or subject it to sterilized filtration.

Sometimes the wines appear to be slightly affected by nube at certain times of the year, but this is usually due to microscopic particles of flor in suspension in the wine, which, when the glass is swirled around, give the smoky impression previously described.

Another disease common to all wines is acetification. When this occurs instant treatment should be given as soon as the symptoms appear in a must or wine, since the condition deteriorates very rapidly, soon making the wine undrinkable. The most effective antidote is fortification with spirit. During the maturing of wines it is normal for acidity to decrease as the flor develops, so that it is necessary, when fortifying wines on which the flor has begun to develop, to be scrupulously careful not to add too much spirit, as if the added alcohol kills the flor any wine which has a natural tendency to acetification will almost inevitably turn to vinegar.

Peste, or 'taint', which simply takes the form of a disagreeable smell, is usually the result of defective fermentation caused by the presence of pathogenic elements.

---

* Some of the bacteria that produces these conditions are aerobic, others are anaerobic. The first type, which includes the acetic bacteria, needs air to exist; the second does not. It is the anaerobic type that produces nube, or *tourne* as it is known in French. Anaerobic bacteria also produce hilo (*grasse* in French). Finally, there are other bacteria which can exist in both conditions: for example, *bacterium maniticus*, which produces *agridulce*, a bittersweet taste occasionally found in the wine.

Sometimes, however, it occurs when the wine has been stored in dirty casks, or in contact with foreign matter. This condition occasionally disappears of its own accord, as it may be caused by an errant piece of sulphur left behind when the cask was disinfected, so that on exposure to air it may disappear completely.

Hilo, or oiliness, is apparently caused by a special consistency of the wine which, due to increased viscosity, makes it appear oily when it is poured. The name *hilo* means literally 'thread', and is undoubtedly derived from the appearance of the wine, which, when it is poured is drawn out into a glutinous thread, a chain of liquid molecules. This disease is more common in some years than in others in the Sherry district, but it is generally a transitory condition and as such does not represent a serious danger. Although the condition does occasionally appear in the wine or must, those experienced in such matters do not attach much importance to it, having perhaps observed that it is sometimes caused by the inherent tendency of these wines to become Finos.

Hilo is often found as a concomitant of nube. Sometimes both can be eliminated by agitating the wine vigorously wth a stirring-rod, or by fining the wine and then filtering it. Another way of stirring up wine is by drawing off several jarras full from the cask and then pouring them back so that the wine is aerated and allowed to 'breathe'.

Whenever the vintage is abnormal, from excess or lack of rain, or any other reason, it is necessary to be extremely alert and take the necessary precautions to prevent these disorders to which the wines are prone. There is a great deal of truth in the saying that the land takes what it needs if it is to yield what is expected of it.

An old story about hilo reflects the Andalusian talent for exaggeration. A Jerez wine-broker was talking to a shipper about the hilo in a certain wine, and to pass it off lightly the broker said to his prospective customer, 'Look, Don José, this is nothing. If you want to see real hilo go and have a look at Don Antonio's young wines . . . . Well, just take a look for yourself: take a sample with your venencia, then put it over your shoulder and start walking, and by the time you've reached the Plaza del Arenal you'll have emptied the butt.'

Chapter 10
The Bodegas

As I have said the original bodegas in Jerez were small and ramshackle buildings, but when the shippers were obliged to start keeping stocks of wine they had to build properly equipped warehouses with facilities more appropriate for bulk storage. The majority of these new purpose-built bodegas were put up at the beginning of the nineteenth century, and some of them are of such dimensions and design that they look like huge temples. These distinctive constructions, peculiar to Jerez, are built of stone and consist of several aisles five or six metres wide, and separated by columns or pillars. These aisles are called *ruedos*, and the central transverse aisle, where the majority of the cellar work takes place, is called in Jerez the *crujía*. The whole way along both sides of these aisles are the tiers of butts (*andanas*) one on top of another. Most of the roofs are supported by beams and wooden battens on which rest layers of thin brick and Moorish tiles, and are almost always of a sloping type. Owing to the height of these buildings and the thickness of their walls, the temperature remains within the limits desirable for the maturing and develoment of wine. The width of the aisles varies: when the aisle is just broad enough to roll one butt along it is called *de un ruedo*; when it is broad enough for two butts end to end it is called *de dos ruedos*; and when a butt can be rolled along and there is room for another to be placed parallel to the axis of the aisle, the breadth of the aisle is called *de ruedo y bretona*.

Temperature Control
The Sherry bodegas are usually situated in the airiest parts of the town, and, owing to this and to the massive thickness of their walls and the height of their ceilings, the internal temperature is maintained between 15°C and 22°C., whilst it is the usual custom to spray the floors periodically with water, thus keeping the temperature lower and reducing the evaporation. The 'cellar instinct', an impor-

tant and traditional characteristic of the Jerezano, influences not only the choosing of the vineyard site—through careful selection of the most suitable soils for planting the vine— but also the location of the bodegas where the wines themselves are matured. It is well known that wines develop better when stored in bodegas on the south or south-west side of the town, probably because the butts benefit from the moisture and aeration of the breeze blowing off the sea.

It is quite extraordinary what an effect position has on the development of Sherry—position, that is, not only of the bodegas themselves, but of individual butts within a single bodega, no doubt because of the variations in temperature, or the draughts that can be set up between doors and windows. Generally, the windows are set at intervals of five or six metres along the side walls; to keep out the heat of the sun the windows are fitted with esparto-grass blinds. If there are other buildings near by they must be at least two metres away, to allow light and air to enter the bodegas: these narrow passages are called in Jerez *almizcates*.

The floor is of hard-packed earth; the aisles along which the butts have to be rolled sometimes have their floors tiled with flagstones, especially on the corners and intersections where the butts have to be turned to be rolled in another direction. In some bodegas the floor of the crujía is made of small blocks of oak, similar to the wedges used for keeping the casks in position, which are made from the trimmings of the oak used by the coopers.

The total capacity of a bodega, assuming that each andana is complete with three tiers of butts, is normally calculated by counting the second tier and multiplying by three. Although it is not an infallible rule, it is approximately true that the number of butts a bodega can hold is equal to the total floor area in square metres.

The workmen employed in a bodega are known collectively as *arrumbadores*. This is a local word, probably derived from *arrumbar* 'to place objects in order'. A distinction should be made between those who handle casks, which is skilled labour, and other workers, who serve only a short apprenticeship. The skilled men usually work in teams of four—foreman, two assistants, and apprentice. There is no team system among the bottlers, as their jobs are constantly changing, so that the only distinction made here is between 'qualified' and 'semi-qualified', according to aptitude, length of service and type of work involved.

The average working day is eight hours, from 8 a.m. till 6 p.m. with a break of two hours for lunch, which is taken from noon to 2 p.m. This timetable varies somewhat from season to season, but never as much as in the vineyards, where the work must be done during the hours of sunshine. Workers in the vineyards are allowed seven short 'cigarette-breaks' a day, each lasting fifteen minutes, together with an hour each for lunch and supper. This generally means seven working hours a day from November to February, eight hours for the remainder of the year.

Workers' Perquisites

It is a tradition in the Jerez bodegas that the workmen are allowed a drink of Sherry several times a day: on starting work, before lunch, on restarting in the afternoon and in the evening before leaving. For this purpose a special cask is provided, mounted on a high cradle. In many bodegas this traditional custom has been abandoned in favour of allowing the workmen to take home one bottle of Sherry a day; those who do not do so are paid extra. Under this system the workmen are forbidden to drink in the bodegas.

The foremen of the Sherry bodegas are not regarded as ordinary workmen; they are known as 'white-collar foremen', and are quite aware of the responsibility they have for seeing that the work of the bodega is properly carried out. Although most of their decisions are taken only with the owners' approval, the latter value very highly their services as advisers, constantly obliged as they are to inspect the condition of the wine and to sample every cask in the soleras periodically.

In the Fino soleras especially it is necessary to sample every cask before the scales are run; and even if it has not been necessary to replenish them every cask should be checked individually at least three or four times a year.

All this brings to mind another story of Alfonso XII's visit to Jerez. One cellar-manager, hearing the King extol the virtues of a wine he had been given to taste, was moved to assure him that 'we have even better wines in stock'. The King, delighted by this outburst, answered with gentle irony, 'You'd better keep them for a special occasion.'

Mechanization Introduced

Since the original version of this book was first published in 1935 some of the activities in the bodegas have been partially mechanized. I have asked my good friend Dr Justo Casas Lucas to contribute a brief note indicating the extent of these changes in recent decades.*

The viniculture of Jerez, steeped as it is in traditional customs, has undergone a slow process of evolution during the last thirty years owing to the universal technical changes with which it has been surrounded. It has however been a very special form of progress, controlled as it is by certain basic principles not easily altered, since they continue to be essential to the existence of the Sherry viniculture.

What has in fact been happening is an improvement in the methods of manual labour, or its mechanization, so as to avoid interfering with or damaging certain factors and conditions, a change in which might be unfavourable to the quality of the wines. For example, from the classical lagar where a carretada of grapes (600 kgs) was pressed by treading we have passed after technological research into the process, to the present vinification.

This has allowed not only high hourly yields but also greater productivity and hence finally, from a social point of view, better wages and an improved standard of living for the workers.

Experience however proved that not all methods of extraction were suitable

* Updated for 1990 edition by Dr Casas Lucas.

for Jerez, nor could one afford to disregard the conditions under which they were employed. The methods now established, which obtain results equal to and, in some cases, better than the traditional ones, are precisely those which work in harmony with the factors and circumstances that an œnological interpretation would find to be most characteristic of the classical treading.

As the methods of extracting grape-juice become industrialized, the small pressing houses, generally situated at the vineyards, are disappearing, to be replaced by vinification plants that can handle large groups of vineyards.

Crucial Innovation

A comparison of the foregoing paragraphs with the author's original notes immediately reveals one important change: the extraction of the juice from the grapes formerly took place in the vineyard, and was considered as a typical function of viticulture, whereas today, to an ever-increasing extent, it takes place in the bodega and is considered a bodega task. This change is one of the steps towards industrialization which are taking place in the development of scientific œnology.

In the period now under consideration the first move has been made towards the study of the 'yeasts' of Jerez, from those that bring about vinic fermentation to those which occur during the wine's biological growth. Additionally some interesting progress has taken place in the œnological understanding of our wines.

A study of the œnological significance of temperature control during fermentation in stainless steel tanks is presently one of the most interesting subjects of research.

There is no doubt that in general today we can assess more correctly and comprehensively many of the phenomena that take place during vinification and growth, as well as those that have an influence on the stability of the wine.

One notices the great progress that has been made in pumps and filters, and in means of transport inside the bodegas themselves; in the stainless steel vats for the fining of wines before bottling, cooling plants, bottling lines, etcetera.

During the last twenty years many wine-growers of Jerez have come to consider œnological research as a natural part of their work. It was as long ago as March 1955 that a Jerez firm set up the first œnological research centre; since then, other firms have decided to carry out research within the company.

Although some interesting œnological studies have been made by the Estación de Viticultura y Enología of Jerez, which is run by the Ministry of Agriculture, the large firms dedicated to the production and maturing of Sherry now carry out their own œnological research.

The application of scientific principles and methods within each firm to its problems and projects and to its individual points of view and commercial 'personality' may turn out to have far-reaching consequences.

Religious Sidelights

I conclude this chapter with a brief note on the special problems involved in the production of altar wine, a substantial quantity of which is made in Jerez.

In Edmundo de Amici's *España* there is a reference which, although almost unbelievable, is none the less of interest: 'During the great years of Seville Cathedral, approximately 500 Masses were said every day at the twenty-four altars, and the wine consumed at these services reached the astounding figure of 10,750 litres a year.'

Dr Lucio Bascuñana, in the second lecture given in the Jerez School of Commerce in April 1933, spoke of the type of wine required for the Holy Mass. Many people are unaware of the precise stipulations laid down in this connection by the Catholic Church, Dr Bascuñana said:

St Thomas put forward this question—if, in case of necessity, grapes are crushed in a chalice, would this juice then be *valid* for use at Mass, that is to say, could this juice perform the necessary act of Transubstantiation? St Thomas answers emphatically yes, on the grounds that this liquid has the *ability to become* wine. To this reasoning I subscribe. Granted that only those wines that are the result of the fermentation of the juice of ripe grapes through the action of *natural yeast* may be called genuine wines, it is clear that the juice of grapes crushed in a chalice has the *ability to become* wine, because it contains the two essential elements: that is must and yeast.

So far, so good—what, then, does the Catholic Church specify about the wine used in the Holy Sacraments?

Leaving aside historical tradition and theological motives, in an instruction given by the Congregation for the Discipline of the Sacraments on 26 March 1929, which summarizes all the past resolutions approved up to that date, it is demanded that *wine must be the natural produce of juice of the vine, and not acid.*

This should be interpreted as expressive of two series of œnological precepts: (a) those which control the production of wine; and (b) those which guarantee its preservation.

(a) As regards the first series . . . I believe that the only means of fulfilling the Church's stipulation is *by using in the production of wine only those grapes that originate from the different varieties of the botanical species Vitis vinifera*, that is to say, any of the vines cultivated in this area; but with the proviso that no natural or artificial sugar product, and chemical or biological product (yeasts) which the juice contained from the pressing of the grape does not naturally contain, may be added to the juice of those grapes.

(b) The precept of the Congregation embodied in the stipulation that the wine *must not be acid* should be interpreted in the sense that the wine must, to conserve its material integrity, have such hygienic properties that it should be incapable of spontaneous acidification or acetification (since it would then obviously cease to be wine, that is, in St Thomas's terms, it would not have the *ability to become* wine and would cease to be valid). The wine also needs these hygienic properties to resist any other disease that might denaturalize it to the point where it has so far altered as to become a different product to that commonly accepted by authorities as the natural wine of the vine.

How can we protect wine against such dangerous changes? The Church allows only one method: fortification with spirit. But this is only *tolerated* and thus subject to the following three conditions. First, the spirit used must be made from grape wine. Secondly it must be added after the start of the violent fermentation, the best time being when this begins to die down. Thirdly, the total alcoholic content including that of the original unfortified wine should not exceed 12 per cent (Congregation of the Discipline of the Sacraments, 25 June 1891), or 17° to 18° Gay-Lussac (Congregations of the Holy Office, 6 August 1896).

The rigour with which these stipulations necessarily have to be enforced demands that the wine spirit should be *distilled by the producer himself*, since it is impossible to distinguish between pure industrial alcohol and wine spirit, and upon which of the two it is depends the acceptability of the product for the purpose for which it is intended.

As regards alcoholic strength, the resolution of 25 June 1891 should be interpreted as referring to 12 per cent of alcohol by weight as measured on the old Richter hydrometer, and the resolution of the Congregation of the Holy Office of 6 August 1896 as referring to 17° or 18° Gay-Lussac, bearing in mind that 12° Richter is exactly equivalent to 17° Gay-Lussac. The indication 17° *or* 18° would clearly refer to the permitted upper limit.

In view of the exalted purpose for which altar wine is intended, it is hardly necessary to underline the importance of adhering strictly to the conditions laid down by the Congregation. There have been many treatises written about the regulations, and I would refer any producer who wants to make any altar wine to the published works of the Rev. Fr Eduardo Vitoria, SJ, Doctor of Chemical Science and a former Director of the Instituto Químico de Sarriá in Barcelona – especially his *El Pan y el Vino Eucarístico* (1944), a technico-liturgical paper. I believe that this extremely learned and pious work satisfactorily answers all the possible doubts that could arise in this field, although what I have said above summarizes the indispensable conditions controlling the quality and quantity of spirit which may be added and the stage at which this can be done. It is forbidden to blend altar wine with other sweet or *color* wines.

For the production of altar wine in Jerez the grapes with the highest glucose-content are naturally selected—that is to say, those which are normally used for the production of Dulces, and these are usually from Chipiona where the grapes are very rich in sugar.

I hope that the Carthusian community which has recently been restored to its ancient Charterhouse of Our Lady of Protection in Jerez* will once again honour the town by evolving a system of production whereby altar wine would be made under their supervision, which would serve as a guarantee not only in the Peninsula but also abroad; it is known that the brand name of *San Bruno* has already been registered with this purpose in mind.

---

* After several years of negotiation Jerez succeeded in persuading the Carthusians to reoccupy the Charterhouse. On 17 July 1948 a small team came to supervise the alterations that were being done to make it possible to establish living quarters for the new community. The first Carthusian Mass was held in the Chapel on the following day, 18 July, 113 years after their expulsion. On the actual anniversary, 19 August 1948, a Solemn Mass was said, although the official opening and entry of the provisional community, which came from Burgos (Miraflores), did not take place until 6 October, the Feast of St Bruno, Founder of the Order. On this day the whole town attended Pontifical Mass at which the Bishop of Kauna, Dom Augustín María de Hospital de la Puebla, Prior of the Charterhouse of Burgos, officiated in the presence of His Eminence Cardinal Pedro Seguro y Saenz, Archbishop of Seville.

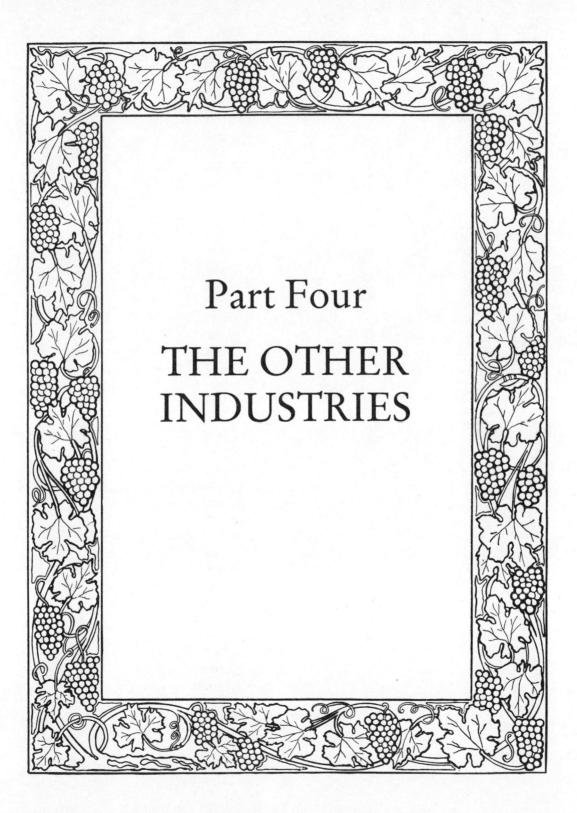

Part Four

THE OTHER INDUSTRIES

Chapter 11

Cooperage

The Bible does not tell us what sort of container or cask Noah used to store the wine he pressed from the grapes in his vineyard. Nor do we know whether the first vessels used by the Greeks and Romans for their wines were earthenware jars or animal skins, treated to render them impermeable and prevent the wines being tainted by the skin. It is probable that in those days the containers most commonly employed for storing wines were large jars made of the less porous clays, from which the wine would be transferred to the amphoras, which held between twenty-five and thirty litres. The Greeks are known to have used the urn, elegantly fashioned and somewhat larger than the amphora. Although it seems probable that skins were also used, especially for the transportation of wine, the earthenware jars were themselves lined with impermeable substances, and those of larger capacity usually had reinforcements or hoops of other materials to prevent their cracking.

Both earthenware jars and goatskins are still used in remote districts of Spain.

It is practically impossible to trace the origins of the wooden cask. In an article in the London *Wine Trade Review* some time ago it was mentioned that Mr George Elkington, a former Master of the Worshipful Company of Coopers and well versed in the history of this ancient industry, offered the suggestion, which appears quite reasonable, that cooperage probably began at the same time as the construction of timber ships. Mr Elkington based his theory on the use of curved and dovetailed planks in shipbuilding, pointing out that the cooper performed more or less the same type of work with similar tools and materials.

The earliest seagoing ships must certainly have needed containers for water, wine and other goods, and wooden ones, being lighter, easier to handle and less fragile than earthenware, would undoubtedly have served best. Although this hypothesis would date cooperage back to the Flood, the earliest specific mention of a wooden cask, according to Mr Elkington's article, was made by Herodotus (900–800 B.C.) in describing the little barques which ran down from Armenia to Babylon, whose cargo he says consisted mainly of wine-barrels. Pliny also writes about cooperage, so that it is possible that the Romans too stored their wines in wooden vessels and transported them to the English coasts in casks, in which case their shape would have been very similar to those we have today.

There is a fine Roman cask in the Römisch-Germanisches Central Museum, at Mainz in Germany. This cask, full of Roman utensils, was found in 1864 in the excavations in the Altmünsterweiher, the moat of the ancient fortress of Mainz, and although it is not possible to ascertain its exact age it is believed to be of about the first to second century A.D. at which time Mainz was under Roman rule.

According to Homer the Greeks in his day (*ca.* 900 B.C.) were familiar with the technique of maturing wines, for which they used wooden casks which they called *pithai*.

Josef Navarro wrote in 1784:

> The towns of Piedmont were the first to invent casks; a truly original invention, which would no doubt cause us much wonder if we had never seen it before. For what industry and loving care must they not have lavished on the construction of these vessels out of small planks joined with strips or bands of bark, which would contain a certain quantity of liquid in an easy and convenient shape for transporting, capable of sustaining the heaviest blows without loss or leakage, and at the same time ideal for the storing of wine?*

Charlemagne, in his Capitularies, enjoined his subjects to use only 'good barrels with iron hoops' as containers for wine. Undoubtedly the success which attended the inventor of the first barrel is reflected in the long time during which these containers have remained in use without any practical substitute being devised.

Germany is famous as a producer of giant-sized barrels: it is said that the largest cask in the world was one constructed by Carl Theodor in 1750, its capacity being 221,726 litres. Some years ago a magazine article referred to one of the biggest casks in the world, built in Hungary in 1802, as the result of a wager, and it has for many years been impossible to repair it for want of wood of the necessary dimensions. Several English nobles, invited to the vintage festivities by a Hungarian Count, bet their host that they could shoot all the pheasants on his property in a fortnight; and as compensation they promised to present him with a cask with a capacity of as many *akres*† as pheasants they shot. Their bag was 2,150 pheasants amd the capacity of the cask had, in consequence, to be 25,800 gallons.

There is evidence that wooden vessels were in use in the Sherry district for transporting wines as early as the fifteenth century. Jerez, like Cadiz, Sanlúcar, Rota, Chipiona, Chiclana, Isla de Léon and other near-by towns, had its ancient customs and regulations for the control of the coopers' craft. In the following

---

* *Memoria sobre la bonificación de los vinos*, p. 87
†A measure equivalent to approximately 12 Imperial gallons.

pages I shall be quoting from some of the more interesting documents relating to vessels for the transporting and storing of wine from the Jerez archives. It appears from these that the first vessels used here for *storing* wines were made of clay lined with pitch, although wooden vessel were used for transporting.

On 21 October 1448 Juan Fernández Barba de Rey, of the suburb of San Miguel, granted to Antón Romero, a sheep-shearer of San Lucas, two aranzadas of vineyard in the district of Santa Catalina del Rio, adjoining the vineyard of Alfonso Martínez de Jaina; his inventory of the stocks in the bodegas refers to 'earthenware jars lined with pitch to accommodate sixty arrobas of wine'.

In the minutes of the Town Council for 9 November 1464 there is a reference to the walnut wood sold in the town, and it seems likely that this was the wood favoured by the carpenters who made the puncheons and butts at that time. As regards the material used, further information is to be found in the Protocol, where there exists an undertaking dated 25 June 1491 by which 'Pedro Martín, cooper, of Xerez, shall pay to Gonzalo González Sarmiento ten casks of good wood, well hooped with hazel and chestnut hoops, such casks in compensation for the sum which the former received in the presence of a notary and witnesses, the payment to be made at the end of the month of July, which ten butts have to go to the vineyards which Gonzalo González owns at the Rio del Portal, where the heads will be removed and replaced and the butts repaired and recoopered'.

On 9 June in the same year 'Anton de Baños, cooper' acknowledges a debt to 'Alonso Diaz, tailor' for ten butts of standard wood.

From previous deeds it can be gathered that the price in 1484, was 300 maravedíes per butt, and that the wood used was Spanish oak.

No doubt there were iron brands and marks for the casks, as appears from a deed in the Protocol, where Fernán López, cooper, signatory to a contract of 27 September 1506, appends between his remarkably legible Christian name and surname a mark, probably an iron stamp, resembling a hand with the index finger extended.

As a curiosity, it is worth noting that in the inventory of the estate of the parents of the famous Jerezano explorer Alvar Núñez Cabeza de Vaca are included, among their assets, their vineyards in the Parpalana district and the value of puncheons and casks of all kinds and sizes. A similar reference occurs in the inventory of the goods belonging to his cousin Pedro de Estupiñán Cabeza de Vaca.

At the council meeting of 10 October 1513 the dimensions and design of the casks were dealt with and it was established that the butts did not bear the brand of the town; nor did they contain thirty arrobas.

In view of the harm and inconvenience caused by the failure to observe the standards followed in Jerez for many years, Señor Jurado Juan López de Arellano brought before the council on 14 April 1567 certain draft ordinances to be sent to His Majesty for approval.

This illustrious town decrees that now and henceforth all master coopers and apprentices and whatsoever other person shall make butts and pipes and puncheons and quarter-casks and barrels to contain must or wine or oil or dyes shall not make bold to construct said vessels with staves or headpieces or any other pieces of wood containing any weakness [*or*, possibly, 'sap rot'] but that all such deficiencies be made good so that the must or wine or oil be safe and the casks do not leak. Similarly, they shall not use nor suffer to be used any tawny stave or broken headpiece or stave, nor should the said vessels have any closed-up pores, and those open pores they do have should be well caulked in the customary manner. And if anything is found contrary to the above, the owner of the wine or oil shall make restitution of the amount which two witnesses shall testify has leaked or been lost from the said vessels or from any one of them. And if there was only one witness to verify the said loss, apart from the oath of the owner, this should be suffcient, and the master cooper whose brand is on the said butt or pipe or quarter-cask or puncheon which has been found with any of the faults above specified be penalized with one-third of the fine, as is customary in this city . . . .

Likewise it is decreed and ordained to all the said justices and any of them, both those who are now and those who shall be hereafter, that they shall not give the town mark to any person for his use but shall themselves mark the said butts and pipes and tubs and other vessels, matching them themselves and seeing they are 'under pressure' as it is said, and measuring their girth and height with the measure and rule which the town has for that purpose, under penalty of a fine of 1,000 maravedíes for each item the said persons contravene anything laid down in these ordinances; the same penalty being imposed upon any master cooper or any other person marking any butt or pipe or other vessels with the town's brand who is not a justice nominated by the said town and its deputies, the said fine to be divided into three parts as herein laid down . . . .

Furthermore, it is decreed and ordained that none of the said justices nor any of them shall make bold to collect the dues for sorting the staves and hoops unless they count them and sort them themselves, entrusting no one else to do so, under penalty that apart from not receiving the dues they shall also lose office, whereupon another person may be nominated in their place by the said town; and likewise it shall be prohibited for such a person to enter again into the said office of justice, on pain of a fine of 1,000 maravedíes, divided into three parts as stated, and he shall remain ineligible to receive and hold office in this town for ten years.

The Guilds

In his collection of documents from the Minutes of the Town Council,* Antonio Fernández Formentani says that in the Corpus Christi procession of 1558 all the Jerez guilds took part, marching under their banners. There were twenty-six guilds in all, and in sixth place was the Coopers Guild. This is further evidence that

* *Costumbres y leyes de antaño – Colección de Documentos extraída de las actas capitulares de Xerez* (Jerez, 1890).

this guild was one of the oldest, if—as tradition has it, and as indeed is likely—they went in order of seniority.

Rallón notes that: 'In 1582 a fleet was being fitted at Puerto de Santa María, and every butt in Jerez was taken to supply it with vessels for water, with evil consequences for local trade, for it caused the ruin of many growers and the loss of a crop, and the price of the cask became almost as much as the price of the wine.'* Agustín de Horozco, writing of Sherry in 1598, said, 'This wine is put into wooden casks for want of other vessels or jars, and these casks are called butts or pipes, which are excessively costly, as the majority of them are used every year for holding wine, or for racking and for exporting outside the Kingdom and to the Indies.'† In that year it appears that the crop was lost entirely, due to the lack of vessels in which to store the musts. Also, Horozco says, at the beginning of the sixteenth century 4,000 to 6,000 28-arroba casks of Sherry were being loaded each year in Cadiz for Mexico and Peru; each cask had ten iron hoops—since the great heat inside the ship caused damage—and each ship carried fifteen or sixteen casks.

It would be rash to speculate on the wood used for the construction of casks in ancient times. Possibly the Romans used Alpine timber and the French their native oak, this being the type of wood which has in most countries proved the most suitable for cooperage, as it is the least porous.

In Spain also many types would certainly have been experimented with; those which seem to have been most used were white oak and chestnut. As to the wood used in olden times by Jerez cooperages there is evidence of several, among them chestnut, hazel, oak, holm oak and cherry. In Portugal, mahogany was used to a considerable extent for constructing large vats in which wines—particularly Port – were blended and stored. Oak from Memel was also much used there.

Antonio Fernández Formentani says that the Council agreed on 10 July 1482:

> . . . that all the butts henceforth constructed by all the coopers of this town for the shipping or loading of wines be made of good wood, as is proper for wine, and that this shall not include wood previously used for sardines or tunny or any other fish, or for oil, or wood which may harm wine; and any butt which contravenes this ruling shall be burnt. And moreover that the offender be fined 600 maravedíes for each offence, the proceeds to go to the civic chest, and that it thus be publicly proclaimed by the town crier, as was done this evening after vespers.

I imagine that the tunny-fishery of Sancti Petri was already using wooden casks for barrelling tunny and other fish, and that some tried to use them afterwards for wine, with the results that one would expect.

Wooden Hoops

No doubt the hoops for the casks would have been made of wood at that time, as in France, where they used chestnut branches. Father Martín de Roa wrote in 1617

---

* *Historia de Jerez.*
† *Historia de Cádiz* (Cadiz, 1845).

that the town 'usually gathers 30,000 butts of wine, a large amount for a single place', and adds: 'A "bota" is the local name for a wooden cask of almost ovoid shape, bound with split willow branches and containing 30 arrobas.'* Nowhere is there any evidence of the type of wood of which the casks themselves were made. The kinds most used in modern times (apart from the local oak and chestnut, and those from Angoulême and the French Pyrenees, which are somewhat difficult to work in) may be classified in three groups: North European Oak (Danzig, Stettin, Lübeck, Riga and Memel); Bosnian Oak (Adriatic Sea); and North American White Oak (Appalachian Mountains).

Esteban Boutelou, writing about cooperage in 1807, says:

> The great wine shippers cooper themselves the casks they require for their trade. They store the woods indispensable for their work, in the firm belief that the good quality of the wood has a special influence upon the conservation of the wines. They use oak almost exclusively; and they esteem more than any that which comes from the United States of America, next the Northern oak, then the Italian and lastly the Spanish. American oak is generally very compact and not at all porous, so that the wines do not leak; nor do even the most volatile and refined spirits filter through. In the opinion of Miller, wines ferment better in butts and wooden vats than in earthenware, which belief is shared by the Sanlúcar growers.

I have not been able to ascertain the exact date when the American white oak shipped from New Orleans and New York was first used in the construction of the Jerez casks; nor who was responsible for the innovation. It is probable that the first American oak came to Europe in the sixteenth century, when the ships provisioning the recently discovered New World needed cargo for their return journeys. This would have been the wood from the forests along the Mississippi, from the information which I have tried to obtain on this point, however, it seems that this trade was to begin much later. It is recorded that among the Pilgrim Fathers—of whom only one-third were adult men, the rest being women and children—there was a master cooper, one John Alden, a native of Southampton, who continued to follow his trade in the New World, fulfilling a most important need in that virgin country. Probably Alden, as an expert in his craft, was the first to appreciate the excellent qualities of the American oak compared with the European woods.

Emigrant Coopers

The demand for their services in the new colony led other coopers to emigrate: it is known that theirs was a well paid craft. At first the barrels made there were for the colonists' own use, but later the development of the fishing and salting industry brought an increase in the construction of barrels for the storage and export of cod and other salt fish, which found a ready market in Europe, principally in Spain, Portugal, France and other Catholic countries where days of abstinence were kept.

* *Santos Patronos de Xerez.*

It is believed that this trade began in about 1640, and that within ten years wines were being imported from the Iberian Peninsula. Although the exact date of the first direct shipment of American staves to Spain is not known, since at first this trade was routed via Liverpool, it is certain that by the second half of the seventeenth century this traffic with western Europe was constant. In those days the price of staves per thousand would be very different to what it is today – Coyne mentions a figure of eighteen pounds sterling, while the current price would run to four figures.

Although both white and red oaks grow in America, the species always used in cooperage has been the white (*Quercus alba*), probably because it is the wood most beneficial to the wine. The red oak, a much faster-growing tree, is very porous.

By 1648 there were already enough coopers in America to constitute a guild; although exportation of staves to Europe was probably still in its infancy, the industry was already of considerable importance, since a large number of casks were used for the locally produced rum and cider.

Although the use of American oak became established in the first instance because of its texture and because, having no knots, it was easy to work with, economic considerations and the need to foster commercial relations between Europe and America no doubt played their part. Later its use became general in almost all wine-growing regions, by virtue of its many excellent qualities: being devoid of resin, it lends itself to the maturing and ageing of wines without transmitting to them any disagreeable taint.

In Jerez no other wood has been used for many years, as American oak has given the best results for the fermentation, maturing, ageing and shipping of Sherry.

Some coopers believe that their ancient guild used to regard St Nicholas as their patron saint.* But a historical record written by Andrés Hidalgo Ortega in 1887 definitely shows that the saint venerated as patron of the Jerez guild was St Andrew. The individual members of this guild, until well into the nineteenth century, used to parade with the statute of St Andrew from the Royal Convent of San Francisco on Corpus Christi, with a red flag bearing the green saltire cross of St Andrew.

The cask most used in Jerez is the butt of 30 arrobas, equivalent to 500 litres, and measuring roughly 1.30 metres in length and 0.90 metres maximum diameter (i.e. through the bung). This is the shipping or export butt, and this is the quantity of Sherry which Jerez shippers are obliged to give their customers as contents of one butt. A 500-litre butt is generally reckoned to produce only 53 dozen ¾ litre bottles (i.e. 477 litres), as the remainder should not be used because of the sediment.

* The Feast of St Nicholas of Myra is celebrated by the Church on 6 December. So far as I know there is nothing to connect this saint with the Guild of Coopers, except that one of his best-known miracles was to bring back to life three children who had been beheaded and whose bodies had been thrown into a vat!

In the old days the shipping-unit used to calculate freight charges to England was the tun of 250 gallons; and probably this is why these charges are still quoted today per *tonelada* of two butts. Today the charges from Cadiz to U.K. ports vary between about £7 and £12 per two butts, which, with insurance and landing fees, averages about £14–15 per butt.

Spanish legislation allows the return of empty casks by the countries importing Sherry. This applies principally to the Scandinavian countries, who generally pay for the wine *nu*, and consequently return the cask. At the time of writing some new casks are exported to Scotland, but undoubtedly Sherry-seasoned casks are preferred.

As well as the butt, various smaller casks are used in Jerez: principally the hogshead of 250 litres, the quarter-cask of 125 and the octave of 62½. There are also barrels of 1 and 2 arrobas (i.e. approximately 17 and 33 litres), and other special measures.

These capacities apply to shipping butts (*botas de embarque* or *de exportación*), but the casks used for the soleras are generally of larger size: the most commonly used are the bodega or large butts (*botas gordas*) of 36 arrobas. Small puncheons of 40 to 50 arrobas are also used in the bodegas for storage, as well as larger puncheons of 60, 90 and even 120 arrobas, equivalent to 2, 3 and 4 butts respectively. The *bocoy*, which is even larger than the bodega butt, is little used in Jerez, except in special cases when casks are in short supply.

The casks used for the racking and blending work inside the bodegas are small bodega butts called *bodegueras*, with a capacity of 34 arrobas.

Finally there is the 'receiving butt' (*bota de recibo*) of 31 arrobas, which is of particular importance as it has always been the standard measure for all buying and selling of musts and wines in the region. Although the *bota de recibo* is still used at the vintage, few are now built to these precise measurements, since all buying and selling can now be done with casks of any capacity; the casks are weighed full, the 'tare' deducted and the specific gravity of the wine measured: the exact number of litres involved can thus be reckoned.

The reason for the receiving butt's holding 31 arrobas instead of the more logical 30 is to allow a margin for loss through evaporation and the porosity of the wood. The origin of this butt appears to date from 1774, when the Vintners Guild resolved to standardize Sherry casks for foreign trade at the Avila standard of 30 arrobas, but cushioned the effect of the restriction by permitting the use of 31-arroba butts for local trade and sales.*

For those who are interested in following the details of this ancient and fascinating process, I have compiled below a complete summary of the cooper's craft as it has traditionally been practised in Jerez, showing the roles of the various cooperage personnel and the tools they employ at every stage from the arrival of the rough staves in Spain to the dispatch of the finished cask.

* A table of the dimensions, capacities and weights of the casks used in Jerez is provided in Part Five (9).

Rough Staves

American oak comes to Spain from the ports of New York and New Orleans in rough split staves. The best white oak has always been considered to be that coming from the Appalachian Mountains, which is fine-grained and compact. In general the lower part of the tree gives the best wood; the upper part is more porous.

The standard trading unit for staves is the *millar de duelas*, or batch of 1,200. The timber is felled in December and January, and the staves reach Spain early in the spring. Before the Civil War the cargoes were generally consigned to firms in Cadiz with warehouses at the near-by station of Segunda Aguada. These firms distributed the staves among the master coopers of the district as required. Since the war, however, due to revisions in the import and export laws, the coopers themselves import the staves and supply the shippers with the finished casks.

The dimensions of the staves, both rough and planed, which arrive in Cadiz from America are all given in English inches, and each American exporter marks on the staves which he sends to the different purchasing markets, apart from his name, the quality of the different lots. Normal practice is to mark them with one two or three dots in one or several colours, which correspond to the different qualities. Thus one red dot generally means 'extra good', two red dots 'double extra', and three red dots 'triple extra'. A white dot means 'good', and other colours generally mean that the staves are not the best. However, each exporter has his own marking and classification code.

When the staves reach Jerez coopers' yards the long process of cooperage proper begins. In the following breakdown of the stages involved, the work is done by the cooper himself unless otherwise stipulated.

Classification (owner or foreman): Each stave and headpiece is graded individually, to see which particular size or type of barrel it is most suitable for. An iron gauge marked with the stave-lengths and head-diameters of the different casks is used to determine this.

Cutting to length (assistant sawyer): The rougher end of each piece is removed and the other end then trimmed to the appropriate length. This is traditionally done by hand, with the piece supported on two tubs, but most cooperages now use the power saw. If necessary, the wood is subsequently left to dry for some time before use.

Splitting (rack cooper): The object of this operation is to obtain a minimum of two usable pieces from each rough stave. Once again, the power saw has largely superseded the traditional method of clamping the stave in a rack and splitting it with the mallet and rack-knife.

Trimming (sawyer): The staves are now trimmed to the correct thickness, the sawyer working away from the ends towards the middle (eventually to be the bulge of the finished cask), where the thickness is reduced by a full 30 per cent. One end is left slightly thicker than the other. The work was normally done by hand, the stave being supported on a cooper's block, generally a tree-stump fixed in the ground and projecting about one metre above it; this too has now been mechanized. Accuracy here is very important: if the finished staves are of unequal thickness, the inside of the cask will be uneven, and hence difficult to clean properly.

Shaping (cleaver): There are four distinct stages to this.

  (i) The sides are split off with a draw-knife, a short-handled knife with a long, narrow rectangular blade set at right-angles to the handle. The cleaver supports the stave on the block and splits it by levering against the knife-handle with the right side of his head and neck; again, the power saw is often used today.

 (ii) Backing the stave is the next stage: this consists of trimming the outside surface down the edges, to produce an external curvature corresponding to that of the finished cask. The stave is held firmly on a shaving-horse and trimmed with the downright shave and backing knife, a straight blade with two handles at right-angles to it.

(iii) Hollowing is the counterpart of backing, the inside face of the stave being hollowed out down its length, producing the same curve on the inside as on the outside. The tool used, a hollowing-knife, is similar to the backing-knife but has a curved blade.

(iv) Chiving is the name given to tapering the width of the stave towards both ends, to give it the shape of the cask. It is passed over a long fixed plane called a chiving-plane.

Grading (assistant cleaver): The prepared staves are now graded again, according to thickness.

Preparing the headpieces (headpiece cleaver): Again, this is a long operation with several distinct stages.

  (i) The pieces are shaved with a backing-knife, on another type of shaving-horse.

 (ii) They are planed with the grain, to give the edges the necessary bevel or chamfer.

(iii) They are planed again, this time against the grain, which serves to make them more solid and compact.

(iv) Finally they are chived, with the chiving-plane, and classified by size. Each head will consist of seven pieces (five, for hogsheads): the midpiece, two intermediate pieces either side of it, and two half-moon-shaped outside pieces known as cantles.

Jointing: This part of the work, also known as 'church-ending', is of vital importance; adjacent jointed surfaces must fit exactly if the cask is to be perfectly formed and watertight. Using a long jointer-plane, like a chiving-plane, the cooper gives the staves their smooth finish and, at the same time, the bevelled edges which enable the staves to fit snugly, the degree of bevel obviously varying in proportion to the width of the stave. This is the final stage in the preparation of the staves, which are now left to dry for several months so that the wood becomes tougher and more durable.

Raising the cask: When the staves are ready, the cooper selects twenty-five or twenty-six for each cask. While these must be of the same thickness, their width may vary considerably, and the even outside curvature of the cask is preserved by careful placing, so that the broadest staves are always next to two narrow ones. Two provisional hoops—a head-hoop and a bulge-hoop—are used for raising the cask; these, together with a measuring-rod giving the head-diameter, control its final size. The first stave is attached to a tiny pin in the head-hoop, and the others added one by one until the circle is complete. The bulge-hoop is now placed over the centre of the staves, the two hoops representing the maximum and minimum circumferences of the finished cask. Now five strong iron truss hoops are placed on the upper half of the cask, so that it is entirely symmetrical and will stand unsupported on the splayed lower ends of the staves. The provisional hoops are removed.

Driving: The cask now has the appearance of a truncated cone, the staves being joined in the upper part but splayed at the bottom; the upper end, where the thicker stave-ends are, is known as the top-head and the lower as the dinting-head. The cask is now taken to the driving-slab—sheltered from the wind if out of doors – and the dinting-head is drawn tight, formerly with more hoops but now more usually with a winch. To soften the staves so that they can be bent a small iron brazier called a cresset is put inside the cask, the wood being damped down from time to time to ensure that it is not scorched. In Jerez, the left horn of a cow has been found to be the ideal shape for sprinkling the water evenly on the inside surface. When the staves have been bent into position, the cask is inverted and the dinting-head set of five hoops are put on and driven home with the thin end of a cooper's hammer (a five pound sledge). The cask is then 'boxed', its curvature being checked on the outside and any uneven staves beaten into shape from the inside with a mallet.

Charring the Casks
It is worth noting at this point what José de Hidalgo Tablada has to say on the subject of the firing of casks:

New woods, unless they are specially prepared sometimes cause the musts stored in them—the action of the alcohol releasing a quantity of tannin—to develop the harsh flavour known as 'woodiness'. To avoid this tainting of the wine, the staves are charred on the inside; and we already know that carbon affects the colour of the wine. The charring thus increases the preservative qualities of both the must and the wood.[*]

Jointing the headpieces: While the driven cask is cooling, the two sets of headpieces are jointed, with a jointer-plane similar to that used for the side staves.

Hooping and planing: Each end of the cask is now fitted with four of its five hoops—reading from the bulge, the bulge-hoop, lower quarter-hoop, upper quarter-hoop, square hoop (set aside for the moment) and chime hoop. The truss hoops are removed, and the outside joints of the staves are shaved with a special

[*] *Tratado de fabricación de vinos en España y el extranjero.*

plane known as a *galga*. The hoops are generally of Spanish manufacture, though some are imported from England; butt hoops are 38 mm. wide by 1.8 mm. thick, hogshead hoops naturally somewhat smaller.

Driving the hoops: The hoops are driven firmly into place with the hammer and driver, a sort of wedge-ended chisel. In the shipping butt the quarter-hoops and chime hoop are each joined by one rivet, the others by two each. The rivets are hammered in on a T-anvil known as a bick iron. To prevent slipping, the chime hoops are affixed to the barrel with screw tacks, the others with tenterhooks. Rivets can be dangerous if the workman rolling a butt in a bodega wears a ring, as a protruding rivet may hook the ring and send the man right over the barrel; a very serious accident of this sort once occurred in Jerez.

Topping: This is a five-part operation.
(i) The first stage is chiming—the cooper bevels the inside edges of the staves, using a large adze with a curved blade called a splaying-adze. The chamfered interior surface thus formed is called the chime.
(ii) The stave-ends are levelled with the long topping-plane.
(iii) The cooper smoothes the inside surface of the staves, where he will cut the croze, using the rounded 'Carthaginian' adze.
(iv) The croze—the groove into which the bevelled edges of the head will fit—is cut with a special instrument (also called the croze), equipped with two cutting blades and a chisel to scoop out the groove.
(v) Finally, the chime is trimmed with the large curved trimming-adze, similar to the splaying-adze but with a sharper blade. The thickness of the stave at the chime varies, but is usually between 30 and 40 mm. for butts, 26 and 35 mm. for hogsheads.

Fixing the square hoop: Once the cask has been chimed, the square hoop can be fitted; the size of this is determined by the chime hoop, over which it must fit exactly. Once it has been driven, the chime hoop itself is tightened, a new rivet being inserted. For the driving of these last two hoops the driver is fitted with a small handle called a *sonajilla*.

Heading: This is another multi-stage process.

(i) The radius of the head is determined by trial and error, the compasses being stepped round the head of the cask until the distance between their points is one-sixth of its circumference. Having thus obtained the radius, the cooper uses it to mark the circumference on the headpieces, which are then sawn to size with a head-saw.
(ii) They are then bevelled, the outside surface with a short, sharp chamfer and the inside with a longer, flatter one. Both jobs are done with a heading-knife, another two-handled knife with a straight blade.
(iii) The heads are now ready to be fitted. The three top hoops at the top-head are loosened, the head is inserted one piece at a time from the inside, and the hoops are tightened again, starting from the upper quarter-hoop and working outwards. Then the cask is inverted and the pieces of the

driving-head inserted, always in the same order, leaving one of the cantles till last. No glue or fixative is used. A hook is buried in the centre of the loose cantle, to enable the cooper to draw it outwards until it slips into the croze, the process being assisted by hammering on the opposite outside surface of the cask with a mallet, forcing the cantle upwards. Fine, damp clay is applied to the joints of the headpieces, and also to the croze where it cuts the stave joints. The hoops are then driven, and the cask at once filled with water—if it is allowed to dry, the joints will work loose. This also allows the casks to be checked for any leakage. As a matter of interest, I believe it is only in Jerez that the heads are fitted piece by piece, a more difficult technique than building the head and fitting it as a whole, but probably producing better results.

Bulrushing: Any leakage revealed by the water is stopped with a bulrush, the staves being prised apart with a flagging-iron and the bulrush inserted with a hammer and bulrushing-wedge.

Bunging: The bunghole is bored in a preselected stave, marked by the line of the rivets and a mark on the heads. The apprentice bores the hole with a gimlet, enlarges it with a taper auger, and smoothes out the inside edges with a special knife known as a thief.

Seasoning: Finally, the cask is seasoned, either with wine or with ammonia and steam.

Weekly Quotas

It is reckoned that a cooperage employing thirty men can produce fifty or sixty butts a week. It was once the custom in the Jerez Coopers Guild that each cooper would estimate a weekly quota for his yard, and would stop work for the week on fulfilling it. This is why piece workers in many yards do not work on Mondays.

The Jerez Coopers Guild has always been recognized as a model of its type, not only by Spanish but by world standards. The work is hard and demands great skill, the membership being relatively small, about six hundred men. The craft is by tradition virtually hereditary; so much so that a workman whose forbears were not coopers is said to be not a 'son of the knife'. Some coopers take young members of their family as apprentices, and these are generally called *lanchas*. The majority of the coopers (about 65 per cent) live in Jerez itself, the remainder being distributed between Puerto de Santa María, Sanlúcar de Barrameda, Cadiz (Segunda Aguada) and Chiclana. All men who carry out the work which has been described in previous pages are called 'new cask coopers' and are paid piece-rate, except the *aviadores* who are paid a daily wage.

Glass Heads

I must record, as a curiosity, a cask which the master cooper M. González Ortega built some thirty-five years ago. It was a bodega butt with heads of bevelled glass 8½ mm. thick; the diameter of the heads was 71 cm. The idea was to make it possible to observe the process of fermentation in the musts, and, above all, to study the development of the flor. The cask has been very useful in both these fields, and has also helped understanding of the evaporation and condensation produced in a Sherry cask.

It is easy to appreciate the difficulties involved in fitting a cask with two glass ends. To do it the cooper built an ordinary butt, taking great pains to ensure it was absolutely right, and left it full of water for several months. The ordinary wooden heads were then taken out and replaced by perfectly circular one-piece iron heads, so that as the wood expanded and contracted the pressure all round the croze would be uniform. If this were not so, these stresses might have broken the glass.

After the butt has been steamed for several days the iron heads were removed and the croze in the chime was cut deeper and filled with damp clay. Then the edges of the glass heads were protected with wet blotting-paper. After that two crossed tapes were fixed on the glass head, and a string tied to them and run through the bunghole. The three upper hoops were loosened and the heads of the staves opened up a bit, the string was pulled through the bunghole to ease the head into position and the edges were fitted into the croze; the tapes were then cut and pulled out through the bunghole, and the hoops were driven carefully, keeping the clay in the croze damp all the time to protect the bevel. Once both heads were in position the cask was slowly filled with water for several days; and eight or ten days afterwards the water was emptied out and replaced by wine to season the cask perfectly.

Coopers are justly famous for their ability to estimate exactly, without so much as a gauge rod, the capacity of the casks they build. Despite this, and despite the reasonably accurate gauge-rod method, the only ways of arriving at the *exact* capacity of a cask are by checking it with water or by weighing it full and empty. Once the casks are measured they are emptied, rinsed, aired and then bunged up tightly. (See Part Five (10) for mathematical calculations of cask capacities.)

Shipping butts should hold 508 to 516 litres, hogsheads 254 to 258, quarter casks 127 to 129, and octaves 63 to 65. The reason for the margin of error allowed is that the measurement systems employed abroad, especially the gauging-rod procedure in the English Customs houses, seem in practice to give a slightly low reading, due to the variation in curvature of the staves in the bouge.

After the cask has been measured it must be seasoned before it can be used for wine because the oak contains tannin and other essential oils soluble in alcohol, which can give a taint to the wine: in extreme cases the wine may be unfit for anything but distilling. It is extraordinary how a single new stave used to repair a seasoned cask can give a taint to the wine; extra staves for repairing seasoned casks must be seasoned beforehand by a long soaking in wine.

The most practical way of seasoning new casks is to use them for storing the musts during the vintage; in this way the cask is seasoned but the must is not spoilt as wine would be. During fermentation the musts absorb the resin content from the wood, while the wood takes in exchange other substances which subsequently form a furry deposit on the inside of the cask, hence the obvious advantage of filling new casks with must during the vintage: both benefit by the system. At times an imperfect young wine can improve by being stored in a new butt. This is probably because, by absorbing the tannin from the wood, it remedies the tannin deficiency which is a general defect of the wines of this part of the world, where it is not the custom (as it is in other parts of Spain) to ferment the musts with the skins, stems and pips.

Nevertheless, if a cask is used to ferment must year after year, the day will come when the wood loses all its consistency; and, if it is dismantled, one look at the joints of the staves will show that the structure of the inner part of the stave in contact with the must is completely different to that of the outer part.

This method of seasoning only began to be practised in Jerez during the last century; in the old days the Jerez growers always preferred to ferment musts in butts which had previously been seasoned with wine. This, of course, was not commercially practical, as apart from losing the wine-seasoned casks it meant tying up capital unprofitably because of the loss by evaporation; moreover, the wine did not improve as it would have done in a new cask.

Because of this the value of a seasoned butt in those days was always about 5 pesetas more than that of one that was unseasoned. Today the difference is almost negligible. Of course, a distinction must be made between a butt that has fermented must during several vintages and one that has been used to store wine in the solera: the former, due to fermentation, will diminish in weight and the wood will finish up by losing its consistency, while the solera butt, saturated with the wine it has absorbed, will increase in weight; large butts which have been used for several years in the soleras sometimes gain up to 25 kilos.

From what I have said it is easy to see that from the economic point of view this way of seasoning is by far the best. Unfortunately, though, it is not always easy to get ready all the casks required for the year by the vintage time: this would be ideal, as the charred insides of new casks further improve the quality of the must, by keeping it as pale as possible.

For wines other than those of the very first quality, for which a butt seasoned first with must and then with wine is desirable, the general custom in Jerez is to treat the cask by a process invented by Francisco Ivison O'Neale. The inventor's explanatory brochure points out that the drier the casks are the sooner the interchange of components between wood and wine takes place. This interchange is also stimulated by heat and motion. The pamphlet adds that the presence of sugar helps the alcohol to dissolve the astringent substances in the wood; thus the sweeter wines tend to become more woody and consequently season the cask more quickly.

The system patented by Sr Ivison, which is followed in most Jerez bodegas, consists of subjecting the cask to a steam jet at a pressure of not more than 7 lb. per square inch, and containing ammonia, for at least forty to fifty minutes.*

Once a cask is seasoned—whether with must, wine or ammonia– it is rinsed out several times, an iron chain being put inside to scrape out any splinters in the joints

---

* Technical details on the use of ammonia are given in Part Five (11).

or staves. If the butts are new they generally require some further attention before they are ready for shipment. This work is generally done by the *repair coopers*, who are paid a daily wage.

Apart from redriving the hoops and replacing any defective staves or head-pieces, the workman generally removes the heads to scrape the inside of the cask and scrubs it out afterwards with strong heather brushes. Once the head is replaced the cask is again washed: this time knotted cords are put inside, and the cask is rocked longitudinally and at the same time turned gently. The cask is rinsed several times, till the water comes out perfectly clear. In many cases the cords will not finish the job, and the chain must be used again.

Generally it is necessary to sulphur a used cask to destroy any acetic germs, and if it has contained vinegar it is sometimes necessary to give it special treatment. If the cask has held acid or nearly acid wines it is generally sufficient to wash it out with soda to neutralize the acidity, but at other times it is necessary to place it on the driving-slab and char it inside, as otherwise it would not take the sulphuring. It is very dangerous to sulphur a cask if there is any possibility that it might have been used for spirits, because there will then be a danger of its exploding when the lighted sulphur is inserted in the bunghole. Even casks that have contained high-strength wines, if they have been lying in the sun for any time, can explode, so it is advisable to leave the tap-hole open when the lighted sulphur is inserted in the bunghole, when there will be no risk of an explosion.

Once this stage is over the cask is virtually ready for shipping: it only remains for the shipper's mark to be burnt on. The port of destination and the initials of the customer are marked in the same way; the rest of the information given on the cask is generally painted on. The heads are then varnished. The cask may also have the wine-marks carved on the stave near the bunghole; this is done with a special tool known as a bung-marker. In some special cases the customer has the whole cask varnished and provided with a protective esparto-grass wrapping; in other cases the cask is given a thin veneer of oak or some other wood. At times a willow hoop (*taparrumo*) is attached to the head end to protect the chime.

The current price of American oak shipping-casks in Jerez can be reckoned at about 80 pesetas per litre of capacity, although with small casks the figure may sometimes be a little higher. It is interesting to note the steady rise in the prices since the beginning of the century. This can be put down to two main factors: one external, the high value of the wood; the other internal, the higher cost of Customs duties, transport and clearing expenses and the expense of labour and the accessories that the cask requires.

1898	40 pesetas per butt
1914	80
1918	100
1931	160
1939	400

1945	725
1962	3,900
1970	4,500
1989/90	40,000

The Sherry casks shipped to Britain have long been very highly esteemed by whisky-distillers for the ageing of their products. Their price on the English market fluctuated a great deal. When there was no demand for empties in Britain butts were sometimes returned to Jerez, either in shooks or whole, taking advantage of the import-licence concessions available on goods destined for re-export; licences were also sometimes given for casks to be imported into Spain free of Customs duty under the temporary-importation system.

The preference for Sherry casks in Scotland* is due not only to their excellent construction, but still more to the beneficial influence which the wine esters retained in the wood have on whisky. The whisky-distillers prefer casks which have held sweet and Oloroso wines, as fuller-bodied wines season the casks better than the lighter Finos; and, naturally, the older the wine the better the seasoning. In consequence casks seasoned with Fino tended to fetch slightly lower prices.

Stainless steel containers have been used for the transport of Sherry to some markets, as has already occurred in the beer industry. Of course, these containers could *only* be used for transport, because wooden casks are absolutely indispensable for the maturing and ageing of Sherry; so it is practically sure that the cooperage industry will never disappear. Any visitors to Jerez who have heard the rhythmic hammering of the casks being driven and smelt the peculiar smell of the charred damp staves will surely agree that it would be a pity to see this traditional industry die out.

Although the ordinary *bocoyes* (reinforced puncheons) for transport are little used in Jerez, some are used when butts are in short supply. These bocoyes, which are not as long as the butts, are very suitable for transporting wines of higher density, such as the *color* wine.

It is reckoned that under normal shipping conditions 40,000 butts require the importation of about 7,000 barrels of staves, equivalent to about 8,000 cubic metres, the average specific weight of staves (counting both green and dry) being approximately 0.900. In recent years some Spanish oak has also been used, due principally to the difficulties of importing American timber, but its greater density and hardness and lower porosity make it less suitable than the American wood.

Wastage and offcuts from both rough and half-planed staves amounts to between 25 and 40 per cent, but all this can be used for small barrels; in former times small olive kegs were also made from these remains. The sawdust and shavings are used for fuel, and the small leftover pieces for making flat and inclined wedges for stacking the butts and for levelling the support of the ground tier.

* A note on the importance of Sherry to the Scotch whisky industry will be found in Part Five (12).

Chapter 12

Bottles & Corks
Labels & Packs

I must now say something about the bottles, packing, and other accessories used in the bottling of Sherry, and brandy, in Jerez.

The discovery of glass is attributed to several civilizations, among them the Egyptians, from whom we have the most ancient containers so far known. In the history of this people mention is made of glass as long ago as 3500 B.C. Other authorities attribute the discovery to the Phoenicians: Pliny mentions an incident which, although in itself it sounds like a fable, at least proves how ancient the discovery of glass must have been. He records that some Phoenician traders were obliged to land their cargo of soda in the desert at the foot of Mount Carmel, and heated their cooking-pots on some pieces of their cargo; the hot soda fused with the sand and glass was produced.

Some historians have said that the Greeks, of whom it can be truly said that they enhanced the beauty of everything they touched, were probably the first to use glass containers, not only for drinking but to store their choicest wines; this is borne out by the existing collections of ancient glass containers. A celebrated painter, Pausias, in the fourth century B.C., painted an image of Methe, the Goddess of Inebriation, drinking from a glass container through which her face could be seen.

Others again say that the first glass bottles were made in the days of Nero, when the use of this product was extended to include, among other things, receptacles for wine. Martial confirms that the best wines of Falerno were kept in small glass bottles.

The industry progressed considerably about the time of the beginning of the Christian era; glass-workers were sufficiently important for the Roman Emperor Constantine (274–337) to exempt them from all taxes.

A visit to the Museo Nazionale in Naples, where over 4,000 pieces of glass are exhibited, mainly from Pompeii and Herculaneum, will demonstrate the hardly believable degree of perfection that the industry achieved in the last centuries of the Roman civilization, above all in the colouring and the cutting of glass.

The principal raw materials used in the modern Spanish industry are silica (sand) from the beaches of Puerto de Santa María and sodium carbonate from Torrelavega (Santander). These two components make up 95 per cent of the total; but other materals are also used in smaller quantities, among them the colouring agents. All these materials are melted together, at a temperature of about 1,500°C.

Glass manufacture has progressed enormously since the time when the melting was done in crucibles and the glass blown through a tube; the development of semi-automatic machines brought it to a level of near-perfection. Nevertheless, the commercial use of the bottle in the wine industry began only with the advent of the cork stopper. The really rapid progress has been during the last fifty years, with automatic manufacture in all branches and careful selection of materials allowing the manufacture of bottles of minimum weight.

Although the glass bottle was widely used in the wine trade during the seventeenth century, the commercial bottling of wines in Europe seems not to have begun till the end of the eighteenth or early nineteenth; I have already observed that the trade in bottled wines from Jerez did not start until the 1870s.

The bottle most commonly used in Jerez is the ¾-litre bottle, with its half bottle of 0.375 litres; there is also a 1-litre bottle, used for export to countries where Customs duties are levied per bottle and, within Spain, for brandies and medicinal Sherries; these bottles are lighter in colour than ordinary Sherry bottles.

As well as these, Jerez also produces a magnum (1.5 litres), quarter-bottles, fifths and miniatures (one-eighth and one-sixteenth of a bottle, generally used for samples and publicity). In recent years most miniatures have been made in the flask shape, which is handier than the traditional round form.

The glass used for Sherry bottles is usually black, as light affects the wine, making it darker. For brandies a greenish bottle (*semiblanca*, or medium white) is used; some of these are shaped like Cognac bottles, others like the standard Sherry bottle.

The First Jerez Factory

Until the first bottle-factory in Jerez was built in 1896, bottles were brought in from other Spanish factories, and some were also imported from abroad. This first factory, called 'La Jerezana', was built by Andrés Bocuze, and the bottles were handblown. Some time afterwards a second factory, 'La Constancia Industrial', was built; here too the bottles were hand blown. This company failed after a short time, due to technical difficulties.

'La Jerezana' later merged with the Belgian Compagnie Générale des Verreries Espagnoles, which replaced the old system of blowing bottles with Boucher machines. Finally, in 1925, the Belgian factory became a Spanish company, and now trades as the Compañía General de Vidrierías Españolas, S.A. There was another factory in Puerto de Santa María, Vidrierías del Guadalete, S.A., but this was absorbed by St Gobain. In 1945 another factory, Vidrierías Palma, S.A. (Vipa), was transferred from the Balearic Islands to Puerto de Santa María, and this now supplies bottles for the Puerto de Santa María and Jerez brandy shipping firms.* In other parts of Spain there are firms—in Barcelona, Badalona, and two in Gijón—which produce containers of all kinds and have from time to time supplied Jerez.

The great majority of the bottles used in Jerez are very similar in shape, and several shippers put their names or marks on the bottles to avoid their being used for other purposes.

The return of empty bottles is a very old custom in Jerez and each firm has its own conditions for the redemption of its empties.

The weight of an empty standard wine or brandy bottle is roughly 750 grammes, but with a new special glass bottles can be manufactured which are equally strong but weigh only just over half this figure; this means a great saving in Customs duties for those importing countries where duties are reckoned on the gross weight of the goods, as the light bottle means a saving of approximately 4 kilos per dozen.

Big glass-manufacturing companies in the United States, I understand, are undertaking research to establish whether the weight of the bottle can be further reduced without making it fragile. Research is also being carried out to find out how oxidation in bottled wines can be eliminated, as it appears that even the conventional dark bottle allows certain light rays through which affect the quality of the wine.

So far only a few firms in Jerez have taken advantage of any of the advances made in the field of disposable bottles; one demonstrable benefit of these would be that they would mean an end to the activities of those who refill empties with their own produce. Many different varieties of disposable bottles and stoppers have been offered to the shippers of Jerez, but none has so far been found to be completely satisfactory, although several types are being used by some of the larger firms.

Cork

Another essential article in the Sherry trade is the cork. Today cork is being used more and more, for many different purposes. In the United States, for example, according to a recent report, as much as 2 kilos of cork per head per annum is being used; it is to be noted that the biggest consumers of this product are the most highly developed countries.

The Iberian peninsula is actually the greatest producer of cork in the world. Spain has about 500,000 hectares of cork woods, a figure which could be still larger, as the cork-tree is highly resistant to the extremely dry climate of Spain.

After Spain and Portugal the principal producing countries are Algeria and Tunisia, followed by France, Morocco and Corsica. Some lower-grade cork is also

* This firm was also later absorbed by Vidrierias Españolas Vicasa S.A.

grown in Japan.

I am indebted for the following details to Mr John Fitzpatrick, late manager of the Manufacturas de Corcho Armstrong, S.A., of Seville.

The ancient Greeks and Romans were familiar with some of the uses to which the bark of the cork-tree could be put. The Greek Theophrastus mentions cork in his famous *Inquiry into Plants*, and Pliny the Elder in his *Naturalis Historiae* mentions its use for stoppers, floats and so on. Horace writes, 'Corticem adstrictum pice dimovebit amphorae' ('Remove the cork sealed with tar from the wine-vessel'): this shows that the cork industry has been closely associated with wine-making for over two thousand years. In all that time no acceptable substitute has yet been discovered.

The word *cork* is probably derived from the Latin *cortex* (bark), and the species producing it are *Quercus occidentalis* and *Quercus suber*. It is around the western end of the Mediterranean that the species are most abundant. They differ mainly in the duration of their foliage, and the structure and maturing-time of their fruit. Both species are evergreens and usually reach a height of 12 to 15 metres and a maximum diameter of about 1.5. Although some attain a very great age the average is about a hundred years.

The first stripping generally takes place when the tree is over twenty years old; thereafter the process is repeated every nine years (sometimes every eight). The product of the first stripping is virgin cork (*bornizo*); that of the second is *primerizo*, and of the subsequent strippings *segunderos*. The stripping is generally done in the early summer (June), leaving the tree protected with another inner bark (called *curtido*, or 'tanned', because it is employed in the tanning of skins). This second bark is always left on the tree: if it were stripped off the tree would perish.

The planned commercial cultivation of cork in Spain did not begin till 1760, when a German agriculturalist resident in Spain, Josef Rumey, rented several cork-woods in Catalonia and started to export the bark to Germany. His example was followed by many other Spanish merchants, and cultivation spread to France, Portugal, Italy and North Africa. Today, world production amounts to about 300,000 tons annually.

One of the most ancient and widespread uses of cork, and the reason why it is a household commodity all over the world, is the sealing of casks and bottles. The number of cork stoppers manufactured each year is of the order of 10,000 million. The manufacture of cork stoppers as an independent industry started in the seventeenth century: Dom Pérignon (1670–1715), the cellar-master of Hautvillers Abbey immortalized as the 'father' of Champagne, is credited with the invention of the modern method of corking wine-bottles.

The principal qualities that favour the use of cork for sealing containers of wine are its elasticity, compressibility and durability, and that it is a bad conductor of heat. It is also impervious, probably because of the climate in which it grows, which makes it necessary for the tree to retain moisture.

The compressiblity of cork is astonishing: tests have been made with samples cut in cube form subjected to a pressure of 14,000 lb. per square inch, which has not proved sufficient to destroy the cells, the samples subsequently regaining up to 90 per cent of their original height. Corks which have been in bottle ten years and more have when drawn regained 75 per cent of their original volume.

Cork contains millions of tiny cells full of air, and this is why it is so light: 53 per cent of its total volume is occupied by air, and it has been proved that each individual cell is in contact with fourteen others. The number of cells per cubic centimetre is approximately 16,000,000. The walls of the cells are of very fine but strong cellulose, hence the low conductivity; and the cells are joined by a sort of natural resin.

When cork is cut a vast number of these cells are split, and when sliding over a smooth surface, such as the glass of a bottle, they produce a vacuum. This explains the high coefficient of friction. Finally, the chemical stability of cork makes it irreplaceable for the stoppering of wine-bottles.

It may be that insufficient importance has been attached to shaping the neck of the bottle to take full advantage of the outstanding qualities of cork, and perhaps it would pay dividends if the two industries concerned were to get together to study the most efficient and durable method, aiming for the least possible contact between liquid and cork.

The corks used in Jerez are cut from the sheets graded *media marca*, the intermediate grade between thin and thick, in the classification made when the tree is stripped. The sheets of bark are boiled—in the open, generally in the cork-wood itself—to remove the sap. As well as giving the slabs the flexibility necessary for cutting, this flattens them so that they can be easily packed and transported.

Some corks are cut by machine and some by hand. They are first cut square, then rounded off; a good cutter can produce between 2,000 and 2,500 per day. The corks generally used in the Sherry trade are from 20 to 22 mm. in diameter and 40 mm. in length. The cork is cut from the sheet in such a way that its axis is parallel to the axis of the tree, and therefore the diameter of the cork can never exceed the thickness of the sheet. The age of the cork can be deduced from the number of stripes visible in the bark when it is cut, each stripe representing one year of growth. Some shippers use completely cylindrical corks, believing that these adapt better to the shape of the bottle-neck and to the machines used for corking; others prefer corks of square cross-section, the corners being rounded, as they consider that this shape produces more pressure on the neck. In the old days, when the bottles were corked by hand, conical (*pontudo*) corks were used.

Sterilization

Some manufacturers, besides sterilizing the corks, bleach them with oxalic acid; others heat them with a solution of cochineal, which gives them a pinkish tinge. After washing and drying the corks are ready for use, but it is essential to keep them in water or wine for some hours immediately before use, as otherwise it is very difficult to draw them.

Most shippers mark their corks with their names, on the side; some also mark the date of bottling.

It is important that Sherry corks should not be too soft, that the pores should be few and small and that the heads should be 'clean'—that is, with as few pores as possible. The cork produced in mountainous regions, is usually better than that grown in the looser lowland soil, which is generally coarser and less compact.

Although the quality of the cork is vital for wines of low strength, it has less effect on the fortified wines, due to their greater alcoholic content, but it remains a very important accessory to the Jerez shippers, who are very careful in selecting cork, particularly for Finos.

For some time now the plastic-topped cork, which can be drawn without need of a corkscrew, has been used in Jerez for both Sherries and brandies. Although this is not yet used by all the shippers it is being adopted by most.

A new development is a plastic-topped cork whose upper part protrudes to cover the outside edge of the neck of the bottle, thus preventing dust from gathering on the neck and coming into contact with the wine when it is served.

Apart from the bottling of wines and other liquids, the main use of cork nowadays is for insulation—60–70 per cent of the annual world production is so used, part as sawdust and part as cork composition sheets. These are made by compressing the dust or particles and heating them in moulds, where the natural gum or resin in the cork melts and the grains adhere to each other, forming a solid compact mass without need of any additive.

There are in Jerez several bottle-cork factories, where the cork is selected and classified for its different uses.

Sealed and Capsuled

Once the bottle is corked the protruding top part of the cork is cut before the bottle is sealed or capsuled.

Nearly all bottling-machines have a special gadget which allows the air to pass out of the bottle as the cork is pressed down, as it is often important that as little air as possible should remain between the cork and the wine. This, however, is less important with Sherries than with other wines.

What is important is that the corks should be well washed before use, as when the bottling-machine compresses the cork it will squeeze out any remaining sap, which, even in a few drops, would affect the wine.

Since the early days of the trade some Sherry bottles have been sealed with special wax, a blend of resin and beeswax (suitably coloured), over the head of the cork; this was invariably done for wines to be consumed in Spain. The sealing is done by hand, the rim of the neck of the bottle being dipped into the molten wax. The principle of sealing the corks to make them impermeable is very ancient: it was done formerly by searing the cork with hot resin or some other substance, as witness the phrase from Horace quoted earlier. More recently, however, the capsule has taken the place of sealing-wax on brandy bottles and also on all exported wines; in fact, the use of wax is now almost unknown, the capsules are fitted either by machine or by hand. They have been used in Europe, especially in

France, since early in the last century. It is important to ensure that the colouring varnishes used do not taint the wine as it is poured. Wax had one advantage: it ensured that no air could get in to cause humidity in the upper head of the cork, as sometimes occurs with capsules, causing the cork to rot and sometimes transmitting a taint to the wine. On the other hand, it had various disadvantages: it sometimes gave a taste to the wines if the corks were too porous; it was very fragile, becoming useless if it cracked; it did not enhance the appearance of the bottle; and, in the great majority of cases, when the cork was drawn from the bottle some fragments of wax fall into the wine, which again could taint it.

Plastic caps with cork discs have been tried in Jerez, but their use has been very limited in the bottling of wines, invaluable though they are for other uses. There is in Jerez a factory for these plastic caps, the Sociedad Limitada de Industrias Plásticas Andaluzas (Calle Méndez Núñez).

I understand that a new process has been patented to increase the efficiency of the capsule system: this consists of frosting that part of the neck, below the rim, which comes into contact with the bottom part of the capsule. The capsule thus adheres tightly to the bottle, allowing no air to enter between the capsule and the cork.

Local Printing

The labels, back-labels and collars which are used in Jerez are practically all printed locally; and the printing and lithographic works in Jerez can produce any sort of label or other paper printing.

For the sake of completeness I give below a brief summary of the history of the paper industry. The Egyptians called it *papyros*, after the papyrus, or paper-reed, from which they manufactured it. The Greeks knew it as *biblos* or *chartos*, and the Romans as *chartas*. Tsai-lun, Chinese Minister of Agriculture in 123 B.C., initiated the manufacture of paper sheets from vegetable fibres. The industry is said to have reached Spain in 1154, when the Moors were making paper at Játiva. Other historians put the date much earlier. In any event, by the fourteenth century the paper industry was certainly established in several parts of Spain.

Printing was invented by Gutenberg at Strasbourg in 1436; lithography by Senefelder in 1796.

A. Rodriguez Monino has observed that Jerez was the fifth town in Andalusia and the first in Cadiz province to start printing, thirty-four years before Cadiz itself did so. The first book printed in Jerez, by Fernando Rey in 1619, is in the Biblioteca Nacional in Madrid.

The labelling of bottles only started half-way through the last century, when multiple printing-presses first came into general use. Very little importance was formerly attached to the outside appearance of bottled goods, the main thing being the contents, but nowadays the label is important, as it attracts the attention of the prospective purchaser. The Sherry shippers have shown themselves as conservative with labels as with bottles, and there has been very little change in the design of Jerez labels for wine or brandy in the last century. There are, however, some firms who go in for more attractive labels which enhance the appearance of the bottle and are easily recognized by the customer; they consider that the label should really *advertise* the contents, and that it is very important to gear the labels to the tastes of the different markets where the wines are to be consumed. Many shippers, especially the older firms, are afraid to change the design of their labels, thinking it might displease their regular customers; but such fears are exaggerated, as in the majority of cases the change can be made gradually. I see no reason why the trend discernible in Sherry publicity and advertising, which in the last quarter of a century has taken a new and much more aesthetically attractive line, should not apply equally to labels, without affecting in the least the different sorts of wine and brandy.

It used to be a practice of certain firms, before labelling the bottles (especialy those destined for South American markets) to cover them with gold and silver foil and sometimes, for special brands, with a silk netting.

The protective envelopes formerly used in Jerez for the packing of bottles were made of bulrush straw, which grows around the town. Today more rice-straw envelopes are used, as these are thought to offer better protection. This rice straw used to come from the east coast, but for some time now the envelopes have been made at two local factories.

For shipment to the United States rye straw is used, as American Customs regulations forbid the importation of rice straw; this also applies to some other markets. For those countries which bar the importation of all vegetable-matter envelopes, corrugated cardboard is used. This is very suitable for the job, though its protective qualities are seriously reduced if a single bottle breaks and the cardboard round the others gets soaked. Envelopes were always used in Jerez before the advent of the cardboard case, except when cases with wooden divisions were used when the envelopes would have been superfluous.

Packing cases

The basic Sherry case holds a dozen ¾-litre bottles; there are also cases for two dozen, and for two and four dozen half-bottles.

Some shippers make their own cases; for the remainder, there are in Jerez and the neighbouring towns several firms specializing in the manufacture of packing cases.

The wood principally used is Galician pine, very suitable for this purpose as it is very hard and resistant. Wood is no longer imported, as it used to be from Portugal and Central and Northern Europe, as apart from the Customs duties now in force to protect Spanish timber, there are other difficulties arising out of commercial agreements between the various countries.

At one time poplar wood was used for parts of the case, because this very light-coloured wood showed up the various markings very clearly, but it is not sufficiently tough to be used for the whole case, as the weight of a dozen Sherry bottles is considerable.

Cases are mechanically stamped with different-coloured inks, never fire-branded as they used to be many years ago. All cases for export, and some for the Spanish market, are strapped or wired for strength and fitted with pilfer-proof seals.

There were at one time patent grooved cases with sliding lids, which were used when it was difficult to get nails, but these have fallen into disuse. A few years ago a nail factory was started in Jerez, where nails of all sizes are made. The nails mostly used in Sherry and brandy cases are of 13 × 35 and 14 × 40 gauge.

Customs legislation in countries where duties were charged by gross weight obliged Sherry shippers to find light packing materials. This affected not only the bottles but also and more markedly, the cases: indeed, willow branch and cane baskets for one, two, three and four dozen bottles used to be produced in Jerez. This represented a great economy in weight, the saving being anything from three to four kilos per dozen, according to whether the baskets held three or four dozen. These baskets, even for South American markets where Customs duties are still reckoned by gross weight, have also fallen into disuse with the introduction of partitioned cardboard packing-cases, which not only reduce the weight but also do away with the need for the envelopes. The cardboard case has practially ousted the wooden, even for shipment to far-off countries, as the cardboard used today is very tough. There are several factories producing these cases in Jerez.

Nowadays all necessary corrugated cardboard is manufactured locally by various companies.

Chapter 13
Jerez Brandy

It seems almost certain that the Greeks and Romans were ignorant of the process of distillation, although they were highly skilled in the art of wine-making. The consensus of expert opinion is that the secret was discovered by the Arabs in about A.D.900 Other authors, however, maintain that the inhabitants of Northern Europe knew the technique even before this date, and that they habitually drank a type of primitive schnapps as an antidote to the cold; and others again put the date of the introduction of brandy into Europe somewhere during the reign of Alfonso VIII of Castile (1158–1214).

In some ancient sources distilled spirit is called 'water of immortality', in recognition of the way it preserved any organic material immersed in it. So fabulous were the properties attributed to the products so preserved that the early distillers used to compare them to the element of fire. According to their ideas the strength and quality of the spirit depended on the length of time the crucible or container was in direct contact with the naked flame, and on the force of the heat applied.

Before dealing with Spanish brandy I must say something of the origin of this drink in the Charente region of France, around Cognac, the first place where brandy was distilled and hence the centre of this important branch of the industry.*

There is no evidence that wines were actually distilled in France before 1313. The original spirit obtained was called *aqua vitae* or *eau-de-vie*—it is interesting to note that this is the same as the Gaelic word *usquebaugh*, from which it is thought that the word *whisky* derives—and was used almost exclusively for medicinal purposes, for which it was highly esteemed.

* For historical comment on Brandy, see Part Five (13).

Extensive wine-production has been a feature of the Charente from early mediaeval times: the wines were well known as early as the twelfth century, and were very much appreciated in England, where there was a mention of them in 1154. Many decrees concerning the sale of wine appear in old English chronicles, and in the fifth year of the reign of Richard II (1377–1400) it was stipulated that the best Rochelle wine should be sold at 6 marks per tun and at 4d. per gallon retail plus 1d. per gallon to cover transport from the English port to the consumer.

It is believed that the first time wine was distilled in the Charente for drinking purposes was a year when the crop was extraordinarily abundant and the owners, finding it difficult to sell their wines, decided to turn them into spirit. It is generally thought that it was a Dutch chemist living in the town of Cognac during the seventeenth century who had the idea of reducing the volume of the wine through distillation to cut transport costs. His native word for the spirit or 'burnt wine' (*vinum adustum*) was *brandewijn*, from which the generic name 'brandy', long used in England and now in many other countries, undoubtedly derives.

It was in 1639 that distillation spread throughout France, especially in the Charente, the brandies of which region, taking the name of the central town of Cognac, have always been considered the best in Europe.

The first commercial firm to develop a regular export in brandies was established at Cognac in 1643, and many other firms quickly followed its example. As a result brandy took the place of wine as the principal export, and many large fortunes were made by shippers.

All the grapes used in the Charente are white, and the wines obtained have an alcoholic strength of only 8–9 per cent. Distilling generally begins in November, the traditional date being the 1st of the month, All Saints' Day.

M. Massé, writing on the Charente trade in 1712, noted that the small owner, if he could raise the necessary cash, preferred to distil his produce rather than sell it as wine, and added that 'the wine obtained in the Charente was really better suited to the making of Cognac than to consumption as vin ordinaire'.

It is important to realize that the spirit obtained by distillation always retains something of the taste and aroma of the essential oils contained in the liquids distilled; the lower the strength at which distillation takes place, the more pronounced this characteristic is. It is only natural, therefore, that the spirit obtained from wine is always better than that from other products; though I should add that, while the qualites of the wine are certainly in evidence in the distilled product, it is nevertheless not always true that the best brandy is obtained from the best wine: to obtain a fine brandy it is more important that the wine used should be full bodied and have a strong bouquet and flavour.

In France the brandies obtained have generally been produced mainly in the Cognac and Armagnac regions, but ordinary *eau-de-vie* and *marc* are made in many other wine-producing centres—Anjou, Angoulême, Bordeaux, Orléans, and so on.

The official definition of Cognac adopted some time ago in France is 'the spirit distilled from grapes harvested within the locally determined boundaries of the

Charente district', and only brandies distilled from wines produced within the said boundaries, as specifically defined in 1909, have the right to the name Cognac.

The Moors As Distillers

As I said at the start of this chapter, it seems probable that distillation was already known to the Arabs in about AD 900—that is, during their rule in the Iberian peninsula—and there is no doubt that we owe the development of the industry to them. This appears to be confirmed by several references, for example:

> . . . during the 553 years that the Moslems were in Jerez they left their mark on the city, rebuilding it and establishing several industries, textile, woodcarving, distillation of spirits and perfumes, flour mills, grain-farming and the cultivation of the vine. They fostered and increased cattle-breeding, built cellars for the wine and silos for the grain and embellished the city with fountains, squares, markets, etcetera.

The Spanish word for a still is *alambique* (*alambic* in French, which is undoubtedly of Arab origin (*al-ambiq*). The same is true of the *alquitara*, a primitive apparatus used for distilling, and of *alcohol* itself.

Not much is known about the use to which the Arabs put the products of their distillation. Nor do we know much about what the early Christians in Spain used alcohol for, although it is very probable that at first they used it exclusively for medicinal or antiseptic purposes and only much later for the fortification of wine.

In spite of the evidence given above some historians consider that the discovery and subsequent exploitation of alcohol can be credited to a celebrated Spanish doctor, Arnaldo de Vilanova (1240–1311), but it is impossible to say whether Vilanova was the initiator and passed his knowledge to the Arabs or vice versa.

As in all wine districts, the production of spirit in Jerez for use in the wine industry is undoubtedly quite old, although at first probably only second grade wines were distilled. It would appear that the industry was already well established in Jerez in the sixteenth century: Portillo writes, 'So as to help in the foundation in Jerez of a Jesuit College the City granted to this Order the revenues from the excise tax on spirits, on 16 January 1580.'[*]

In those days wine spirit was used in the Jerez district only for the fortification of wines, although there is no doubt that it was later exported to other countries, especially to Northern Europe. A production list of the various Jerez distillers gives some sales figures for 1798–9. At the top of the list are Messrs J. Gordon & Co., with sales of 37,396.5 arrobas.

The Gremio purchased the right to the spirit excise tax of Jerez and its district from 1759–67 inclusive.

Although, in the early nineteenth century, only inferior wines and pomace were distilled (good-quality wines naturally being reserved for sale in Spain and abroad), Cyrus Redding, writing in 1833, considered the Spanish spirit second

[*] *Noches Jerezanas*, II, p. 57

only to the French in quality.* Probably this was what decided the shippers to go in for the commercial export of brandy, which was first matured in oak casks.

Many Jerez firms at that time were receiving orders for spirit from the countries of Northern Europe, and sometimes, due to shipping delays, these orders remained for some time in the bodegas. Under these circumstances the shippers were bound eventually to notice the fine bouquet the spirit developed and the flavour it took on from the oak casks during the time it was maturing in them, so that it was not long before many firms decided to age the spirit in their bodegas instead of exporting it as soon as it was distilled.

A Pioneer Exporter

Extensive research into the origins of the brandy trade in Jerez suggests that the spirit was not marketed until the end of the last century, and that the establishment of the trade was very largely the work of a Jerezano whose name has occurred several times before in these pages, Francisco Ivison O'Neale, who, in 1880, owned a very substantial stock of spirit which he was maturing along the lines followed by the firm of Otard Dupuy of Cognac. At first he concentrated mainly on the export of brandy to England, under the brand-name of La Marque Spéciale, without mentioning either his name or the trade name under which his firm then operated, F. G. Cosens & Co. A couple of years later, in 1882, Juan Hernández Rubio, after studying the production of Cognac in the Charente, started producing and ageing brandies in Jerez, and on 1 April 1884 formed the firm Riva y Rubio y Cía, which, officially, was the first company established with this specific object. Since 1903 the tradename of Riva y Rubio has belonged to the shipping firm of Díez Hermanos.

Although in the official handbooks to Jerez, which list details of the principal wine firms, no reference is made to production of a Cognac-style brandy earlier than 1890—beyond a bare acknowledgement that the business had started on an experimental basis some years before—the foundations of the industry were solidly laid between 1880 and 1886, when the most important Sherry shippers decided to modernize the production and maturing of their brandies more or less on the lines followed in France; French stills were imported, and the help of French experts and technicians sought.

Among the firms that did most to foster the new business and launch the product on the market was the house of Domecq, always well to the fore not only in the Sherry trade but in everything else that could be beneficial to the town and in every undertaking of cultural or social significance launched in Jerez.

Other firms, also, amongst them those of Marqués de Misa (who started using Endrivet stills), Bertemati, Juan V. Vergara, González Byass and some others who already had distilleries, set aside a proportion of their produce for the establishment of stocks, and thus contributed to the well-earned reputation Jerez enjoys for the distillation and maturing of brandy.

* *A History and Description of Modern Wines.*

In later years many other firms turned their attention to the new trade, and today nearly all the Sherry shippers are also shippers of Jerez brandy, and belong to the Sindicato Oficial de Fabricantes Exportadores de Aguardientes Compuestos y Licores, which was formed in 1931, at the same time as the Sindicato Oficial de Criadores y Exportadores de Vinos. At present all firms must belong to the Sindicato Nacional de la Vid, Cervezas y Bebidas, as membership is an essential condition of qualifying for the rebate of the excise tax granted on exported spirits.

International Law

Although the trade in low-strength brandies had existed in Jerez many years before, at the date when the bottled brandy business began there was no international wine legislation in force, possibly because of this the word *coñac* was adopted to define the brandy distilled in Jerez, which had some similarity to the French product and was at that time the only brandy known in Spain. The earliest reference I have found to the word *coñac* is in Miguel M. Lerdo de Tejada's *Comercio Exterior de México desde la Conquista hasta hoy* (1853 edition), where there occurs the phrase '*109 arrobas aguardiente coñac*'. It was not until 1914 that Antonio Maura incorporated the word in the fourteenth edition of the official dictionary of the Spanish language, although this had been approved on 19 November 1908.

The importance of the brandy industry in Jerez has since grown day by day to the point that the amount of French or other brandies imported in Spain has been reduced to insignificance. Jerez brandy has also sold well on other foreign markets, especially in Latin America, although the international commercial treaties between Spain and other countries do not always favour the brandy trade. The Spanish Government has this matter in hand, but there is still a long way to go.

In the United States the Federal Alcohol Control Administration (FACA) some time ago adopted officially a generic definition of *brandy* as: '. . . the alcohol distillate obtained solely from the fermented juice of fruit and distilled in such a way that the characteristic bouquet, i.e. the volatile elements of taste and aroma, remain in the distilled product. Grape brandy is that distilled from grape wine. Apple brandy, peach brandy or that of other fruits is obtained by identical processes from the fermented juices of the respective fruits.' According to the rulings in force in the United States all Spanish brandy exported to the American market must be described as *Spanish Brandy* and must meet certain requirements.

On the Spanish market 'alcohol' is generally understood to mean ethyl alcohol (C_2H_5OH), obtained by the distillation of wine, of its residues or of the pulp of beet or cane molasses, and having a strength of more than 95 per cent alcohol volume. Alcohol is colourless and has an agreeable smell and a fiery taste. Its specific weight at a temperature of 15°C. fluctuates between 0.800 and 0.815. It boils at a temperature of 78.4°C., and when it is mixed with water its temperature rises and it contracts by nearly 4 per cent.

The Spanish Wine Statute defines alcohol in Article 4: 'The name of *ordinary* or *ethyl alcohol* is given to the product of distillation of any liquid which has previously undergone alcoholic fermentation.' The name *wine alcohol* is employed exclusively for the product of the *distillation of wine*.

As regards spirits, the Wine Statute defines them in Article 5: 'Spirits [*aguardientes*] in general terms (leaving aside the excise differentiation between simple and compound) are the product of the direct distillation of any liquid which has previously undergone alcohol fermentation and the strength of which does not exceed 80 per cent. Also, blends of ethyl alcohol with water in various proportions, with or without aniseed, flavourings, sweeteners and caramel colouring agents.'

Spirits distilled at low strength (60–70 per cent) are called in Jerez *Holandas*,* and are obtained only from the distillation of wine. Today the law demands that *Holandas* should be distilled at not more than 70 per cent alcohol by volume.

Distillation processes have naturally been modernized with time and experience, in Jerez as elsewhere, and while at the start the spirits obtained were only of low strength (proof spirit, which is about 56.9 per cent), Jerez distillers can today obtain, through rectification, alcohol up to a strength of 96 per cent.

Spanish law today allows only the distillation of ethyl alcohol, divided into two classes: wine alcohol, which comprises both that made from pure wine and the product of grape pulp and winery residues; and industrial alcohol, distilled from molasses of beet or sugar-cane. Although Spain has for centuries had some form of legislation controlling the making and use of spirits and alcohol, the first comprehensive ruling was that known as the 'Ley de Osma', of 10 July 1904. This law later underwent many modifications under different Governments, until 4 October 1924 when complete legal control over alcohol manufacture was established by Primo de Rivera's Government. The manufacture of alcohol for drinking purposes from such materials as grain and figs was suppressed on 29 April 1926.

The taxes levied on the manufacture of the different classes of distillates have changed many times during the past years, but all legislation passed on the subject has been aimed at avoiding speculation in this branch of industry, no easy matter in view of the high price of alcohol in the last few years.

For drinking purposes Spanish legislation allows the two classes of alcohol mentioned above, with certain restrictions depending on the size of the vintage. A proportion of the molasses alcohol obtained in Spain goes to the lacquer industry, which prefers rectified, neutral spirit, free from impurities, to wine alcohol, which always retains something of the bouquet of the wine. These industrial alcohols are also used in the perfume industry, and some, intended for fuel and other industrial uses are made undrinkable, or 'denaturalized', by the addition of substances such as acetone, benzine, methylene or fluorescene, as it is difficult to separate these components by chemical or physical processes.

* The name derives either from the fact that the perfector of distillation was a Dutchman or, more probably, from the mediaeval trade with Holland whence low-strength spirits were imported for the fortification of wine.

The low-strength Holandas, 64 per cent to 65 per cent, may only be used for the production of brandies, and may only be obtained from pure and wholesome wines.

The law stipulates that wine and residue spirit may not be manufactured simultaneously in the same building and also that the pure wine alcohol should have a red transport voucher, wine-residue alcohol a green and molasses alcohol a white, to avoid any blending of these different classes of spirit and to protect the consumer.

There are various provisions made by the Ministry of Finance for the refunding of tax on wines and spirits not consumed in Spain, though any wine exceeding 24 per cent alcohol by volume is deemed not to be wine (as in other countries) and does not qualify for the export rebate.

Wine distillation can be carried out all the year round, but it is natural that the busiest period should be when the wines are racked after their second fermentation.

Apart from the quality of the wine distilled which should be drinkable and of low acidity, various other factors affect the quality of the brandy obtained. These are, principally, the distillation system, the cask in which the brandy is matured and the period of time for which it has been ageing in cask.

For the manufacture of Jerez brandy only wine spirit is used, especially Holandas. As the aroma of the final product of low-strength distillation depends entirely on the components and impurities of the wine that remain in the spirit it is naturally most important that the wine should be clean: if it is, an excellent Holanda can be obtained, even though the wine itself may not have been first class.

The wine used for Holandas generally has a strength of approximately 10–13 per cent and as the alcoholic strength at which the Holanda is obtained is between 60 per cent and 70 per cent by volume, it takes five or six hectolitres of wine to produce one of brandy. The colourless Holanda produced is stored in oak casks, from which it gradually gains colour, and kept in the bodegas for maturing.

These Holandas really contain 0.015–0.020 per cent of esters and 0.001–0.0012 per cent of aldeydes, which impurities do not exist in high-strength alcohol and account for the difference between broken-down high-strength alcohol and low-strength spirit.

Some of the Holandas used in Jerez are distilled in the town itself, and pure wine alcohol is also produced in small quantities, but as alcohol is a neutral product used principally for the fortification of wines it is generally brought in from other districts of Spain (principally Ciudad Real and La Mancha) where wine can be obtained more cheaply than in Jerez, Sherry being naturally considerably more expensive than ordinary table wines.

There have been several schemes for planting vineyards specifically for the production of alcohol in the arenas, where the yield per hectare is higher and the tilling much cheaper. These plans have recently been revived and I hope there may yet be a chance of putting them into practice.

The Holandas used in the brandy industry should not contain any iron, nor should the alcohol used for the fortification of Sherry contain iron or methyl alcohol, as this would make the spirit unsuitable for drinking and affect the quality of wines to which it was added.

The legislation of most countries prohibits drinks containing methyl alcohol, above certain limits. The Spanish Wine Statute however admits up to 2 grammes per litre of alcohol.

The iron which the Holandas sometimes contain is harmful because it combines with the tannin from the oak cask or the cork to produce iron tannates, which give a grey-green colour to the brandy, though before this chemical process takes place the iron can be extracted by decanting.

Apart from analysing the spirits and Holandas for iron and methyl alcohol and testing them for strength, the principal test is that of the nose and palate. In order to be able to sample and compare without the sense of smell becoming dulled by repetition, it is usual to blend one part of spirit or alcohol with two of water; and it is then much easier to appreciate the aroma and other qualities, as it becomes less pungent.

The process of distillation is quite simple, consisting of heating the wine either by steam or over direct heat and condensing the evaporated liquid by passing it through a coil in a refrigerated tank.

In the early days in Jerez the stills had boilers, and the wine was evaporated over direct heat. Some of these old-fashioned apparatuses were modernized and equipped with accessories which allowed the regulation of the distillation temperature, and consequently of the exact strength of the distillate. With primitive stills the only way of obtaining a higher or lower strength was by adjusting the temperature of the boiler by increasing or reducing the fuel and regulating the flues, and in many cases several successive distillations had to be made. The strength is sometimes controlled by means of rectifying discs placed near the outlet of the boiler; these are refrigerated externally by running water, the flow of which can be increased, reduced or suppressed at will.

Recommendations for a Still
Amongst the stills used today for brandy, I would single out the one marketed by the firm of Deroy, of Paris. The manufacturers' own advice to users of their product gives a good idea of the workings of a modern still.

White wines produce the best spirits because, not having been fermented with the skins and stems as red wines are, they are free of the essential oils that come from the skin and pips of the grape and are dissolved in the alcohol produced during fermentation. Once the fermentation is finished the wines may be distilled; it is preferable to work with new wines rather than to let them mature.

Distillation can be single or double, according to the quality of the wine: that is, one can obtain a spirit of the strength required in one or two successive distillations. Wines of strong bouquets are generally distilled twice: the first distillation produces *broullis* (very low-strength spirits) which are then distilled again to produce a spirit of the requisite strength.

In the first operation the entire distillate is collected in a single container; in the second it is broken down: first the esters, or *head*, which give a bad taste to the brandy and appear at the beginning of distillation, and then the *tail*—the heavier components condensed at the end of distillation when the strength is down to approximately 40 per cent or even 50 per cent—being separated off. The only part classified as good brandy is the 'heart': what is left when the head and tail have gone. The heads and tails are redistilled with the next lot of wine. Certain wines of less bouquet give better results when distilled only once, and the spirit obtained has a nicer bouquet: this is the case with almost all wines but the special ones made in the Charente. The wine spirit should be distilled slowly, because the smooth and gradual action of the heat is what later produces the taste and aroma so esteemed by connoisseurs.

The stills known as 'triple stills' have a wine-heater plus an extra boiler divided into two compartments. Their method of operation is something between the processes of intermittent and continuous distillation.

The process in the triple stills is as follows. First of all the wine-heater is filled, then the contents are passed to the double boiler, the bottom part being filled first, then the top. Once this is done the wine-heater is refilled and distillation can start. The vapours produced in the lower part of the double boiler, instead of passing direct through the coil to condense the spirit they contain, pass through the wine in the upper part, thus starting its distillation. This operation continues until the hydrometer reading for the contents of the lower boiler falls to zero. Then the residue is drawn off and the lower boiler refilled with the contents of the upper. This in turn is filled with the contents of the wine-heater, which is then filled with fresh wine.

Thus the successive distillations follow rapidly one upon the other, with no appreciable reduction in strength. The lower boiler finishes up the process and produces the steam, the upper boiler is where distillation takes place, and the wine-heater replaces the heat lost by the alcohol vapours condensing in the interior coil through which they pass before reaching the refrigerating coil.

Distillation in this still, though not continuous, is very rapid, and allows easy breaking down: this makes it particularly suitable for very busy producers. The upper compartment, which is fed with the liquid from the wine-heater, distils while the strength does not go below what is desired, and its contents pass to the lower compartment when this is empty. Thus the distillations continue uninterrupted, producing spirits from 50 per cent up to as much as 75 per cent if desired.

Ageing Brandy

The Holanda to be stored and aged for brandy is put into casks which have previously held Sherry, and the spirit absorbs the tannin from the oak and thus develops its colour. Holanda undoubtedly acquires a certain flavour from the wood, more pronounced as the surface with which the liquid is in contact increases. Hence, probably, the distinctive oval cross-section of the casks used in the Cognac district, which give a higher surface-capacity ratio than the traditional circular-section casks.

Probably because of the porosity of the wood other changes take place in the liquid, and oxidation produces esters and aldehydes, notably acetic ester and acetic aldehyde.

As for the alcoholic strength of the spirit, no fixed rule can be given to correlate changing strength with increasing age. In the Charente cellars, where there is a mean temperature of about 15°C., a significant reduction in strength takes place during the first ten years if new casks are used for maturing the brandy; this reduction becomes gradually less marked as the spirit matures. I know of no specific research undertaken into the variations in alcoholic strength of the brandies relative to their age. Holandas, like the majority of alcoholic liquids, generally decrease in strength as they get older, but some experts consider that in special conditions, depending on the cellars and casks, the spirit can actually increase in strength: this is attributed to, amongst other causes, the relative humidity and temperature of the cellar.

Gonzalo Fernández de Bobadilla, who has done so much work on Sherry, has also written some interesting reports on Jerez brandy. From one of these I take almost intact the section dealing with production and ageing.

> Holanda is the principal ingredient of Jerez brandy, being a spirit which has not undergone rectification, as the high-strength spirits do and is therefore richer in vinus esters or aldehydes (impurities).
>
> The two sorts of spirit may be blended, the high-strength spirit first being broken down, but the higher the proportion of Holanda the better the brandy: fine brandies are made entirely from Holanda.

Piquant Flavour

The principal components of a spirit when it leaves the still are ethyl alcohol and water, plus certain extra substances which give it its piquant flavour.

These substances are what give brandy its special character, and constitute what are known as the 'impurities'. They include different types of alcohol (amilic, propiolic), furfural, acetic and butiric acids, aldehydes (principally the acetaldehyde), ethylacetic ester, and so on. With age the spirit and other components undergo oxidation, some of the resulting products remaining in the liquid and others going to the sediment. Also, the oak yields tannin, sap and aromatic resins which, when hydrolysed, produce reducing matters. Some very interesting chemical ester reactions take place, the principal discernible result being a regular increase in acids and aldehydes and a darkening in colour.

Two basic processes are used in Jerez for the ageing of brandies: one which might be called a blend between the French and Jerez systems, and one typical of Jerez. The first process, used for the higher-quality brandies, involves ageing the Holanda in oak casks, as in France, until a reduction in strength is achieved, varying according to the capacity and age of the cask which has a great influence on quality. In small casks the increase in colour and loss of strength are much higher than in larger casks during the same period of time; as between two casks of the same capacity, the age is the deciding factor. The majority of the brandy firms age some of their brandies separately for an indefinite period to preserve them as special brands, but the general procedure is to break the strength of the spirit down with distilled water to about 44 per cent after a certain time. A small quantity of syrup is added and the ageing of the brandy is continued, on the solera system.

The system of ageing the brandy is in fact the same as is used for Sherry—soleras and criaderas. For each type of brandy there are several scales, sometimes as many as fourteen, each consisting of a certain number of casks in three or sometimes four tiers. The first scale—like the solera scale for Sherry—is the brandy ready for sale, and each of the remaining scales contains a younger brandy than its predecessor, so that the last contains the youngest. The brandy drawn from the first scale is replaced, when the scales are run, by that drawn from the second, the ullage in the second is made up with the brandy from the third, and so on. In this way the new brandy passes through all the criaderas and soleras, during which time it is constantly being aired and oxidized. This encourages the maturing process and the uniform quality of the first scale is maintained from one year to another.

Of the other procedure, used in Jerez for ordinary brandy, Fernández de Bobadilla writes:

It consists of breaking down high- or low-strength spirits, or a blend of both, with water soon after distillation, leaving them at a strength of 44 per cent. As the high-strength spirits are more 'neutral'—that is, they are less rich in those elements that give the brandy its bouquet—the quality obtained in this way is not as choice as that obtained by the first procedure. After the reduction in strength syrup and, if the colour is not dark enough, a little caramelized sugar are added. After this, ageing continues along the lines followed in the Sherry bodegas.

The following of this ageing process is of great importance, because, as the product for sale is drawn, as I have said, only from the solera, the quantities drawn from this being replaced by an equal quantity from the next scale, and so on till the last scale is reached, the two principal objects are achieved: first, the ageing; secondly, and very important, the maintaining of the characteristic qualities of each brand. Moreover this sequence of operations facilitates oxidation, with favourable results for the maturing.

It can be clearly seen that this Jerez system is completely different to the classic French system of leaving the brandy for several years in the same oak cask, and so it is logical enough that the effects of ageing should also be different. In effect, when a brandy is aged by the French system, the spirit cannot undergo any perceptible change: the furfural and the esters do not alter beyond a certain specific limit—the furfural cannot exceed what the wood supplies, and the esters cannot change beyond their state of equilibrium. It is only the acids and aldehydes which continue to increase with age, and the analysis must therefore show, year by year, an increase in the coefficient of oxidation, a definition of which I shall give later on. The tannic matter, sap and resins do increase with age.

In the brandies aged by the Jerez system everything happens differently. The spirit increases or decreases in passing from one scale to another according as the brandy to which it is added contains more or less; the same happens with the furfural, and when the blend takes place the equilibrium of the ester reaction is upset—as this reaction is reversible there can be either an increase or a reduction; as regards the acids and the aldehydes, their increase may not be as noticeable as they are influenced by the quantity contained in the blend. The tannic matter, sap and resins cannot increase constantly, as the casks used are always the same and the quantity of tannin they yield is limited by age, and, therefore, the reactions do not increase as the years go by.

Impurity coefficient: I said earlier that ethyl alcohol, the product obtained from the distillation of wine, is not pure but contains esters, aldehydes, furfural, acids, etcetera, these impurities being what gives quality to the brandy. The quantitites of these impurities are expressed in the analysis in milligrammes per cent, and for the purposes of comparison they are reckoned in 100 cc of pure alcohol. The sum of all these figures reckoned above is known as the coefficient of impurity or 'non-alcohol'.

Oxidation coefficient: this is the percentage that the oxidizing products, acids and aldehydes, constitute of the impurity coefficient and is expressed as:

$$\text{Oxidation coefficient} = \frac{(\text{acids} + \text{aldehydes}) \times 100}{\text{impurity coefficient}}$$

This is the figure that can give us an idea of the age of a brandy from the analysis. But if we look at the figures representing it we see that for a brandy aged on the French system, in which the only appreciable variations produced by age are due to acids and aldehydes, this increase appears only in the top part of the fraction, multiplied by 100 and not in the bottom part; the top part increases 100 times more than the lower part, and the oxidation coefficient therefore increases very rapidly and constantly with age.

On the other hand, in the ageing according to the Jerez system, as I have said, all the figures which constitute the *impurity coefficient* are subject to positive and negative variations and, therefore, the oxidation coefficient is a less accurate yardstick for determining the age of a brandy than in the French system.

Essential Oak

As I said earlier, one of the most influential factors in the maturing and ageing of Jerez brandy is the oak cask in which it is stored. The new Holanda naturally takes on more colour in less time, and also a stronger flavour of the tannin and the rosins, from new casks than from those which have already been seasoned or have contained wine or brandy. Seasoned casks can also be used, though not if they have been used for several years to store fermenting musts, as the fibre of the wood is adversely affected by the chemical reactions of fermentation.

During the past forty years, due principally to the occasional difficulty of getting American wood, other timber has once or twice been tried, especially oak from the north of Spain. Unfortunately this is undeniably inferior to American oak, not only because it adds about 5 per cent to the weight of a butt, but also because it has more knots and, being a harder wood, is much more difficult and costly to work. Nevertheless, if it is completely dry and has been worked properly, it can be used, although the quantity available is insufficient to meet Jerez's needs.

The butts used for the brandy soleras are carefully chosen and frequently have to be replaced, as the high strength of the liquid undoubtedly attacks the wood and shortens the life of the cask.

Success of Jerez

The Jerez brandy trade grew rapidly from the beginning, thanks to the fine quality of the product. Today it has a virtual monopoly of the home market and is also much appreciated in other countries, though it is only exported to those where import duties have not made the price prohibitive.

Within Spain Jerez brandy is generally sold in bottle, under its various brand-names, but bulk orders have also been supplied. In Spain these generally take the form of glass demijohns with a protective cover of esparto grass, willow, cane or wood. Legislation is now under way which will prohibit these bulk sales, as it is considered that the brandy should be sold only in bottle. The only process to which the brandy is subjected before bottling is filtration. The filters mostly used in Jerez are those with cellulose pads.

Export of brandy to foreign markets is generally in bottle, but some shipments are also made in cask, especially to Northern Europe. The shippers have a separate solera for each grade of brandy, marked with 1, 2 or 3 stars or some similar distinguishing mark; they also have other brands of extra or superior quality, each with its registered name and trademark.*

The strength of the various types of commercial brandies can be anything between 36 per cent and 45 per cent alcohol by volume, although brandy is also exported to certain markets at a higher strength, between 58 per cent and 60 per cent, to save Customs duties in the importing countries, where it is subsequently broken down to the normal strength.

The success Jerez brandy has had on different markets can be attributed to the climatic conditions, which foster the development of esters, and to the distillation and selection of the Holandas by the brandy shippers, who are expert tasters. The

* See Part Five (13).

tonic properties of the brandy, its smoothness, mellowness and fragrance—which in wines and brandies can be attributed to age—and its delicate bouquet, so much enhanced when it is drunk from the traditional balloon-shaped glasses, have won Jerez brandy many devotees, not only in Spain but also abroad.*

Brandy de Jerez, the name registered by the Jerez shippers, should not be considered as an imitation of Cognac; in fact they are not really very similar—if Jerez brandy resembles any French product it is Armagnac. If only the brandy industry in Jerez had adopted a special name for the product from the beginning it would have been no less successful, and our French neighbours would have had no complaints that Jerez was trying to cash in on their great reputation.

The Spanish consumer generally seems to prefer brandies of low strength, and sweetened; but in the export trade it is generally up to the customer to specify the type preferred, stipulating not only the degree of sweetness, generally much lower than in Spain, but also the age and colour, and finally the strength, which, as I have said, can be as much as 58 per cent to 60 per cent. All these data are recorded in the Shipping Register, and reference samples are kept, so that should the customer want a repetition of the order an exact sample will be on hand.

Most countries—including Britain and the United States—have legislation stipulating minimum standards for imported brandy. These conditions can be tested by analysis, the impurity content varying in proportion to the period of ageing which the Holanda has had.

The United Kingdom has legislation covering different classes of brandy, although this word used by itself can be applied to the trade only to the 'distilled product of the fermented juice of fresh grapes without the addition of any other alcohol'. (This description incorporates what should be the definition of the word 'wine', but Britain is one of the few countries that have not officially defined this word.) Other fruit brandies are described in England as 'the product of the distillation of the fermented juice of different fruits, apart from the grape.' Spirits distilled for drinking purposes from the skin or pomace of the grapes, after the juice has been drawn off, are called in England 'Marc Brandy', and any blend or imitation of any of these can be sold only as 'Imitation Brandy'.

---

* According to the experts, the three rules for good brandy are that it should be fiery on the tongue, velvety on the throat, and warm on the stomach.

La Penúltima*

It has always been said that Sherry can be enjoyed at any hour of the day. Certainly it has no rival as an apéritif: a meal that starts without a glass of Sherry is like a day that begins without sun.

There are few things in life so pleasant as to give something to a friend: and if the something is a glass of fine Sherry the pleasure is doubled, for not only does the host see his friend enjoying the offering, but he can have one himself. Now, as I cannot offer the reader a glass of Sherry, as I would if he were leaving a Jerez bodega—*la penúltima*, 'one for the road'—I think it is my duty to say a few words of apology for having made the road so long. I can only put it down to what Frates Sureda said about Sherry: 'It gives recklessness to the prudent and scholarly confidence to the ignorant.'

When I started writing this I had four objects in view. The main one was to collect in a book, and offer to Jerez, my lifetime's notes on the various branches of the principal industry and commerce of Jerez, in the hope that the result would be of some interest and that at least some of the information I had collected would be new to many of my readers. After all, every wine-production district of any importance in the world has at least one book presenting all the data relating to its viticulture and viniculture; yet, so far as I knew, nothing on this scale had then been done in Jerez, although various firms have published very interesting material which deserves to be more widely distributed and read. I would not claim that my work is complete, but I hope it may at least serve as a basis, and perhaps even as a stimulus, for others with more knowledge and information to improve and complete the picture.

* In Jerez there is no such thing as the last glass of Sherry—it is always *la penúltima*, the last but one. (It is also a Jerez custom to say not, 'Have another Sherry,' but just, 'Have a Sherry'—it may well be at least the second, but it is not necessary for any new arrival to know that.)

My second object was to put an end once and for all to the misapprehension which has been fostered by interested parties from time immemorial, and still persists in the face of all official attempts to discredit it, that the name *Sherry* is a generic denomination, representing a *type* of wine. It is difficult to understand how this legend has survived when the word *Sherry* (unlike, say, *claret*) has no more general meaning in the English language.

My third object in writing these notes was to remind all my fellow-citizens of the importance to Jerez of the plantation and continued care of the vineyards, and the vital necessity of reducing producion costs in albariza vineyards.

My fourth aim was to stress to the younger generation in the Sherry industry and trade that they should know as much about it as possible. Now, with the publication of this English edition, another factor arises to make my labours seem well worth while: with the increasing mechanization of vineyard and bodega, some of the old techniques are passing—the product remains the same, but the methods change.

The road I have made my reader travel has been longer than it was ever my intention to make it; but if I have been successful, even if only in part, in some of the objects I had in mind, in interesting some of my readers in the study of Sherry, then I am completely satisfied and can consider my efforts crowned with success. As for the Jerezanos, I shall have done my duty by them if I have shown them that they should all, especially those who are now starting in the business, understand that the welfare of Jerez and of those fortunate enough to live there depends on the wine industry. The Jerez viti-viniculture is perhaps one of the most complex of all, due in part to the multitude of types of Sherry that exist, and therefore it is not easy to acquire the necessary knowledge of the different branches of the trade.

It is a comfort to see that the Spanish Government, in fostering the study of the different industries in this country, has not forgotten the wine industry, and that several colleges and practical schools of viticulture and viniculture have been founded where young Spaniards can obtain the necessary knowledge of these branches of industry.

I know that many more things could have been said about Sherry in this book which I may have forgotten. The same thing happens in everyday life: very often, after saying goodbye to a friend, one remembers what one has forgotten to say in the pleasure of meeting.

There are so many people—including many Spaniards—who are ignorant of the wealth of some of our regions that it is only natural that those who come from abroad and from other parts of Spain should be surprised by their first visit to Jerez—the prosperity and gaiety of the town, the zest for life of the people, perhaps attributing the gaiety of the prosperity. Thinking about this recently, I was struck by the thought that no one should be surprised by the happy atmosphere of Jerez. The stocks in the Sherry bodegas are well over 600,000 butts —that is 300,000,000 litres—and normal evaporation here is at least 5 per cent per year; which means that every year there are some 15,000,000 litres of wine vapour floating around to be inhaled by the Jerezanos. Undoubtedly there *are* people in

Jerez who don't drink wine, but they cannot say they don't breathe it and feel the wellbeing it produces. This happy state of affairs has its drawbacks: the Spanish Treasury is convinced that Jerez shippers live in clover and have no financial hardships.

So many friends have helped in this work, and so many business colleagues have provided me with information required for this book, that it is impossible to mention all the names, and I prefer not to give a list for fear of forgetting someone. But I must express my deep gratitude to all my friends for their valuable help: as members of the Sherry trade they have been the principal architects of this book.

Undoubtedly Sherry has many points in common with man. I have shown how the wine is born when the must ferments, and how its development continues to approximate to the human life-cycle until it reaches maturity; but from then on Sherry has the advantage over us, because old age brings us aches and pains, whereas the older Sherry gets the greater grow its vigour and strength while it always retains the fragrance of youth: it can be said, as of no other wine, that decrepitude never afflicts

SHERRY: THE NOBLE WINE

Part Five

SUPPLEMENTARY NOTES, ADDENDA & APPENDICES

1. Part One, chapter 2

A POETIC CONNECTION

In 1986, the Sherry Producers of Jerez generously revived a lapsed tradition linking Spain and England.

King James I of England (James VI of Scotland) in 1619 formalized the post of Poet Laureate to the Crown by granting letters patent to Shakespeare's contemporary, Ben Jonson, with a salary and an annual 'Butt of Sherris-Sack'. In 1688, the salary was increased, as were the poetic duties, to the then handsome sum of £300 yearly. This continued until 1790, when the debt-burdened Henry Pye became Port Laureate, an appointment received with literary ridicule. (Not a line by him appears in the massive *Oxford Dictionary of Quotations*, against seventy extracts from Jonson's works.) Pye asked for cash instead of Sherry and thus the wine was commuted to a payment of £27. Over the ensuing years the salary remained the same, as Poet Laureates' potential earnings grew, and £27 was the sole perquisite of office until 1972. Then the Queen partially reinstituted the old custom by donating a small quantity of wine of the poet's choice.

It was to supplement this and to restore, if not annually, the proper wine association, that the Sherry Producers presented to the Poet Laureate, Ted Hughes, a Butt of Sherry. The gift also commemorated the notable success of a recent State Visit to Britain by the King and Queen of Spain, and their country's full entry into the EEC. Mr Hughes went to Jerez to sign the Butt ceremonially: its contents, some 700 specially labelled bottles, were delivered to him the next year, 1987.

J.D.

This section contains certain technical topics originally appearing in the main text: they have been transferred in the interests of literary flow. Much of the other material is also from the first edition, amended and updated where necessary. There is some fresh ancillary information. Where this did not derive from the author, initials are suffixed.

2. Part One, chapter 4

USE OF GYPSUM IN PRODUCTION OF SHERRY

The amount of gypsum added depends on the condition of the grapes at the time of the vintage. If prospects are good, only a small quantity is used; if the grapes are in poor condition the amount is increased to guard against defective fermentation. The gypsum used in Jerez is obtained from the province of Cadiz and is purified calcium sulphate; it does not contain the high proportion of alum encountered in other countries. In the past larger quantities have been used than are normally required these days, when the usual proportion is about one kilo to each carretada of grapes, (that is, about seven hundred kilos, producing one butt of wine).

According to the *Lancet*,* which published the findings of a committee appointed to examine the production, composition and characteristics of Sherry, the analysis of the gypsum used revealed the following composition (by percentages):

Insoluble matter	2.30
Calcium sulphate	83.57
Calcium carbonate	4.57
Potassium sulphate	1.48
Water, etc.	8.08

Dr Revueltas states in his report that:

Gypsum which has been baked and ground beforehand has a physical and chemical effect on the wine, since it undoubtedly absorbs some of the moisture of the grapes, and this is the sole effect it has before the skin of the grape is broken. Afterwards, as it is mixed with the must at the moment of pressing, the calcium sulphate reacts on the potassium bitartrate which the liquid naturally contains to give insoluble calcium tartrate and soluble potassium sulphate. The apparent effect of this is to moderate the rate of fermentation, and . . . there has never been the slightest indication that the gypsum can in any way transmit any harmful characteristic to the wine itself . . . . Less than half the gypsum added actually takes part in the reaction, and the ensuing must is passed through a sieve before reaching the butt, so that the amount of potassium sulphate (soluble anyway) which may be found in a butt is insignificant and can have no deleterious effect at all on the wine.

* 29 October 1898

The investigating committee sponsored by the *Lancet* carried out a detailed study of this pertinent question. Furthermore the report sees in the custom of adding gypsum to grapes a throwback to the ancient practice of centuries ago, when it was found that the wine produced was better when grapes still had particles of albariza sticking to them (probably brought by the wind). Later gypsum was added instead. Whatever the origin of the practice—and it is difficult to be dogmatic about it today—experience has proved that it has decided advantages. The reaction between the gypsum and the potassium bitartrate in the musts may be expressed by the chemical formula:

$$2C_4H_5O_6K + Ca\,SO_4 \quad = \quad C_4H_4O_6\,Ca + K_2\,SO_4 + C_4H_6O_6$$

$$\text{potassium bitartrate} + \text{gypsum (or calcium sulphate)} = \text{calcium tartrate} + \text{potassium sulphate} + \text{tartaric acid}$$

Thus a fraction of the potassium bitartrate converted into potassium sulphate, whilst the insoluble calcium tartrate is precipitated into the lees, so that the wine is left bright and clear, though it still contains a proportion of the original tartrate in the form of free tartaric acid. As a result of this the wine undergoes an increase in its potassium sulphate content.

The committee then analysed the lees of identical musts with and without the addition of gypsum, and then the respective musts after they had been racked off the lees. The conclusion reached was that the lees from the wines treated with gypsum contained more organic matter than those that were not so treated. The practice is therefore useful since the use of gypsum reduces the risk of subsequent alterations in the composition of the wine, a greater part of the foreign matter having already been displaced. Another conclusion was that musts treated with gypsum produce a larger quantity of lees.

The report also deals with the esters present in Sherry, the stable ones being those responsible for the characterstic flavour of the wine whilst the volatile ones are responsible for its aroma or bouquet. The committee demonstrated that the addition of gypsum stimulates the formation of ester development, freeing tartaric acid which combines more effectively with alcohol to form ethyl tartrate and other wine esters responsible for Sherry's aromatic bouquet.

The same subject was dealt with in a paper published in 1934 and compiled by José Ramón Garćia de Angulo, an agricultural engineer and director of the Bureau of Viticulture and Œnology in Jerez. He lists as the advantages accruing from the addition of gypsum to the must: an increase in the factor of the potential acid energy, which is favourable to the fermentation of the musts, an increase in the acidity of the wine, which keeps it well balanced; a reduction in potassium bitartrate content, which makes it improbable that the limit of solubility would be exceeded, which could cause turbidity by precipitation; a reduction in the phosphate content, which in turn diminishes the risk of 'white casse'; and certain organic and volatile changes that encourage the production of the distinctive aromas characteristic of Sherry. Señor Angulo advises that the addition of gypsum should not exceed 150 grammes per hectolitre—that is, 750 grammes per butt – and that it should be as pure as possible.

This view, it should be added, has been confirmed in practice by my own experience, acquired from a close associaton with this wine for over half a century.

The effect of gypsum on musts was investigated by Juan Moreno Luque in 1917, when he was in charge of the Central Army Laboratory (Artillery). His conclusions were also favourable. As a result of his experiments he maintains: that gypsum increases the free acidity of the wine, thus helping to combat disease; that, due to the increase of total acidity, the development of fatty components is arrested, avoiding oiliness in the wine; and that the brilliance of the wine as well as its alcoholic strength is increased (by the introduction of potassium sulphate), thus improving the bouquet and vinification.

Francisco Germá, M.Sc., former director of the Analytical Laboratory in Jerez, commented on this same topic: 'The Jerez musts are generally deficient in dry extract, and in the minerals indispensable for the development of the vital yeast cells, which is known to be the real basis of Fino Sherries. This alone would be sufficient to justify the addition of gypsum; and it also helps to preserve the wine and increase its body.'

Francisco Ivison of Jerez, who undertook much valuable research into Jerez œnology, strongly supported the practice of adding gypsum at an international conference in Paris in 1909.

In France the maximum permitted content of potassium sulphate was at one time two grammes per litre, but this limit was later increased to four grammes, bearing in mind that the sulphate content increases as the wine becomes older owing to evaporation. In any case, no such legislation should prescribe the same standards for ordinary table wines as for those of higher strength, as these are normally consumed in smaller quantities and there is no evidence to suggest that the potassium sulphate has any harmful effect on the consumer.

3. Part Two, chapter 5

NOTE ON ENGLISH WINE

There are now some twenty English vineyards of true commercial status. There are also well over 200 small growers who only sell, if they sell at all, from their own premises. Some are farmers who planted vineyards as a hobby, profit being of minor importance. The total area devoted to vines does not exceed 400 hectares. Around two million bottles of English wine are sold annually: there is a small export trade.

Vineyards are mainly in the South, South-East, East Anglia and West Country but extend as far as Lincolnshire where there is what is thought to be the most northerly of all productive vineyards, White grapes are grown almost exclusively, The best English wines have received high praise in recent years.

English wines must never be confused with 'British wines'. The latter are based on reconstituted concentrates and EEC authorities have expressed doubts as to whether they are entitled to be labelled as Wine.

J.D.

4. Part Two, chapter 5

ALBARIZA VINEYARDS & MAP

THE ALBARIZA VINEYARD PAGOS OF JEREZ

Key to Map on following pages

1. Barrameda	37. Anaferas
2. Martín Miguel	38. Torrox
3. Salto Grillo	39. Parpalana
4. Haza Pozo	40. Gibalcón
5. Callejuela	41. Alfaraz
6. El Peral	42. San Julián
7. Marimacho	43. Zarzuela
8. Santillana	44. Cantarranas
9. El Hornillo	45. Orbaneja
10. Cabeza Gorda	46. El Corchuelo
11. Evorilla	47. Cerro Pelado
12. Haina	48. Valcargado
13. Cabeza Vaca	49. Tizón
14. La Jara	50. Marcharnudo Bajo
15. Hato	51. Cerro de Santiago
16. Bohorca	52. Amarguillo
17. Doña Elvira	53. Marcharnudo Alto
18. El Senõr	54. Almocaden
19. Medidora	55. Espartinas
20. Atalaya	56. Martinazo
21. Cabezudo	57. Manzanillos
22. Paganilla	58. Carrascal (Jerez)
23. Ferianes	59. Capirete
24. San Borondón	60. Raboatun
25. Carrascal (Sanlúcar)	61. Algarrobo
26. Miraflores	62. Montealegre
27. Campix	63. Montegil
28. Los Cuadrados	64. Alijar
29. Garañina	65. Alcantara
30. Balbaína Baja	66. Burujena
31. Montana	67. Capita
32. Añina	68. Cuartillos
33. Mari Hernández	69. Isletes
34. Balbaína Alata	70. Montecorto
35. Carrahola	71. Casarejo
36. Los Tercios	72. La Florida

213

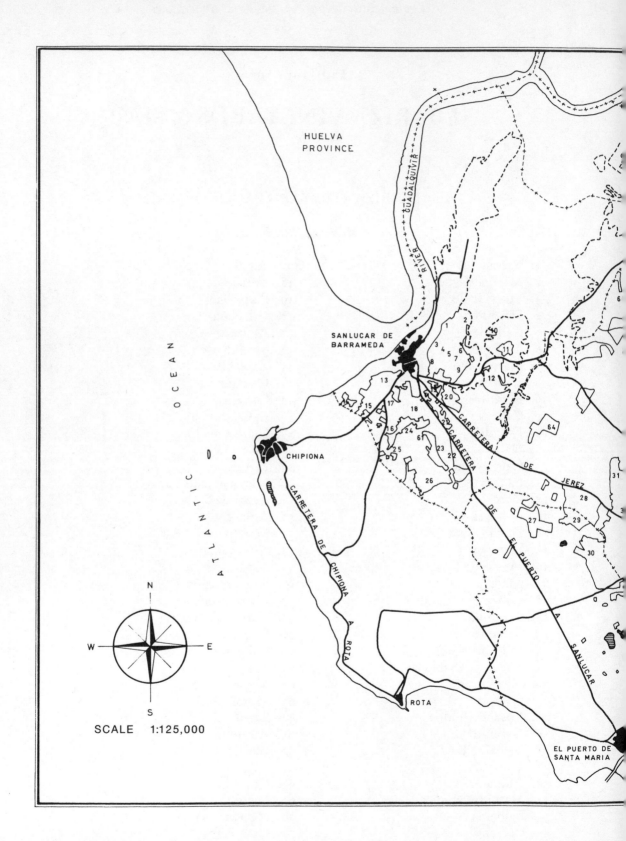

HUELVA
PROVINCE

SANLUCAR DE
BARRAMEDA

CHIPIONA

ROTA

EL PUERTO DE
SANTA MARIA

N
W   E
S

SCALE   1:125,000

O C E A N

A T L A N T I C

CARRETERA DE CHIPIONA A ROTA

CARRETERA

CARRETERA

DE

EL PUERTO

A

SANLUCAR

DE JEREZ

1 2
3 4 5 6
8
9
11
12
13
15
17 18
20
16 24
25
23 22
26
27 29
28
30
31
64

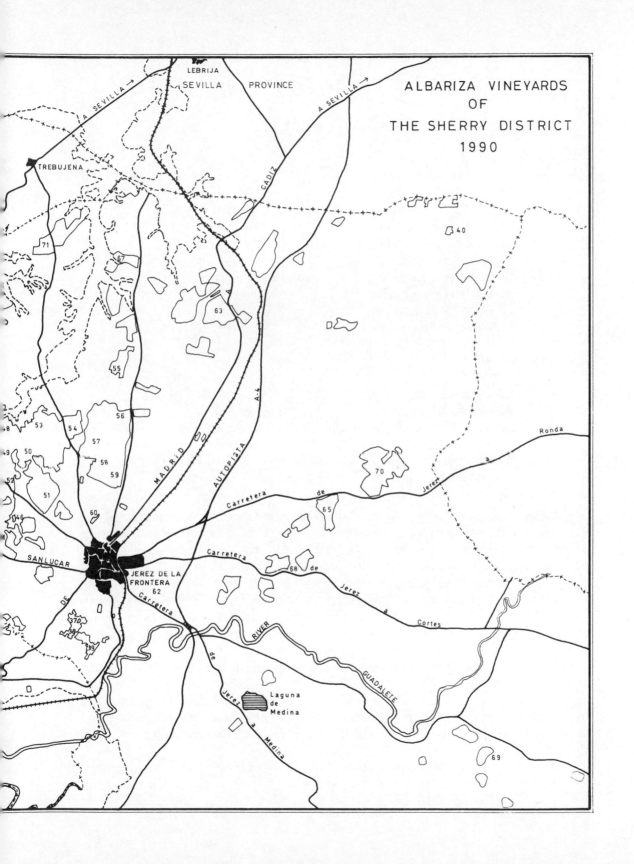

ALBARIZA VINEYARDS
OF
THE SHERRY DISTRICT
1990

5. Part Two, chapter 6

VINE STOCK

The most suitable vine stock for albarizas are:

Berlandieri × Riparia	420 A
Berlandieri × Riparia	157/11
Berlandieri × Riparia	34 E
Riparia × Berlandieri	161/49
Berlandieri × Rupestris	99 and 110 Richter
Berlandieri Resseguier 2	–
Chasselas × Berlandieri	41 B
Cabernet × Berlandieri	333 E

and for arenas:

Rupestris del Lot	–
Riparia × Rupestris	3306 and 3309
Berlandieri × Novo-Mexicana	31 Richter
Riparia × Rupestris	6736 R
Aramon × Rupestris	9
Gloria de Montpelier	–

All these are pure American stocks, except the Chasselas × Berlandieri, the Cabernet × Berlandieri, and the Aramon × Rupestris, which are crosses between a European (French) variety and an American. The average price for these plants per thousand varies according to the demand and the variety used and is now (1990) well over 45,000 pesetas.

At present the Chasselas × Berlandieri 41 B is planted in 90% of the Sherry vineyards. Another variety, Riparia × Berlandieri 161/49, is also used when the calcium carbonate content does not exceed 40%, and another, Cabernet × Berlandieri 333E, is preferred when it exceeds 60%.

Other varieties of American roots which have found some favour in recent years are: Berlandieri × Colombard No. 1; Berlandieri × Vinífera Desconocida 19/62; and Berlandieri Estación de Viticultura y Enología Jerez (EVEX 13/5), which are more resistant to calcium carbonate than the 41/B; they also mature quicker and are more productive and easy to graft, although it is said that the first two have a shorter life.

These three varieties are being planted widely now in long-estabished vineyards, and also to replace dead vines, as it is good policy at times to change the variety on land which has been planted with vines for many years.

6. Part One, chapter 3 &
Part Three, chapter 8

BAUMÉ

The degree Baumé is the scale unit on a type of hydrometer, which takes its name from its inventor. The scale was originally based on a comparison of the specific density of water with that of a 10 per cent solution of sodium chloride. Taking the density of distilled water as 0, the saline solution was given an arbitrary value of 10, and the interval between them on the scale divided into ten equal parts each designated one degree. When the hydrometer is immersed in the wine the presence of alcohol causes it to give a slightly inaccurate reading, known as the 'apparent density'; to correct this, the alcohol is evaporated and the liquid then brought up to its original volume by the addition of distilled water. A second reading now gives the 'true density' of the wine, free of alcohol.

7. Part Three, chapter 8

MAIN REACTION IN ALCOHOLIC FERMENTATION

$$C_6H_{12}O_6 \quad = \quad 2(C_2H_5OH) \quad + \quad 2(CO_2)$$

(grape-sugar)   (ethyl alcohol)   (carbon dioxide)

The fermentation also changes part of the sugar into other compounds, some of which appear in the following analysis of the product of the fermentation of 100 grammes of grape-sugar:

Carbonic acid	46.67%
Ethyl alcohol	48.46%
Glycerol	3.20%
Succinic acid	0.61%
Other substances	1.06%

8. Part Three, chapter 9

VINEGAR (chemistry)

The principal reaction in acetic fermentation may be expressed in chemical terms as:

$$C_2H_5OH \quad + \quad O_2 \quad = \quad CH_3CO\,OH \quad + \quad H_2O$$

| ethyl alcohol | + | oxygen | = | acetic acid | + | water |

On 31 May 1935 a law was passed in Spain defining vinegar as 'the liquid resulting from the acetic fermentation of wine, of wine alcohol or of one of the by-products of wine, having a minimum of 40 grammes per litre of crystallizable acetic acid'. The same law also established, among other stipulations, that vinegar should not exceed 1 per cent of alcohol by volume nor be under 0.1 per cent. *Vinagre de yema*, made from the *mosto de yema* before it is fortified, is the vinegar generally preferred in Jerez for domestic use, and particularly for the pickling and canning industries.

9. Part Four, chapter 11

STAVES (details)

The table below shows the dimensions of the staves, their commercial names, and the usual application of each different size.

	Dimensions in inches	Commercial name	Purpose for which used
Rough staves	60 × 5 × 3½	Pipes	Large bodega, small bodega and shipping butts. Hogsheads and their headpieces.
	42 × 5 × 3½	Orleans	Hogsheads
	35 × 5 × 3½	Barrels	Quarter-casks (7½ arrobas)
Finished staves	54 × 5 × 2	Pipes	Butts; hogsheads and their headpieces
	42 × 4 × 1⅛ 44 × 4 × 1¼ 46 × 4 × 1½	Hogsheads	Quarter-casks Hogsheads
	35 × 4 × 1⅜	Barrels	Quarter-casks (7½ arrobas) and their headpieces
	28 × 4 × 1½	Headpieces	Butt headpieces
	24 × 4 × 1⅜	Headpieces	Hogshead headpieces

10. Part Four, chapter 11

CASK CAPACITIES

There are innumerable mathematical formulas for calculating the capacities of casks, but due to the variations in the curvature of the staves the results cannot be relied on. Amongst these rules a few may however be mentioned:

$$V = 0.268 \, L \, (D^2 + d^2 + Dd)$$
$$V = 0.3927 \, L \, (D^2 + d^2)$$
$$V = 0.15 \, L \, (d + 1.27 \, D)^2$$
$$V = 0.012 \, L \, (5D + 3d)^2$$

and the formula I regard as the most accurate, Lapparent and Jasseron's:

$$V = \frac{\pi L}{60} \, (8D^2 + 4Dd + 3d^2)$$

where L represents the length of the cask, D its interior diameter through the bung and d the head diameter; linear dimensions in metres give volume in kilolitres.

Another formula, probably the simplest, involves taking the diagonal R from the bunghole to the most distant point in the circumference of one of the heads; then:

$$V = 0.635 \, R^3$$

11. Part Four, chapter 11

AMMONIA IN CASK SEASONING

The *minimum* quantity of ammonia (of a specific gravity of 0.92 to 0.94) required per cask should be:

Butt	1.60 litres
Hogshead	1.00
Quarter-cask	0.60
Octave	0.38
2-arroba barrel	0.18
1-arroba barrel	0.12

As the commercial ammonia generally available in Jerez has a specific gravity of 0.88, water has to be added to get it down to the right level. According to Sr Ivison's pamphlet, if a special seasoning is required better results can be obtained by adding spirits to the quantities of ammonia listed:

Butt	1,000 cc.
Hogshead	600
Quarter-cask	200
Octave	180
2 arroba-barrel	50
1 arroba-barrel	30

Sr Ivison notes that ammonia gives a dark colour to the inside of the cask; and adds that low-quality must or wine can be added instead of spirits. The ammonia is poured into the casks, and the steam is applied by means of a piping system with numerous copper nozzles which fit snugly into the bungholes of the casks. To prevent the head of a cask being displaced by excessive pressure, the heads are reinforced during the steaming.

12. Part Four, chapter 11

IMPORTANCE OF SHERRY TO SCOTCH WHISKY

When the use of Sherry casks for maturing Scotch whisky first started cannot be dated with any precision. Probably its benefits were an accidental discovery. Historically, the Scots are lovers of Sherry. To re-use casks rather than return them to Spain would have appealed to a nation with a reputation for financial astuteness—and what better than to employ them to store the national product.

The peculiar virtues of Sherry casks over any others was first noted in writing by William Sanderson, a noted distiller and pioneer blender of whisky, in 1862. Their use became standard practice with all important malt distillers, and the improvement in matured whisky was certainly one potent factor in the global growth of the Scotch whisky industry.

With a huge increase in trade and decrease in bulk wine shipments, supplies of Sherry casks proved inadequate, but the Sherry connection remained. The practice grew up of importing from the USA staves from casks that had held Bourbon whiskey (which may be matured solely in new casks). These American casks are reassembled, charred and treated with *paxarete** (a Sherry concentrate from the Pedro Ximénèz grape). These casks perform an essential role in the production of Scotch malt whisky, similar to that of true Sherry casks, of which old examples are prized and carefully maintained by Scotlands's top distillers.

With the decline in exports of Sherry in cask, in favour of bottling in Jerez, whch is likely to become the sole manner in which Sherry is shipped, leading Scotch distillers now buy new casks coopered in Jerez and pay shippers to season them with Sherry before sending them (empty) to Scotland.

J.D.

* See main text.

13. Part Four, chapter 13

COMMENT ON BRANDY

Historical Aspects

Though it is true to say that Cognac was the pioneer in commercializing Brandy, that the Charente was the spirit's original home would be hotly contested by the Gascons who give seniority to their Armagnac.

Yet it may be that Spain should lay claim to evolving the spirituous nectar of the grape! In supporting Gascony's assertion of precedence, Pamela Vandyke Price[*] points out that there are much earlier references to Armagnac brandy than to that of Cognac. She surmises with some justification that Gascony's proximity to Spain may well have brought to that region Moorish knowledge of distillation from wine before it spread further North.

For a long time the English employed the term Brandy to cover any spirits, not simply those of vinous provenance. Today, Brandy is, with few exceptions, internationally recognized as indicating a spirit solely based on wine, with occasional permitted derivatives (closely defined by EEC rules) such as cherry brandy.

Brandy de Jerez

Although Brandy has been made for centuries in the same area as Sherry, it has been granted legal status of a geographically delimited producing area (*Denominacion Especifica*) under the supervision of a Control Council (*Consejo Regulador*) embracing government officials, qualified scientists and members of companies belonging to the Register of Brandy-making and Ageing Bodegas.

The Council conducts regular inspections and tests. A Tasting Panel takes samples of all Jerez brandies: without its approval the essential Certificate of Denomination cannot be granted. The Council recognizes three categories of Jerez Brandy:

The youngest is *Solera Brandy de Jerez*, aged not less than six months. Formerly the most popular, demand for this style has recently fallen as consumers switch to superior grades.

Solera Reserva Brandy de Jerez must be matured for over one year. The finest Brandy comes into the category *Solera Gran Reserva Brandy de Jerez*, aged for at least three years—often much longer. All brandy exported must carry an official certificate of analysis.

J.D.

[*] *Spirits & Liqueurs* (Penguin Books, 1979).

APPENDIX A

Details of Sherry Exports from 1800

YEAR	TOTAL EXPORT IN BUTTS	COMMENTS
1800–21	Average 7–9,000. (1809–15,000; 1811–4,000.)	Average local price 34 pesos per butt. In 1809 crop reached 40,000 butts, but average for 1817–23 only 15,000.
1822	11,509	During this period capital was invested by Spaniards returning from Latin America. Popularity of Sherry greatly stimulated by George IV in England. In 1824 must fetched 90 pesos per butt.
1823	12,477	
1824	11,669	
1825	14,809	Very poor crop: similar prices.
1826	9,190	Prices rose to 100–20 pesos.
1827	13,719	
1828	16,744	
1829	13,268	
1830	12,245	
1831	12,728	Slight fall in prices
1832	12,628	Fall in prices continued.
1833	15,341	Good crop. Prices dropped to 60 pesos.
1834	15,563	Vintage of inferior quality – cholera epidemic.
1835	13,787	Good harvest. Stocks accumulated and prices fell: 25 pesos for musts coming from the outlying areas (albariza), 12 pesos for musts from the arenas.
1836	16,512	Abundant crop of good quality. Prices maintained at low level.

YEAR	TOTAL EXPORT IN BUTTS	COMMENTS
1837	13,175	Crop similar to 1836. Slight rise in prices. Musts were quoted at 34 pesos from the albariza vineyards and 22 from the barro areas; arena musts fetched 16 pesos.
1838	15,977	Exceptionally large crop. Large surplus of unpicked grapes. Prices as low as 8 pesos.
1839	18,861	Stocks increased due to abundant vintage. 30 pesos paid for albariza musts, 9 for others.
1840	17,001	Rainy year. Medium quality. Albariza musts 24 pesos, and arena musts from 14 (white grape) to 22 (black grape) according to quality.
1841	14,778	Plentiful vintage, generally of good quality although rain fell during harvesting. Prices for albariza musts unchanged from 1840 and those from the arenas quoted at 15 pesos. At this time Fino Sherry was not separately classified.
1842	12,413	Lean crop of indifferent quality owing to spring frosts. Prices for best qualities rose to 41 pesos; musts from the arenas still 15. Import duties into England £30 a butt.
1843	14,296	Plentiful crop of good quality. Prices fell to 26 pesos for the barro musts and 14 pesos for the arenas.
1844	17,508	Small crop owing to exceptionally hot July. Poor quality. Albariza and barro musts quoted at 31 pesos, arenas at 12.

YEAR	TOTAL EXPORT IN BUTTS	COMMENTS
1845	18,134	Normal crop. 28 and 14 pesos.
1846	17,641	Abundant crop but poor quality. 36 and 16 pesos.
1847	16,276	Abundant crop. Rain during vintage. Contrary to expectations quality good. Wines developed a much sought-after nutty flavour. 33 and 14 pesos.
1848	17,369	Crop of good size and quality. 35 and 11 pesos.
1849	20,585	Musts of low strength. 38 and 13 pesos.
1850	21,457	44 and 13 pesos. Threat of oidium.
1851	20,647	The practice started of selling musts *a la piquera* or just as they are run off at the lagar. Lees usually sold at 1 peseta per arroba. Ten years before it had cost the same price to have 30 arrobas of lees carted away as useless and valueless. Price of albariza musts rose to 50 pesos.
1852	20,530	Vineyards of Chiclana attacked by oidium. 59 and 34 pesos.
1853	30,101	Smaller crop. Musts from the best areas at 50 pesos; others unchanged.
1854	29,270	Oidium atacked the Jerez vineyards. 55 and 35 pesos.
1855	26,620	Lean crop of inferior quality. 65 and 40 pesos.
1856	30,407	Oidium continued to ravage the vines. 87 and 40 pesos. Musts imported from Trebujena and other areas in the district. However, owing to oidium musts sold at much lower prices than quoted.

YEAR	TOTAL EXPORT IN BUTTS	COMMENTS
1857	26,588	Crops depleted by oidium. Prices for albariza musts ranged from 90 to 110 pesos per butt and arenas from 36 to 70.
1858	16,187	Lean crop owing to drought. Export of Fino sherries to England began. Oidium less prevalent. Prices down to 69 and 38 pesos.
1859	25,324	Coarse-quality musts. 70 and 38 pesos.
1860	30,725	Quality generally satisfactory.
1861	29,799	Average yield, prices higher – 100 and 68 pesos.
1862	32,789	Lean crop, coarse quality. Prices again rose to 150 and 80 pesos. The beginning of an era of great prosperity for Jerez.
1863	38,720	Abundant crop, excellent quality. Prices rose again and reached 230 and 130 pesos. Wages and other costs also rose.
1864	36,941	Prices fell to 150 and 60 pesos with less activity in the trade. Crop of medium size and good quality.
1865	30,431	Abundant crop and good quality. Drop to 100 and 40 pesos.
1866	36,638	Average-sized crop of inferior quality. Musts of low strength. 80 and 45 pesos.
1867	42,186	Lean crop deficient in quality. 105 and 50 pesos.
1868	47,068	Lean crop owing to drought. Average quality. 80 and 40 pesos.
1869	49,272	Similar crop to 1868. 90 and 45 pesos.

YEAR	TOTAL EXPORT IN BUTTS	COMMENTS
1870	49,597	Good crop. 85 and 44 pesos.
1871	55,668	Small crop of poor quality with 50 per cent 'rejects'. 80 and 40 pesos.
1872	61,811	Average quality and quantity although two-thirds lost. 80 and 35 pesos.
1873	68,467	Fall in prices. Announcement of tax on exports to come into effect the following year accounts for increased volume of exports. Scant crop of medium quality. 70 and 30 pesos.
1874	46,134	Small crop. Full-bodied wines above average quality. Prices stable. Albarizas 66–70 pesos, arenas 24–30.
1875	44,134	Lean and bad crop due to drought. 65 and 25 pesos.
1876	42,662	Small crop of medium quality. 60 and 30 pesos. Considerable activity in exports to Russia.
1877	42,047	Average quantity and quality. 60 and 30 pesos.
1878	35,007	Fair crop, although quality better than expected. 45 and 22 pesos.
1879	34,858	Average quantity but good quality: albarizas 50–2 pesos, arenas 26–30.
1880	38,955	Large crop of good quality. 36–40 and 20–8 pesos.
1881	40,822	Less than half 1880 yield. Musts of low strength.
1882	40,579	Average size; very good quality.
1883	39,713	Average but variable quality. Some musts sold at around 400 pesos.

YEAR	TOTAL EXPORT IN BUTTS	COMMENTS
1884	35,214	Lean crop of middling quality. Some musts very thin.
1885	35,354	Plentiful crop of good quality.
1886	40,588	Copious crop but very low-strength musts.
1887	40,055	Reduction of 33 per cent in crop musts of high quality and strength.
1888	42,138	Good crop, Low strength.
1889	47,712	Smaller crop. Low-strength musts.
1890	50,217	Average yield, good quality.
1891	66,258	Medium-sized crop of good quality though musts had little body.
1892	42,452	Identical to 1891. Predominance of Fino musts.
1893	41,730	Lean, only fair quality.
1894	42,270	Reasonable quantity, better quality than 1893.
1895	44,539	Satisfactory quality and quantity.
1896	40,075	Good quality but disappointing quantity.
1897	41,568	Same as 1896.
1898	45,825	Sparse crop due to spreading of phylloxera, which started to attack the vines. In spite of this quality was good.
1899	39,155	Less quantity than 1898 owing to intense heat. Quality generally poor.
1900	42,489	Good quality but lean crop due to phylloxera.
1901	31,037	Small yield. Medium quality.
1902	41,240	Small crop, reasonable quality.
1903	42,565	Relatively small quantity and mainly good quality.

YEAR	TOTAL EXPORT IN BUTTS	COMMENTS
1904	30,272	Good quality and quantity.
1905	26,639	Average quality and quantity.
1906	32,872	Fair.
1907	29,017	Average quantity. Good-quality wines.
1908	26,380	Abundant crop of good quality.
1909	26,078	Good quality although crop small.
1910	31,262	Small quantity. Good-quality musts.
1911	25,535	Reasonable quantity. Good-quality musts.
1912	26,541	Small quantity but good quality.
1913	27,315	Crop again small. Average quality.
1914	20,570	25 per cent more than 1913. Fine quality.
1915	21,108	Low crop due to heat. Good quality.
1916	31,123	Medium quantity and good quality.
1917	19,312	Medium size, good quality.
1918	20,305	Sparse crop. Quality fair.
1919	41,006	Very indifferent quality—small quantity.
1920	20,260	Abundant crop and medium quality.
1921	17,216	Improvement on 1920 quality.
1922	16,107	Lean crop. Good quality.
1923	16,117	Same as 1922.
1924	32,083	Lean crop but good quality wines.
1925	32,150	Same as 1924.
1926	32,832	Very lean crop but good quality.
1927	31,136	Again very lean crop, but poor quality.
1928	30,542	Fairly plentiful crop, good quality.
1929	33,183	Same as 1928.

YEAR	TOTAL EXPORT IN BUTTS	COMMENTS
1930	32,967	Same as 1928–9.
1931	30,735	Medium quality and quantity.
1932	25,344	Abundant crop and satisfactory quality.
1933	32,687	Fair quantity. Good quality musts.

TOTAL SALES

*1934**	40,618	Very abundant vintage but gathered by inexperienced workers owing to general strike in vineyards and bodegas. Nevertheless musts quite satisfactory. Crop very large, exceeded normal by 33 per cent. Musts of high strength, unusual when crop is large. Prices approximately 100 pesos for the albarizas and 50 for the arenas.
1935	43,514	Normal crop of good quality, average strength musts. Albariza grapes reached 5.35 pesetas per arroba, equivalent to 107 pesos per butt.
1936	54,551	Crop 70 per cent of normal. Fair quality but high strength. Prices remained almost unchanged.
1937	57,236	Good crop; about 20 per cent more than in the preceding year. High strength. Prices higher—135 pesos.
1938	55,699	Crop still larger than 1937 but musts of low strength. Albariza musts around 165 pesos.
1939	65,373	Fair-sized crop of good quality. 180 pesos.

* Sales figures from 1934 onwards are provided by the Consejo Regulador (official Sherry Control Board) which was set up in that year and these figures include both exports and sales within the Spanish Peninsula.

YEAR	TOTAL SALES IN BUTTS	COMMENTS
1940	75,909	Small crop of good quality. About 190 pesos.
1941	44,012	Prices underwent 100 per cent rise (374 pesos), as crop not large but of good quality.
1942	40,329	Highest price ever for albariza grapes was reached. 25 pesetas per arroba (about 500 pesos per butt). Quality good but volume approximately half normal.
1943	49,076	The albariza vineyards of Jerez, Sanlúcar de Barrameda and Puerto de Santa María produced about 22,000 butts of must. Prices fell slightly to about 423 pesos, off the lees. The year was dry, strength of musts 13.75 per cent alcohol by volume. Crop normal, quality very good.
1944	51,098	A larger albariza crop in the above-mentioned area which exceeded 30,000 butts. Prices around 440 pesos. Another dry year; quality fair, strength only 11.5 per cent.
1945	42,410	Crop much reduced owing to extreme drought throughout the two previous springs; reached only 27,000 butts. Rainfall half average over the past 20 years. Quality good, strength over 12.5 per cent. Albariza 400 pesos.
1946	64,328	Heavier rainfall. Crop of good quantity and quality.
1947	67,128	Crop 25–30 per cent larger than in 1946.
1948	48,890	Abundant crop of good quality; strength normal.

YEAR	TOTAL SALES IN BUTTS	COMMENTS
1949	51,233	Early vintage due to excessive heat, but quality good and strength high. Price of a butt of must 1,425 pesetas.
1950	57,246	Medium quality, due to mildew during spring. Strength low but quantity abundant.
1951	65,481	Early vintage due to east winds. Alcoholic strength normal, but quality only medium. Price of musts 1,975 pesetas.
1952	51,574	Mildew and rot prevalent during spring; late vintage with some rain. Although strength normal, a lean vintage of bad quality.
1953	58,007	Normal vintage and good quality with high strength, due in part to excessive heat.
1954	62,476	Late and lean vintage, but good quality and high strength. Price per butt 2,000 pesetas.
1955	78,001	Early and normal vintage of good quality. Price per butt 2,050 pesetas.
1956	75,100	Some rain during the vintage and strength low, but crop abundant and of good quality. Price per butt 2,205 pesetas.
1957	77,774	Some mildew in spring and some rain during the vintage, but normal crop of good quality. Price per butt 2,440 pesetas.
1958	76,832	Early vintage, poor in quantity and quality, although strength high. Price per butt 2,500 pesetas.
1959	81,834	Some mildew, but average vintage in quantity and strength, of good quality. Price per butt 2,650 pesetas.

YEAR	TOTAL SALES IN BUTTS	COMMENTS
1960	86,182	Early vintage. Strength high, but lean crop of very bad quality due to rot. Price per butt 2,850 pesetas.
1961	93,632	Early vintage, normal quantity and strength and good quality. Price per butt 3,150 pesetas.
1962	101,202	Normal vintage all round, good quality. Price per butt 3,475 pesetas.
1963	113,019	Some rain during the vintage, mildew late in the season. Quantity abundant but quality not good and strength low. Price per butt 3,660 pesetas.
1964	113,185	Average crop of good quality. Strong, very hot east winds; vintage early. Alcoholic strength was average. Price per butt 3,660 pesetas.
1965	126,536	Crop larger than average. Rainy winter, dry spring. Price per butt 4,140 pesetas.
1966	133,423	Very low crop. Average rainfall. Price per butt 4,140 pesetas.
1967	149,593	Excellent though very dry weather. Low crop. Price per butt 4,140 pesetas.
1968	166,139	Average rainfall, late vintage and low crop. Price per butt 4,315 pesetas.
1969	168,837	Very heavy rainfall and late vintage. Very abundant crop.
1970	176,940	Generally rainy year though dry spring. Average crop. Price per butt 4,695 pesetas.
1971	221,872	Very rainy Spring. Late though plentiful vintage of average quality. 6,067 ptas per butt.

YEAR	TOTAL SALES IN BUTTS	COMMENTS
1972	282,538	Less rain than average. Ideal spring. Very cool summer. Largest vintage of the century. Rained during picking. Average quality. 7,070 ptas per butt.
1973	271,209	Less than average rainfall. Very hot and dry summer. Production above average. Healthy, good quality. 12,650 ptas/butt.
1974	203,916	Less than average rainfall. Very hot, dry, windy summer. Average quantity. Good quality.
1975	218,190	Less than average rainfall for the fourth consecutive year. Average quantity. Good quality.
1976	266,030	Less than average rainfall (fifth consecutive year). Hot and dry summer. Very small quantity. Good quality. 11,250 ptas/butt.
1977	289,394	Normal rainfall. Very cool summer. Above average quantity. Excellent quality. 13,750 ptas/butt.
1978	306,286	Average rainfall. Very hot and dry summer. Quantity below average. Good quality. 16,252 ptas/butt.
1979	322,021	Very wet winter. 4 inches of rain at the beginning of the vintage. Some hail. Later cool and dry. Average quantity. Variable quality. 18,585 ptas/butt.
1980	287,710	Little rain. Hottest summer of last 30 years. Quantity somewhat below average. Good quality. 19,360 ptas/butt.

YEAR	TOTAL SALES IN BUTTS	COMMENTS
1981	281,638	Very dry year. Vines suffered last year's excessive heat. Very small crop (less than 50% of normal). Average quality. 21,360 ptas/butt.
1982	259,402	Very dry year (third consecutive). Enough rain. Extraordinarily mild summer. Vintage late because of strike. Small quantity. Good quality. 21,360 ptas/butt.
1983	292,450	Driest year of the century (after 3 dry years) but adequate rainfall in November and April. Exceptionally cool summer: moist sea breezes. Early vintage. Very small quantity. Good quality. 21,360 ptas/butt.
1984	260,108	Normal rainfall. Good weather during vintage. Small crop. Good quality. 22,950 ptas/butt.
1985	301,654	Normal rainfall. Normal summer. Late vintage. Average crop. Excellent quality. 25,720 ptas/butt.
1986	252,149	Less rain that normal. Virtually no spring, freezing in April and great heat in May caused very bad flowering. Crop below average. Rained during vintage. Quality poor. 28,155 ptas/butt.
1987	239,489	Normal rainfall. 3 inches of rain on 28th August (exceptional) followed by fogs. Later great heat and dry wind dried many bunches. Late vintage because of bodega strike. Average quantity. Quality variable. 29,640 ptas/butt.

YEAR	TOTAL SALES IN BUTTS	COMMENTS
1988	237,940	Normal rainfall extended to June. Very late summer. Dry hot vintage avoided spread of Botrytis which had commenced in Summer. Large crop. Average quality. 29,640 ptas/butt.
1989	194,028	Very dry year. Hottest June and July of the century. Very small grape. Small crop. Excellent quality. 30,125 ptas/butt.

APPENDIX B

The Sherry Casks

Types of cask	Capacity in arrobas	Capacity in litres	Approximate weight in kilogrammes (empty)	Approximate weight in kilogrammes (full)	Approximate number of staves	Thickness of chimb in millimetres	Length of cask in metres	Bung diameter in metres	Inner diameter of head in metres	Outer diameter at edge of chimb in metres	Outer circumference of bung in metres	Width in millimetres and calibre of hoop used (and number of hoops)
Bodega butt	36	600	140	740	27	40/50	1.38	1.00	0.67	0.75	3.14	50/16 (10)
Bodeguera butt	34	550	130	680	26	35/40	1.35	0.95	0.66	0.73	3.00	45/17 (10)
Shipping butt	30	500	95	595	25	30/38	1.28	0.90	0.63	0.69	2.85	38/18 (10)
Hogshead	15	250	54	304	23/24	30/35	1.00	0.74	0.53	0.59	2.30	35/18 (8)
Third	10	167	40	207	22/23	30	0.87	0.65	0.46	0.52	2.05	34/18 (8)
Quarter cask	7½	125	30	155	21/22	26	0.78	0.60	0.42	0.47	1.90	32/18 (8)
Octave	3¾	63	17	80	20	22	0.60	0.48	0.34	0.38	1.50	28/18 (8)
Sixteenth	2	33	10	43	21/22	20	0.50	0.39	0.28	0.32	1.22	25/18 (6)
Thirtieth	1	17	5	22	23/24	20	0.40	0.32	0.22	0.26	1.00	22/18 (6)

APPENDIX C

Comparative Production Costs Since 1898

Date	Case for 1 dozen bottles	Bottles per mille	Corks per mille	Capsules per mille	Sets of label, back label and collar per mille	Tissue-paper envelopes per mille	Straw envelopes per mille	Daily wage of bottling-department labourer
				(Pesetas)				
1898	0.85	200	17	13	15	5	24	3
1918	2.60	483.70	20	25	22	6	25	4
1939	3.50	492	35	45	50	25	75	12.75
1945	6.60	914.10	65	88	91	45	135	15.50
1970	25	3250	400	500	140	120	—	296*
1989	135	21000	4000	—	5000			11000* (average)

* Figures include certain social benefits.

APPENDIX D

DECREE RELATIVE TO THE WINE STATUTE
(Law No. 25/1970 of 2 December 1970. Official *Gazette* of 5 December 1970)

PART III, (i) OF THE DECREE
Denominations of Origin

Article 79: For the purposes of this Law by *Denomination of Origin* is understood the geographical name of a region, area, place or locality, used to designate a product of the vine, wine or spirits, of the respective zone which has differentiated qualities and characteristics principally due to the natural environment and human factors.

Article 80:
(i) In respect of denominations of origin, they are given the names of:

(a) *Zone of Production*—the wine-producing region, area, place or district which due to characteristics of the natural environment, the varieties of vine and systems of cultivation produces grapes from which are obtained wines of different and particular qualities by means of specific methods of preparation.

(b) *Zone of Preparation*—the region, area or locality in which the bodegas are situated and where the processes of preparation and ageing which must give them their character are applied to the wines of the appropriate zone of production.

(ii) The zones of production and preparation of products supported by each denomination of origin will be delineated by the Minister of Agriculture in accordance with Article 84 of this Law.

Article 81:
(i) The protection afforded by a denomination of origin extends to the exclusive use of the names of areas, limits, localities and districts which compose the respective zones of production and preparation.

(ii) In wines protected by denominations of origin those names to which the previous paragraph refers can be used as a subdenomination in accordance with what the Regulation may establish.

Article 82:
(i) The use of the denomination of origin and of those names to which the previous article refers will be exclusively reserved for those products which, in accordance

with this Law and the rules of each denomination, have the right to use of the same.

(ii) Only natural or legal persons who have their vineyards or installations registered in the Register of each denomination of origin can produce grapes destined for the production of wine protected by the denomination or produce or mature wine so protected or use the relevant denomination or subdenomination. The Ministry of Agriculture can declare obligatory the registration of assets of the nature indicated situated in the zones of production or preparation, provided tbat more than 75 per cent have been voluntarily registered.

Article 83:
(i) The use of names and brands which because of phonetic or orthographic similarity with protected names can cause confusion as to the nature of origin of the product is forbidden, excepting established rights which may be duly recognized by the Instituto Nacional de Denominaciones de Origen.

(ii) In the case of products not protected by denomination of origin, geographical names so protected cannot be used on labels, documentation or advertisements, even though such names be preceded by the terms *type, style, stock, bottled in with bodegas in* or other analogous titles.

(iii) Trademarks, commercial names or company titles which refer to the . . . denominations of origin can only be used for the merchandizing or advertising of products which actually correspond to the conditions which this Law or supplementary legislation establishes.

(iv) For the maximum protection of the denominations of origin herein referred to these will be communicated to the Registros de Propriedad Industrial and to the register of companies and to this end the Consejos Reguladores and Instituto de Denominaciones de Origen may promote the action officially.

(v) The rulings of each denomination or origin may forbid the use of trademarks, symbols or advertising copy in the merchandizing of other products of the same sort.

APPENDIX E

Sales of Jerez Brandy, 1909–89

Although the Jerez brandy trade really began between 1880 and 1886, I have been unable to find any sales figures from earlier than 1909, and it is very probable that no accurate records were kept before that date. The figures given in this table are from a reliable source, and include both home and export sales. But it has not always been possible to determine whether the figure for any given year refers to the town of Jerez alone or to the whole district. Certainly figures from 1945 on include sales from Sanlúcar and Puerto de Santa María.

Year	Litres	Year	Litres	Year	Litres	Year	Litres
1909	2,900,000	1935	4,603,500	1955	20,351,826	1975	117,006,192
1915	1,441,628	1940	7,952,419	1960	21,831,370	1980	64,141,300
1920	4,492,000	1945	7,592,021	1965	61,312,231	1985	119,588,493
1925	4,351,464	1950	20,708,800	1970	103,703,202	1989	75,490,807
1930	4,407,667						

APPENDIX F

The Sherry Shippers

The following is an official list of the shippers in Jerez de la Frontera, Puerto de Santa María and Sanlúcar de Barrameda, 1990.

JEREZ DE LA FRONTERA

Tómas Abad, S.A.	Cuesta del Palenque, 1	Aptdo. 337
Manuel de Argueso, S.A.	Pozo Olivar, 16	Aptdo. 6
Antonio Barcena Blanco	Avda, Sanlúcar s/n	Aptdo. 349
Hijos de Agustin Blazquez, S.A.	Ctra. de Cartuja, s/n	Aptdo. 540
José Bustamante, S.L.	Lealas, 28	Aptdo. 63
Coop. Ntra. Sra. de las Angustias	Vtra. Circunvalación s/n	Aptdo. 253
Croft Jerez, S.A.	Ctra. Madrid-Cádiz	Aptdo. 414
Diez Merito, S.A.	Ctra. N.IV Km. 645	Aptdo. 2
Pedro Domecq, S.A.	San Idelfonso 3	Aptdo. 80
José Estevez, S.A.	Cristal 4, 6 y 8	Aptdo. 167
M. Fernández, S.A.	Ctra. Circunvalación	Aptdo. 217
Garvey, S.A.	Guadalete 14	Aptdo. 12
M. Gil Galán, S.A.	Ferrocarril 14	Aptdo. 111
M. Gil Luque, S.A.	Ctra. Arcos, Km.2	Aptdo. 26
González Byass, S.A.	Manuel Mª. González, 12	Aptdo. 294
Juan González Sillero	San Marcos, 2 – dptdo.	
Luis G. Gordon, Sucr.	Huerta Pintada	Aptdo. 48
José Mª Guerro Ortega	Picadueña Alta 135	Aptdo. 10
Grupo Harvey, S.A.	Don Juan, 4–10	Aptdo. 36
John Harvey & Sons (España) Ltd.	Alvar Nuñez, 53	Aptdo. 494
John Harvey, S.A.	Colón 1–25	Aptdo. 1
Emilio M. Hidalgo, S.A.	Clavel, 29	Aptdo. 221
Bodegas Hurgo, S.L.	Ctra. Lebrija, Km.3	Aptdo. 827
Bodegas Internacionales S.A.	Ctra. N-IV, Km 645	Aptdo. 140
Jiménez González, S.A.	Pl. de la Serrana, 8	
B.M. Lagos, S.A.	Banda Playa, 46 y 48 (Sanlúcar)	
Emilio Lustau, S.A.	Plaza del Cubo, 4	Aptdo. 193
Antonio Nuñez	Armas de Santiago, 3	
Luis Páez, S.A.	Banda Playa, 46 y 48 (Sanlúcar)	
A. Parra, S.A.	Plaza de Orbaneja, 3	Aptdo. 501
Cayetano del Pino y Cía., S.L.	Cardenal Herrero, 6	
Bodegas Rayón, S.A.	Rayón, 1 y 3	
Hros. Marqués del Real Tesoro, S.A.	Pajarete, 3	Aptdo. 27
La Riva, S.A.	Alvar Nuñez 44	Aptdo. 493
Sánchez Romate Hnos., S.A.	Lealas, 28	Aptdo. 5
Sandeman Coprimar. S.A.	Pizarro, 10	Aptdo. 53
José de Soto, S.A.	Mª. Antonio Jesús Tirado, 6	Aptdo. 29
A.R. Valdespino, S.A.	Pozo Olivar, 16	Aptdo. 22

Juan Vicente Vergara, S.A.	Carretera Cartuja, s/n	Aptdo. 9
Viñas, S.L.	Lealas, 28	Aptdo. 63
Williams & Humbert, Ltd.	Nuño de Cañas, 2	Aptdo. 23
Wisdom & Warter, Ltd.	Pizarro, 7	Aptdo. 20

PUERTO DE SANTA MARIA

Luis Caballero, S.A.	San Francisco, 24	Aptdo. 6
Mª Loreto Colosía	Enrique Martínez, 40	Aptdo. 129
Jesús Ferris Marhuenda	Avda. San Fernando, 116 (Rota)	
Miguel M. Gómez, S.A.	Avda. de la Libertad	Aptdo. 73
José Luis González Obregón	Santa Fé, 22	
Osborne y Cía., S.A.	Fernán Caballero, 3	
Portalto, S.A.	Postigo, 14	Aptdo. 68
Bodegas 501	Valdés, 7 y 9	Aptdo. 90
Fernando A. de Terry, S.A.	Santísima Trinidad, 2 y 4	Aptdo. 30

SANLUCAR DE BARRAMEDA

Hros. de Argüeso, S.A.	Mar, 8	Aptdo. 6
Manuel de Argüeso, S.A.	Bolsa, 18	Aptdo. 25
Antonio Barbadillo, S.A.	Luis de Eguilaz, 11	Aptdo. 25
Bodegas Barón, S.A.	Molinillo, 2	
C.A.Y.D.S.A.	Avda. del Puerto	Aptdo. 102
Delgado Zuleta, S.A.	Carmen, 26	Aptdo. 4
Ana Mª. Escobar Suárez	Santiago, 16	
Gaspar Florido Cano	Santa Brígida, s/n.	Aptdo. 29
Bgas. Infantes de Orleans-Borbón, S.A.	Baños, 1	Aptdo. 31
José Medina y Cía, S.A.	Banda de la Playa 46, 48 y 50	
Hijos de R. Pérez Marín, S.A.	Banda de la Playa, 28	
Hijos de A. Perez Megía, S.A.	Fariñas, 56	Aptdo. 21
Pedro Romero, S.A.	Trasbolsa, 60	
Miguel Sánchez Ayala, S.A.	San Juan, 34	
Vinícola Hidalgo y Cía, S.A.	Banda de la Playa, 34	Aptdo. 127

APPENDIX G

MIXED DRINKS WITH SHERRY

That Sherry was much favoured by Charles Dickens is witnessed by the contents of his well-filled cellars at his home, Gad's Hill. The list of wines in the catalogue for the sale after his death in 1870 commences with

> 12 dozen brown Sherry—a dry golden Sherry,
> 18 bottles Sherry 'Solera',
> 1 dozen Sherry, very delicate—old dry pale 'Preciosa',
> 1 dozen Amontillado,
> 13 Magnums Golden Sherry, very old, full-flavoured.

The great novelist's taste in drink was catholic. He was fond of mixed drinks, and took pride in personally concocting them. References to Sherry drunk by some of his wonderful fictional characters feature such things as Sherry Negus and Sherry Cobbler.

Though purists may grumble, we live in an age when mixed drinks are again much in demand. There is nothing new in this. Since the earliest times of civilized wine-drinking, the social scene has been enlivened by amalgams of different wines or admixture of wine with other ingredients. Only the style and popularity of certain potions have changed: some have given way to new inventions, others have endured for generations. Let us start with the two classics mentioned above, remembering Sherry has a long history.

The Negus is named after an early eighteenth-century minor English celebrity, Colonel Francis Negus, who evolved and popularized in London a hot wine drink for which no original recipe survives. An attractive Sherry Negus, a sound warmer for winter hospitality: rub 75 g/3 ozs. lump sugar with a lemon until yellowed and place in a warmed punch bowl; add juice of two large lemons and one bottle of medium Sherry; pour in 575 ml/1 pint boiling water and sprinkle powdered nutmeg on top. Ladle into warmed glass or china mugs.

Sherry Cobbler is a complete contrast, a summer cooler. Cobbler is an ancient description for a cold alcoholic drink containing citrus fruits. The infinitely respectable Mrs Isabella Beeton (1836–65), in her celebrated *Household Management* (1861) included a Sherry Cobbler. Her liqueur-reinforced recipe for three persons—total cost the equivalent today of 6p—does not coincide with modern practice. One can probably not improve on the version given by the Association of Spanish Bartenders (ABE): nearly fill a wine glass with crushed ice; add 4 dashes of sugar syrup; fill to halfway with preferred Sherry; add any fruit to personal taste, and serve with straws. Look in six drink books and you will find six different

Sherry Cobblers. No more than in cooking with Sherry are Sherry-based drinks subject to rigid rules.

Sherry Punch is capable of many variations: say, 125 ml/4 fl. ozs. medium Sherry; 1 teaspoon each of lemon juice and caster sugar; shake with ice, strain into large goblet containing cracked ice; serve with straws, after topping with soda-water.

The ABE published eight Sherry mixed drinks out of the nine it contributed to the *International Guide to Drinks* (compiled by the UK Bartenders' Guild). It revives another old name of British origin, Sangaree—possibly a corruption of Sangria, quite a different drink. The Spanish Sangaree consists of a heaped teaspoon sugar, 125 ml/4 fl. ozs. Sherry, stirred with crushed ice in a wine glass; a slice of lemon and a sprinkling of nutmeg.

Simplest of ABE mixes is the Jerez Cocktail: 75 ml/3 fl. ozs. dry Sherry stirred with ice and 2 dashes each of orange and peach bitters; strain into cocktail glass. A drink very similar to this is given in a book published in New York in 1882 by the then well-known bartender Harry Johnson. Sherry cocktails are not a novelty.

The Scandinavian devotion to Glögg deserves attention. It can be highly complicated. A straightforward version: 1 bottle of medium Sherry, 1 bottle of brandy, 75 g/3 ozs. sugar, teaspoon powdered cinnamon, a few dashes of Angostura, half-bottle ordinary red wine. Heat without boiling. In warmed mugs put a few seedless raisins and an unsalted almond, and pour Glögg on to these.

The most comprehensive of all drink books, the American Stan Jones's monumental *Complete Bar Guide* contains 110 recipes for mixes based on Sherry. A number of these contain spirits and some experts aver that possibly only brandy goes well with Sherry. There are those who maintain that dry gin (or vodka) are wholly acceptable, as in Straight Law: 2 parts dry Sherry to one of gin, stirred with ice and strained, with a zest of lemon rind squeezed firmly over the glass; a cultured mutation of the Dry Martini cocktail. In fact Sherry is an excellent and versatile mixer.

Dry Sherry is the perfect alternative for those who by choice, or on medical advice, avoid spirits. In circles where mixed drinks are socially popular, there is a growing interest in low-strength drinks both on health grounds and because of the drink-drive factor. Here Sherry excels.

Vogue magazine epitomizes the fashionable and modern. In his contributons to its pages, the American authority, Henry McNulty, resident in London, praises the merits of very dry Sherry on-the-rocks (poured over ice cubes) in place of anaesthetizing cocktails.

There follows a short selection of Cocktails containing Sherry. Some date from over a century or more ago; others evolved in modern times.

It is important to reiterate that drink recipes are not holy writ. Frequently, different authorities give marked variations in ingredients and proportions under the same title. Personal initiative is half the fun of mixing drinks: recipes are only guidelines.

To avoid tediously excessive repetition, it should be taken that 'stir' or 'shake' always mean *with ice*. The terms are virtually interchangeable.

Instructions have been kept to a minimum. All recipes are for single servings. Obviously, quantities of liquid in mixes dictates size of glasses: it is best to employ glasses which will not be filled to the brim.

Please note:

To obviate constant cumbersome references to amounts, figures represent units of 25 mls/1 fl oz. Thus: 2 dry Sherry = 2 fl. ozs. or 50 mls. J.D.

BARBARA WEST

1 medium Sherry
1 dry gin
teaspoon lemon juice
dash of Angostura

Stir and strain

BARCELONA

1 medium Sherry
1 dry gin
teaspoon lime juice
half-teaspoon sugar

Pour over ice in tall glass, top with soda.

BUCK JONES

1 medium Sherry
1 white rum
teaspoon lime juice

Pour on ice in tall glass, top with ginger ale.

CUPID

2 dry Sherry
one egg
teaspoon sugar
pinch of Cayenne pepper

Shake and strain.

DIZZY IZZY

1 dry Sherry
1 Bourbon (or Scotch)
teaspoon each pineapple and lemon juice

Shake and strain.

DRY BOSTON

1 dry Sherry
1 Bourbon
teaspoon sugar
one egg yolk

Shake briskly, strain into goblet.

HAVANA

2 sweet Sherry
1 white rum
teaspoon lemon juice

Stir and strain.

HUDSON'S BAY

1 dry Sherry
1 dry gin
1 orange juice
teaspoon lemon juice and dark rum.

Shake and strain

SHERRY FLIP

2 dry Sherry
one egg
teaspoon sugar
2 dashes Angostura

Shake briskly, strain into stemmed glass, top with grated nutmeg.

SHERRY SPRITZER

3 medium Sherry

Pour over ice in tall glass, top with soda-water (club soda), add twist
of lemon peel.

SHERRY TWIST

2 dry Sherry
2 orange juice
1 Scotch whisky
dash of Cointreau

Shake and strain.

APPENDIX H

Sherry in the Culinary Arts

By its unique and decisive character, Sherry can enhance many dishes. Where it is customary to use ordinary wine, partcularly white wine, a smaller quantity of appropriate Sherry should result in marked improvement, indeed ennobles many a simple recipe. There are honoured precedents for cooking with Sherry, or its addition to food.

When that supreme clear soup, turtle, was more usual than is now the case, Sherry was invariably added to it. All consommés benefit from Sherry. This should be poured in just before serving—not during heating, or the bouquet will be dispersed. Cold soups are much enhanced by Sherry. Jellied consommés prepared with Sherry are more interesting than ones not thus improved.

A most useful sauce that is little appreciated outside Spain is Salsa Española: it deserves wider circulation, for it is highly adaptable. Salsa Española is of unknown antiquity and has evolved over the years.

There is no single way with most sauces. It is not our intention to give rigid recipes—rather suggestions on which discerning cooks may exert their own expertise. Thus for a basic Salsa Española: 2 finely chopped large onions; 2 deseeded, diced red peppers; 500 g/18 ozs tomatoes; a clove of garlic crushed in salt; pepper to taste; 225 ml/8 fl. ozs. Sherry. Gently fry onions and peppers in oil until tender; remove excess oil; add tomatoes and cook until totally soft; add salted garlic and pepper. Pass all through a blender and then mix in the Sherry.

Salsa Española can also be employed as a marinade for most meat to be used in stews and casseroles. It goes especially well with lambs' kidneys: *Riñones al Jerez* is a classic dish. Wash and prepare 1 kg/2 lbs. kidneys and soak for an hour in cold water with Sherry vinegar added. Slice thinly and fry briefly in butter to seal; place in casserole containing 275 ml/1/2 pint Salsa Española; add 250 ml/9 fl. ozs. dry Sherry, and cook slowly, without boiling, for one hour or until tender. Serve with saffron rice or warm crusty bread.

White meats that are to be used in recipes calling for frying at some stage—veal escalopes, breast of chicken for instance—may with advantage be marinated in a mix of dry Sherry, olive oil, lemon juice, powdered coriander, brown sugar and herbs (proportions to individual discretion) for twenty-four hours, being turned occasionally.

After the vogue for *nouvelle cuisine* in Britain, there has been revived interest in more solid traditional fare. Amongst these is Trifle, favoured as a sweet course by all ages, at all levels of society, for two centuries. Old recipes differed from those of today in that they called for none of the plain sponge cake that is the base of the modern version. For Sherry Trifle: push (fat-free) sponge cake or biscuits into a bowl and soak for twenty-four hours in about 150 ml/1/4-pint of medium-dry Sherry. Then cover with a layer about half-inch thick of preferred jam or conserve. Pour one inch/2.5 cms or more of custard on top and allow to set. Top this with a stiff sauce on these lines—120 ml/8 tablespoons of same Sherry as used for soaking, grated peel of a lemon, 2 tablespoons lemon juce and sugar, a little powdered nutmeg and cinnamon, 275 ml/1/2-pint double cream. Adding cream last, whisk these ingredients slowly but thoroughly and, after spreading them over the trifle, decorate to taste with chopped candied fruit. Chill before serving.

A lighter sweet dish is *Gelée au Xeres*. Heat, without boiling, 575 ml/1 pint medium Sherry with grated peel of a lemon and 30 ml/2 tablespoons white sugar. In a half-cup of water, standing in near-boiling water, dissolve 15 ml/1 tablespoon gelatine. Stir the dissolved gelatine, plus a cup of hot water, into the wine. Pour into jelly mould. Chill thoroughly, turn on to a dish and decorate with whipped cream.

In nearly all fish dishes involving white wine in their preparation—such as *sole bonne femme, coquilles St. Jacques*, Lobster Thermidor—half the amount of Sherry as a replacement of the usual wine will produce exciting results, or flavour may be added to conventional wine by mixing it half and half with Sherry.

That Sherry has a place in many national cuisines is demonstrated by an expert's opinion that, in Oriental dishes calling for rice wine, Sherry is a wholly acceptable, refined alternative.

Experienced and enterprising cooks, domestic or professional would do well to understand the merits of Sherry and to experiment with its enrichment of their craft, while the less expert should be encouraged to venture into what Cervantes called 'The Elysian fields of Jerez'.

For more complete recipes for cooking with Sherry, see *El vino de Jerez en la cocina universal*, by Lalo Grosso (Espasa Calpe S.A., Madrid, 1982).

J.D.

Index

Index